DESIGNING FUTURE-ORIENTED AIRLINE BUSINESSES

Dedicated to Angela, Matthew, and Sophia

Designing Future-Oriented Airline Businesses

NAWAL K. TANEJA

ASHGATE

Published by
Ashgate Publishing Limited
Wey Court East
Union Road
Farnham
Surrey, GU9 7PT
England

Ashgate Publishing Company
110 Cherry Street
Suite 3-1
Burlington, VT 05401-3818
USA

www.ashgate.com

British Library Cataloguing in Publication Data
A catalogue record for this book is available from the British Library

The Library of Congress Cataloguing-in-Publication Data has been applied for.

Printed in the United Kingdom by Henry Ling Limited,
at the Dorset Press, Dorchester, DT1 1HD

Contents

List of Figures

List of Tables

List of Abbreviations

BI	–	Business Intelligence
CASK	–	Cost per Available Seat Kilometer
CMR	–	Customer Managed Relationship
CRM	–	Customer Relationship Management
DVR	–	Digital Video Recorder
FFP	–	Frequent Flyer Program
GDP	–	Gross Domestic Product
GDS	–	Global Distribution System
HIFTs	–	High Income Frequent Travelers
IAG	–	International Airlines Group
IATA	–	International Air Transport Association
IFE	–	In-Flight Entertainment
IFEC	–	In-Flight Entertainment and Connectivity
IPO	–	Initial Public Offering
JV	–	Joint Venture
LCC	–	Low Cost Carrier
NEATs	–	New Emerging Affluent Travelers
NDC	–	New Distribution Capability
NFC	–	Near Field Communication
NPS	–	Net Promoter Score
O&D	–	Origin & Destination
OTA	–	Online Travel Agent
PFC	–	Passenger Facility Charge
PNR	–	Passenger Name Record
POS	–	Point of Sale
PPP	–	Purchasing Power Parity
PRASM	–	Passenger Revenue per Available Seat Mile
PwC	–	PricewaterhouseCoopers
R&D	–	Research & Development
RFID	–	Radio-Frequency Identification
SEO	–	Search Engine Optimization
VFR	–	Visiting Friends and Relatives

Acknowledgements

I would like to express my appreciation to all those who contributed in different ways, especially Angela Taneja, an experienced analyst of best global business practices, Peeter Kivestu (Global Program Director for Travel and Lodging at Teradata), Dr. Dietmar Kirchner (formerly with Lufthansa and now a Senior Aviation Consultant), and Rob Solomon (the former Senior Vice President and Chief Marketing Officer at the Outrigger Enterprises) for discussions on challenges and opportunities facing the global airline industry and related businesses.

The second group of people that I would like to recognize, who contributed their Thought Leadership Pieces in Chapter 9, include: Dieter Brandes (formerly with ALDI); Nils Brandes, Hard Discount Retail; David Trimm, the Hertz Corporation; Jonathan Kletzel, PricewaterhouseCoopers LLP; Vaughan Chandler, Qantas; and Stan Boyer, Sabre Airline Solutions.

The third group that I would like to acknowledge includes the Foreword writers who took valuable time out of their extremely busy schedules to provide global insights on the airline industry. They are: Alex Cruz, Chairman and CEO, Vueling Airlines; Alexandre de Juniac, Chairman and Chief Executive Officer, Air France-KLM; Tom Klein, Chief Executive Officer and President, Sabre Corporation; Temel Kotil, Chief Executive Officer, Turkish Airlines; Christoph Muller, Chief Executive Officer, Aer Lingus; Fernando Pinto, Chairman and CEO of the Executive Board, TAP Portugal; Marty Salfen, General Manager, IBM Global Travel & Transportation Industry; John Slosar, Chief Executive, Cathay Pacific Airways; Jeff Smisek, Chairman of the Board, President and CEO, United Airlines; Rob Torres, Managing Director, Google, Inc.; Erik Venter, Chief Executive Officer, Comair Limited; Wang Yingming, Chairman, HNA Aviation Group Company Limited; and Juan Carlos Zuazua, Chief Executive Officer, VivaAerobus.

The fourth group of people to whom I owe thanks includes: at Affinity Capital Exchange—Atanas Christov; Aimia—Evert De Boer and Sandra Diem; Airbus Group—Eduardo Galicia-Roquero and Jan Reh; Air China—Zhihang Chi; Alitalia—Michel Coumans; Boeing Commercial Airplanes—Fariba Alamdari and David Gamrath; CAPA—Centre of Asia Pacific Aviation—Peter Harbison, Derek Sadubin, and Susan Tran; Cathay Pacific Airways—Ivan Chu; COPA Airlines—Joe Mohan; Etihad Airways—Peter Baumgartner; Google—Rob Torres; Hawaiian Airlines—Avi Mannis; Hipmunk—Adam Goldstein; IATA—Brian Pearce and Eric Leopold; IBM—Tom Liebtag and Steve Peterson; JetBlue—Martin St. George; KLM—Michel Pozas-Lucic; Lufthansa German Airlines—Christoph Klingenberg and Andrea Pernkoph; PricewaterhouseCoopers—Jon Glick, Jonathan Kletzel and Bryan Terry; Sabre Airline Solutions—Angela Berry and Jonathan Tong; Siegel+Gale—Jason Cieslak, Kristin Metcalfe, Margaret Molloy and Brian Rafferty; Southwest Airlines—Michael Delehant, John Jamotta and Pete McGlade; Teradata—Ralf Wittiber; United Airlines—Alex Savic and John Slater.

There are a number of authors whose work and ideas have been referenced in this book. They include: Angela Ahrendts, Barry Berman, Gordon Bethune (with Scott Huler), Luc de Brabandere (with Alan Iny), Linden R. Brown (with Chris L. Brown), Ralph Browning, Erik Brynjolfsson (with Andrew McAfee), Thomas H. Davenport, Niraj Dawar, Matthew Dixon (with Karen Freeman and Nicholas Toman), Matt Egol (with Michael Peterson and Stefan Stroh), Michelle Fischer, Henry H. Harteveldt, Loizos Heracleous, Eric V. Holtzclaw, Cindi Howson, Thomas M. Koulopoulos, Nirmalya Kumar (with Jan-Benedict E.M. Steenkamp), Matthias Krust, Josh Leibowitz (with Kelly Ungerman and Maher Masri), Harley Manning (with Kerry Bodine), Kelly McDonald, David Meer, Idris Mootee, Jeanne Meister, Christopher Morace (with Sara Gaviser Leslie), Rajat Paharia, Bryan Pearson, Martin Raymond, Michael E. Raynor (with Mumtaz Ahmed), Fred Reichheld, Howard Rheingold, Viktor Mayer-Schönberger (with Kenneth Cukier), Gary Shapiro, Eric Siegel, Brian Solis, Jay Sorensen (with Eric Lucas), Reza Soudagar (with Vinay Iyer and Dr. Volker G. Hildebrand), Jim Stengel, and Laurence Vincent.

There are a number of other people who provided significant help: at The Ohio State University — Joshua Fisher, Jim Oppermann, and Seth Young; and at Ashgate Publishing, Guy Loft — Publisher, Gillian Steadman — Production Editor, Nikki Selmes — Editorial Manager, Charlotte Parkins — Proofreader, Lianne Sherlock — Assistant Editor, and Luigi Fort — Senior Marketing Executive.

Finally, I would so like to thank my family for its support and patience.

Foreword

Alex Cruz

Chairman and CEO
Vueling Airlines

Sustainable returns in the commercial airline industry—oxymoron or within our grasp? I vote for the "people" factor

Nawal has been studying our industry all his life. He has interviewed everyone of significance and has listened to everyone gripe about our problems. When faced with a foreword on this new book, *Designing Future Oriented Airline Businesses*, I could only do one thing which I do very seldom: reflect over history and focus on what has made some operators more sustainably successful. It is a simple analysis, actually. The challenge, as usual in life, is *people*.

Vueling is a young airline. This year, 2014, we will celebrate our 10th birthday. In industry terms, we are just starting. Yet, we are intimately aware that if we want to make it to our 20th birthday with a strong ROE, we have to continue focusing on the basics. Our world is short-haul; it is competitive; it is intense; it is dynamic; it is multi-cultural; it is inundated with many regional, state and European Union regulatory and legislative demands set in a political system that does not sufficiently incentivize growth or innovation. Our world is based in the Old World where only the emerging, younger, professional work force accepts that there is still much to be learnt in order to increase enterprise and social competitiveness, and is willing to work hard to achieve it. And Europe is a world where airline capacity discipline is not a priority for all involved; though controls have tightened, direct and indirect subsidies are still a reality—for many governments, it is simply not an option to let its national airline die regardless of cost.

In that world, day by day, Vueling staff live and breathe by a sense of "urgency" and a sense of "proving" to our shareholders, to our competitors, and to ourselves that we can achieve what very few others have in the past: grow profitably without penalizing those that feed us, our passengers. Today's now formula "du jour" is clearly key for success for short-haul operators; more and more are adopting it. We have been going at it since 2004. It is a simple formula to articulate, but difficult to deliver: lower your non-growth-related costs and improve the quality of your product and service, year on year, every year.

But if we look at history, as I promised, we can see a few airlines that have been consistently profitable and deliver a reasonable ROE over long periods of time, say, more than 20 years. Putting aside those smaller operators that have miraculously operated in near-monopoly markets, these successful airlines have three attributes in common which I believe are key to sustainable return on capital. I will call them my very own "Three "C's" of Success":

- **Capacity**: no successful operator can survive without flying in routes with the right level of capacity; too much and you lose money; too little and you invite competitors and then you enter the "too much" category. Capacity discipline is often not a factor which you can control, but as we have seen in the US over the last five years, everyone comes to understand the benefits behind progressive capacity cuts; it has clearly been under everyone's control to pursue it. As mentioned before, this is more difficult in continents with multiple countries and agendas—but the signs of small market shifts are encouraging. But at the end, *don't you have control over how many extra flights to put or remove in a given route?*
- **Customer**: topical or not, most revenues are generated by passengers. Passengers are today best placed to make choices and they are also the most informed that they have ever been. Those that acknowledge this sophistication are always in a better position to successfully capture those revenues. It is not easy but the penalties for not doing it are large— in Europe, a giant operator has recently acknowledged

this fact. And frankly, it has become easier and cheaper to address Customer's needs because they are more and more accessible via Internet and mobile channels. *When was the last time you were told your flight was delayed and offered two alternative boarding passes for other flights, all within your airline app, automatically? Why not?*

- **Culture**: airline teams and the culture they embrace is the final glue to this list. Airlines with strong, consistent, clearly articulated cultures have led the market place for years. The nature and "tone" of the specific airline culture could be debated, sure, as some have had more negatively perceived internal cultures (*"you are not allowed to charge your mobile phone in the office"*) whilst others have put transparency and personal development first (*"press releases always first in the Intranet"* or *"you are allowed to make mistakes"*). In addition, industry consolidation has resulted in companies with multiple internal cultures which have not been properly addressed. *How often do you measure your strengths and weaknesses in your internal culture and what are your weekly actions to maintain it?*

I can hear some people being shocked at my exclusion of the "C" for Cost in my list—there is no speech or presentation that I have made over the years where I do not highlight the virtues of operating with a very low cost structure. This is because for me, "cost control" is something which you either have in your DNA or you don't. It is part of capacity decisions (*"compete better if you have lower costs?"*), customer strategy (*"how can I improve without spending?"*) and finally, of course, company culture development (*"am I thinking about costs all the time?"*).

But at the end, acknowledging that people are the ones that drive success (or "less failure" as in some cases) and acting on it, is the cornerstone of all airline strategies. The "people factor", for me, is the simple most important driver for delivering success in our industry. This does not mean paying above market salaries for office jobs or "giving in" to unreasonable union requests; in fact, part of the "people culture" is acknowledging that many things that need to be done in order to survive in our industry are basically not easy or comfortable, and then, being transparent about it and building the right "expectation management" processes around it. This is not an industry for everyone.

Of course, there is much more. Our industry is very Complex. In this book, Nawal visits many of the evolving operating and commercial models of our airline peers. It exposes how and why some of those airlines have chosen to evolve. It explains what models appear to be more "survivable" and why. Altogether, it provides an ample view of how airline leaders have dealt with our standing challenges.

Yet, it's people who create the problem, and it will be people that will solve the problem. Investors are waiting...

Barcelona, Spain

Foreword

Alexandre de Juniac

Chairman and Chief Executive Officer
Air France-KLM

"Even if you don't have a vision on their industry, they will certainly have it on your industry"

Last October, Nawal Taneja peeked my interest when he presented at the International Air Transportation Association's World Passenger Symposium and argued that there are many more opportunities for achieving growth in revenue and margins from innovation in customized products and services than in network/ fleet and airport innovation.

As a relative newcomer to the industry I cannot help but, at times, be still amazed by the tremendous complexity of the forces acting upon the airline industry. While organizations like the Air France-KLM Group do an astounding job addressing these daily complexities, there is also a need to reflect on the structural changes taking place in our industry and rethink the strategies and business models that we employ.

This is nothing new; it's not the strongest that survive, but the most adaptable to change.

However, Taneja is asking the question: Could incremental change be enough or do we need to make transformational changes?

Let's look at the speed of technological change. The digital age has completely changed the relationship between customers and the airline. Today, 99% of our frequent passengers use a mobile, which they have close to them 24/7. Every day more devices are connected to the global digital network, creating a "hyperconnected world" that is combined with the rise of true machine intelligence.

These technological developments are game changers. They provide an opportunity for information-rich, technology-savvy, and analytics-driven companies to serve customers by knowing them better and to retail tailored products and services. Should airlines become such companies and offer, for example, seamless door-to-door travel? And what if they don't? Especially those airlines with high cost-bases in low-growth markets, open to competition, will be asking themselves this strategic question; as I know many of my European colleagues have.

I believe pursuing such a change will be a tall order for most companies. Transforming the focus from seats to (guest) solutions—as Taneja is suggesting—requires not only dissolving borders between sales, services, marketing, and operations, but changing the culture and skillset of the company. This is no incremental matter and requires leadership.

Clearly the airline industry has got to do something to be better rewarded for the risks it takes on the one hand, and provide a higher level of customer experience, on the other hand. This book will show airline practitioners the aspects they need to consider in redesigning their future airline business.

Profitability buys you freedom and as Nawal states, innovation is the key to this. Other industries have shown that higher quality and lower cost *can* go hand in hand. I believe that the airline industry can achieve the same.

Paris, France

Foreword

Tom Klein

Chief Executive Officer and President
Sabre Corporation

Even after nearly 30 years in airline and travel technology, nothing is more exciting to me than the innovations that continue to drive our industry forward. In recent years, I've been deeply involved in the development of technologies and strategies to support ancillary products and services, or as many call it, airline merchandising.

Ancillary services have grown dramatically over the past several years—these services represent a critical revenue stream for many airlines today. To excel in this important growth category, however, airlines cannot simply put their ancillary strategy on autopilot. To generate the desired additional revenue, airlines must evolve their merchandising strategies to meet or exceed customers' expectations for more personalized and diversified products and services. In doing so, airlines must think more like retailers, offering the right products to the right customers at the very time those customers are most likely to buy. That means starting with understanding the customer need without bias to where and when you will promote, sell, and deliver the service while paying close attention to the customer's view on the price to value proposition. And, that's only a fraction of what's required to achieve exceptional airline merchandising.

In the case of airline customers, one size definitely does not fit all. Therefore, segmentation is a critical factor in successfully selling ancillaries. For some customers, price is the primary driver. For others, it's all about comfort, convenience and user experience. Data-driven customer insights enables airlines to understand discreet customer psychographic profiles to accurately segment customers by purchase drivers—all of which enables the development of more personalized—and more successful—offerings. And, having the right product or service is not the whole answer. Today's consumers—and especially today's savvy airline customers—are all about "on-demand" delivery, so airline merchandising must be convenient for the customer to access whenever they want it and airlines have to be confident, and flawless, on their ability to deliver the service in a consistent way.

A successful retailing strategy can strengthen an airline's brand while also differentiating it from competitors. It offers substantial financial benefits to the airline, enhances the customer experience and ultimately leads to more loyal, long-term relationships between an airline and its customers.

While I have simply touched on a few of the more important factors to consider, it is essential that airlines develop and implement a comprehensive, end-to-end retailing strategy that is in harmony with their core mission of safe and efficient air travel. While complex, airline retailing is quiet manageable. Advances in technology combined with experience and best practices gained from successful retailers can position airlines to become successful retailing practitioners. Without a doubt, retailing has become a critical success factor for many profitable airlines, and when properly executed, retailing also offers great value and convenience to create a better travel experience for customers.

I applaud Prof. Nawal Taneja for addressing airline retailing in his book, and I am confident that his ideas and concepts on this topic will greatly enhance any airline's retailing strategy.

Dallas, USA

Foreword

Dr. Temel Kotil

Chief Executive Officer
Turkish Airlines

In a very competitive environment consisting of many leading airlines, Turkish Airlines has positioned itself as the world's fastest growing airline with the largest international network. Turkish Airlines, reaching today nearly 250 destinations worldwide in 105 countries with its young fleet, has been transformed into a truly global brand as a consequence of significant investments implemented during the last decade. Turkish Airlines achieved a 17% annual average growth in the last decade, approximately 3 times of the industry average growth rate. By the end of 2014, Turkish Airlines' revenue is expected to reach 11.4 billion dollars while it was only 1.9 billion dollars in 2003. Turkish Airlines is currently the 10th largest airline in the world in terms of international passengers, serving more international destinations to its customers than any other airline in the world.

Turkish Airlines has strategically turned its geographic advantage into a success story by offering a wide range of origin and destination choices with a high quality product and a worldwide famous service culture as well as by bursting innovative marketing campaigns all over the world. As an important player within the global aviation community, we are proud to win distinguished awards which encourage us to achieve further accomplishments, and this is a depiction of Turkish Airlines' wise growth strategy. Turkish Airlines, Europe's best airline based on passenger votes, became the 2nd largest airline in Europe, a region with more than a billion travelers and one third of the world's aviation industry's market share.

Even though many European and American carriers are decreasing capacity and losing market share, with its growth rate,

Turkish Airlines has been continuing to increase its market share. By the end of 2014, Turkish Airlines is expected to offer 1.9% of world passenger capacity, increasing its market share by almost 4 times in 10 years. Keeping up the average annual growth by 10%, by 2023, we will reach 120 million passengers, more than 450 aircraft, and a 24 billion dollar revenue.

Customer preferences and the aviation industry have been changing. Over the next years, the market potential of passengers who tend to fly will develop more but some regions would grow more rapidly than others, changing the passenger gravity center of the world, shifting it more to the south and east. In 20 years, traffic to/from and within Europe and America will almost be doubled, but traffic to/from and intra-Asia will be more than three times of today's traffic exceeding Europe and America. The Middle East and Africa will also grow about 3 times. One important point in this picture is Europe will still be the most powerful driving region for international traffic. To keep the growth sustainable, we have to keep in mind this power change and manage the capacity accordingly. Growing profitably in these markets among other strong competitors, one needs to be different, be most cost efficient and exceed expectations of customers. While planning cost efficiency and high customer satisfaction, not only the traditional methods, but also innovative methods will be needed.

Turkey is in the middle of the growing traffic flows, making a natural hub of the world. Reaching airports with billions of passengers in a couple of hours presents huge cost efficiency and product variety. By using narrow and wide body fleet efficiently, we achieve cost efficiency, offer better connectivity and more destinations. With the construction of a new airport in Istanbul, which will be the world's largest airport, and using the geographical detour advantage, Turkish Airlines can transfer more and more passengers with shorter travel times, effecting the gravity change.

Aviation has been growing but the growth has some constraints up front. The industry has to go through the liberalization process, overcoming limited international traffic rights, new taxes, regulations, change in customer preferences, limited human, asset and capital resources, infrastructure capacity problems, and changing price elasticity.

Global economic growth will shape future aviation. Prospects for long term growth remain bright. An intensely competitive industry continues to drive innovation and out-of-the-box thinking. Intractable global policy issues and a highly regulated industry, covering both technical, economic and customer service dimensions will be main points of the future. Further steps are needed to truly liberalize this most global of industries. Airlines have to well manage the risks and carefully allocate capacity growth in order to continue to grow profitably.

Today, the airline business is at the beginning of a new era which will carry it to a new level of transformation together with its customers despite existing extra ordinary limitations in the horizon. With technological connectivity widespread, the passenger is at the center of the airline business, and the innovative ideas generated will certainly keep Turkish Airlines at the forefront of that trend. Competitiveness will be sharpened at the edge of innovation and touching the customer. New brand and service concepts invite everyone to explore new horizons and bring the passenger experience to a new level by making each feel special and valued throughout the travel by developing new experiences at each stage of travel, offering pleasant surprises in a diverse and memorable travel experience.

Superior service is the distinguishing mark of Turkish Airlines, separating it from its competitors. By upgrading its already excellent offerings, it is, in essence, competing with itself as it continues to upgrade and enhance the passenger experience, trying to move customer satisfaction to an even higher level and increasing the differentiation between Turkish Airlines and its competition.

In this evolving era, airlines should be more transformative and innovative than before in developing skills to capture the markets rather than being only cost or revenue oriented. Customer Service and Product Quality will make a difference while achieving growth and leadership. Some dimensions that would improve competitiveness in growth are revenue enhancements through tailoring products to markets, dynamic capacity allocation, yield management and improvement of cost competitiveness through asset utilization, productivity, and fuel efficiency.

In this book the author is trying to highlight some edge points of airline business as the future brings new questions on the horizon. As in his previous books in this series, Prof. Taneja once more brings forward the most important and contemporary issues with a fresh approach. He gives the secrets of surviving in this new era to the airlines with a taste of descriptive narrative.

On behalf of Turkish Airlines and personally, I would like to express my special thanks to Prof. Taneja for his great contributions to airline business with this new book and previous books of this series. This book will help the airline practitioners through showing the necessary steps towards the future. Wishing great success to him, I am looking forward to his next book eagerly.

Istanbul, Turkey

Foreword

Christoph Muller

Chief Executive Officer
Aer Lingus

The Legacy of Aviation

Ever since the first flight by the Wright Brothers, aviation has evoked a deep sense of romanticism in people worldwide. The pursuit of aviation has won wars, delivered aid to the needy, enabled business across boundaries, created burgeoning tourism industries, connected people, and has made the world a smaller place. Suffice to say that we should expect to see the commercial aviation industry constantly evolving and reinventing the travel experience.

Recognizing the Power of the Internet

Technology has been a huge enabler for the commercial aviation industry, and the influence had run the gamut, from airframe design, to efficient engines, to computer-aided cockpits and flight management systems. Over the recent years, we have experienced a marked shift in technology utilization—from it being a tool for cost control and optimization, to technology morphing into a competitive weapon for increasing revenue generation, creating new revenue streams, and increasing customer satisfaction.

Commercial aviation suffered several setbacks over the years with most recent major aberration precipitated by the events on September 11, 2001. Legacy airlines had to rethink their business models as they faced increasing fuel and overhead costs, and competition from scrappy low cost and hybrid carriers who had optimized their cost models and passed on some of the savings to their customers. Legacy carriers had entrenched business processes, decades of rot that had built-up, and simply did not understand how the traveling public had changed over time with respect to what drove purchase decisions and loyalty.

At around the same time, the age of Internet Commerce impacted world markets with a never before seen rate of change. Technology was evolving at breakneck speed, and for the first time, consumer technology was outpacing the enterprise. Consumers were experiencing the power of contextually relevant and timely data, and as a result were affecting a wholesale change in purchasing decisions.

Smart businesses foresaw this shift in decision-making patterns and raced furiously to build up their Internet presence and present their products on the digital store shelf, which was available to any consumer who had access to the Internet, anywhere on the planet. At first glance, it is hard to comprehend the extremely rapid and seismic shift in the relationship between businesses and consumers that the Internet brought forth.

Today, we take Internet commerce for granted, and *value* carriers that straddle the market between legacy and low cost carriers, have been at the forefront in recognizing and exploiting the power of the Internet.

Businesses have grudgingly acceded to the power of the Internet Powered Consumer.

A Lethargic Oligopoly

It is notable that legacy airlines have been slow to recognize and ride the incessant technology waves during the last decade. This lethargic reaction to the most radical change impacting businesses in a generation was partly due to being out of touch with the customer and partly due to decades old processes and systems.

It is important to note that a great degree of this lethargy can be attributable to Computer Reservations System (CRS) and Global Distribution System (GDS) providers, and indeed, the CRS providers who are also GDS platforms. For decades, these system providers delivered an invaluable service to airlines by supplying computing platforms to manage reservations, airline operations and enabling the distribution of airlines' products to partners and physical store fronts like travel agents. But, over time, these technology providers chose the comfortable position of collecting Passenger Booking and coupon fees instead of investing in technology and in the enablement of airlines and their customers. They took this stance despite the incredible innovation in technology that surrounded them, and it is little wonder that airlines and their customers alike suffered in myriad ways as a consequence of this lack of investment.

While it is hard to gauge the true impacts of the CRS/GDS industry's lethargy thus far, it is not hard to imagine the cost of ignoring commerce in a digital economy. The Internet has ushered in the business-to-consumer model and the business-to-business commerce model is now increasingly relegated to core, invisible (to consumer) interactions like supply-chain and logistics. Airlines and their customers have recognized the benefits of direct relationships and conversations with each other, and the call for change is now loud and clear.

Yet, the CRS/GDS industry has been slow to respond, and has instead created a comfortable oligopoly that continues to tighten its commercial grip on airlines and consumers alike, has consciously ignored the digital economy, and has constantly battled the tide of positive change that will benefit consumers.

The Vicious Circle

An incredibly confounding aspect of the relationship between legacy airlines and the systems' providers is that the airlines continue to pay the providers hefty premiums for access to greatly deficient products marketed by the CRS/GDS providers. These deficiencies span multiple dimensions including availability, dynamic packaging, pricing, and merchandising and retailing opportunities. The airlines then attempt to pass the cost on to the consumers, and where they cannot do so, they further compromise the quality of their already deficient products to keep costs under control. This vicious circle involving legacy airlines and CRS/GDS providers is constantly perpetuated and the biggest losers are the consumers followed closely by the airlines. It is important to note here that the CRS/GDS providers continue to profit, similar to any industry that suffers the blight of intermediaries more commonly known as "middle-men".

To break out of this legacy mold and to counter the slow pace of change by the CRS/GDS providers, IATA and forward thinking member airlines are working diligently on initiatives like Simplifying the Business (StB) and New Distribution Capability (NDC), both of which are aimed at helping the airlines jettison inefficient and irrelevant business processes, maximize revenue potential and customer loyalty, and in providing consumers with wide varieties of product choices and transparency in pricing. These initiatives have been designed from the ground up to bring airlines closer to their customers than ever before, and to help them wrest control from the intermediaries where necessary. It is therefore little wonder that the intermediaries are opposed to initiatives like NDC, simply because it is a giant first step in chipping away at their relevance. In addition to the IATA initiatives, like-minded airlines are now actively engaged in discussions to jointly develop modern technology platforms and solutions that will benefit airlines and their customers, by allowing the airlines to dynamically present contextually relevant products that the customers need, and by providing customers choices that they haven't had before.

Re-Thinking the Business—Customer Centricity

There is little doubt that airlines have to reinvent themselves to grow their market share and to remain relevant to the traveling public. The fastest way to achieve this goal is to massively re-engineer airline business processes to fulfill the needs of the consumers of today and the future—the theme of Nawal Taneja's new book. The computing systems and platforms available today are cheaper, faster and far more scalable that those developed sixty years ago. Technology has made multiple quantum leaps in the last decade and aviation technology needs to address this widening gap rapidly before the chasm is too deep and wide to address economically.

The retail industry, for example, long recognized the value of the data they held and the data generated by their customers' behaviors. Today, the retail industry is a pioneer in big data crunching and in understanding, affecting and predicting consumer behavior. The airline industry can use many of the lessons learnt by high-street retailers and can greatly accelerate the initiatives to re-engineer their business processes, and use modern technology as a sustainable and scalable enabler for the new way of doing business. Again, Taneja discusses both the data and analytics aspects in Chapter 7 and provides, throughout the book, numerous examples of multi-industry insights from a broad array of non-airline businesses, including retailers.

Any shift in the airline business model will be an exercise in futility unless the business model has the customer at the core, and the technology that enables the business model is designed around the customer. Today, airlines generally find it difficult to meet their customer centricity goals because customer focus has to be retrofitted into their legacy business and technology environments, with numerous compromises made along the way. Ultimately, in the current environment, neither the airlines nor the customers experience any real benefits, and the inefficient status quo is maintained.

The Travel Experience of the Future — Powered by Technology

It is undeniable that the travel experience expected by different segments of the traveling public has rapidly evolved in the last decade. And most if not all of the expectations are centered on the utilization modern technology. Responsive websites, smartphones, apps, wallets, 4g LTE mobile networks, near field communications, one click purchasing etcetera, are all huge innovations in their own right, but when brought together, yield the ultimate power to the traveler. It is estimated that in 2015 $36 billion will be transacted for travel on mobile devices in North America, and that number is increasing exponentially.

As mobile devices and supporting networks have become more powerful and less expensive, the adoption rate has sky rocketed and more consumers are making purchases while on the move. This has obvious implication for airlines and the larger travel industry because that's exactly what we do — we move people. We, the airlines, have to lead the industry in reaching our current and future customers where they are, with the products they need, at the price points they can sustain.

Airlines and airports have to work closely together in enhancing the traveler's experience, despite competing for the traveler's business at various touch-points. Without active collaboration between these two elements of the travel experience, the traveler's experience will be left wanting and unsatisfactory.

A critical factor informing customer behavior is Social Media, and the ever-decreasing attention span of those utilizing this medium. Social Media interactions need to be woven into most if not all aspects of the travel experience in order to attend to customers' needs expeditiously—another topic covered extensively in this book.

There are many aspects of the travel experience that can be enhanced by employing technology. Today's traveler wants a very high degree of personalization. Airlines need to provide highly integrated and personalized services using modern technology in order to satisfy the modern traveler's incessant drive for individualization.

Dublin, Ireland

Foreword

Fernando Pinto

Chairman and CEO of the Executive Board
TAP Portugal

I've been following with great interest all the literature published by Nawal Taneja. This 8th book of the series gives us impressive insights on "designing future-oriented airline businesses". I consider Taneja's books a "must read" not only for airline executives and managers, but also for everyone working or interested in this industry.

Reading this book, I noticed that in line with Nawal's vision, there are several steps for future-oriented airlines that TAP has already undertaken.

TAP is positioned as a niche airline. We found out several years ago that the best path for passengers flying from Latin America and East Africa, to Europe, and vice-versa, is through Portugal and our hub in Lisbon.

When we realized this and adopted the necessary operational and market strategies, many other airlines, including major European Low-Cost Carriers, started looking to Portugal as an interesting and developed market. Soon enough, many of these airlines launched or incremented their operations, or even established bases in the country.

This has been an extremely important challenge for TAP, since the newcomers, with different business models in our home turf, keep us on our toes, continuously evolving to be more efficient and competitive. We understand that clients flying with Low-Cost Carriers are open to flying TAP if we can provide them the offer they want. In order to shape that offering, we have, for instance, unbundled our product, offering several different levels of service at different prices. As a result, we've gained access to a new type of customer that we had to interact in a different and much more dynamic way.

We also found that one of the most crucial aspects in this business is to know how to listen and interact with customers. Actually, we strongly believe they can show us what an airline should become in the future.

Therefore, in TAP, we do our best to engage customers through technology. We want to hear what customers have to say, and we want to be where they are. And they are on the web, on social networks, using their smartphones, anywhere, anytime. So, we are evolving and working hard to be in the same places, at the same time, listening, helping, providing and taking care of customers.

It is obvious that customers today are highly price-sensitive, but we also realize they are more emotional than ever in their relationship with companies and organizations. They are more open to be surprised and to demand things beyond the expected level of service. They also have all platforms at their fingertips to share their experiences and emotions with other customers. We believe that purchasing decisions are more and more based on these emotions and how they are shared, in addition to pure and simple pricing.

We try to have a transparent relationship with our customers, doing all we can to avoid a simple transactional one, where we sell and they buy. We are establishing partnerships with them.

I believe this is the path for future-oriented airlines.

Lisbon, Portugal

Foreword

Marty Salfen

General Manager
IBM Global Travel & Transportation Industry

There has been a great deal of sound and fury around the dual promises of big-data and analytics in the airline industry in the past several years, and for good reason. Readers of this book will no doubt be interested in reading the examples of airlines that are using these powerful tools to transform their businesses. The intense interest in these topics, and the very appropriate focus Nawal has placed on them in this book, stem in part from the obvious and transformative impacts these capabilities can have on the core operational and customer facing aspects of the airline business, but I suspect an equal measure of the interest in these topics grows from industry practitioners – the tens of thousands of airline executives, analysts, advisors, and consultants – who know how hard it is to deliver on these two important promises. All too often airlines struggle in vain to convert the compelling vision of more analytic-driven operations into reality. Similarly, stories of large but futile investments in projects that purport to funnel customer insights from 'big-data' into each and every customer touch point are legion. In other words, big-data and analytics adhere to the time-tested dictum that success in the airline industry is 1% strategy and 99% execution; knowing what to do is relatively easy, but making it happen is what separates the leaders from the laggards.

As I started to digest the eighth installment in Nawal's airline series, I took particular note of the three powerful examples of successful airline transformations he describes in chapter one. Even the casual industry observer will be struck by the stark differences between JetBlue, Qantas, and Singapore, but for me one powerful commonality between these three diverse but successful players was obvious: they are all IBM clients. Perhaps that is why I was asked to write this foreword; when airlines get serious about turning the grandiose visions that are propagated in the popular press into reality, often IBM is among the first companies they turn to for help. What is more, the airlines we help, especially in the areas of big-data and analytics, are those that the rest of the sector are now looking to for examples of how to make productive change happen. In other words, based on extensive and relevant experience, the IBM team understands not just the challenges that airlines want to overcome with investments in big-data and analytics, but also the opportunities that overcoming the barriers of tricky implementation can reap when success is achieved.

The challenges faced by air carriers from each geography are well documented and widely understood. Perpetual growth in capacity and a relentless focus on price among many key customer segments make success in key profit corridors, be they trans-oceanic or within sub-regions, essential features of the strategies for most carriers. As Nawal notes in Chapter 3, this translates into razor-thin margins on the majority of flights that take place outside of the most valuable routes. Loyalty programs, route structure, and above all consistently excellent service delivery account for success within these profitable sectors, but creating a competitive advantage in the rest of the network prompts most carriers to consider other, more creative solutions. A central theme of this book which is proven and re-proven in these pages through dozens of compelling examples, is that success demands a customer-centric orientation across all aspects of airline operations, and delivering the experiences customers desire turns on an airline's ability to derive insights from the sea of data that customers make available. Indeed, this theme is also a key organizing principle of our entire airline practice because we believe, and by the examples Nawal has included in these pages the industry agrees, that airlines need to select partners that can deliver against the complex objective of personalizing service delivery for customers through data-driven insights.

Of course if rising to the challenge of data-driven personalization were easy it would cease to be a worthwhile goal, and many of the companies like ours that work to bring this goal to life would need to shift focus. As Nawal rightly observes in Chapter 6, and again in Chapter 8, most airlines have a long way to go before they deliver on the promise of personalization. In prior decades the data needed to satisfy customer demands was held almost exclusively within databases and systems that the airlines controlled. Today, however, a much more diverse set of inputs are needed to truly understand the customer and their unique preferences. Partners and other collaborators have slices of insight based on the data they harvest from customers, so sharing that data across firm boundaries remains a very real challenge with very tangible rewards. Of course, additional insight resides in unstructured formats found in social networks, travel review sites, and other traveler forums. Airlines that are not focused on extracting insights from all these diverse data sources are missing a huge opportunity to customize interactions and personalize service delivery.

In addition to the examples Nawal notes of airlines that are using data analytics to deliver more personalized customer experiences, other industries and sectors also offer compelling illustrations of the opportunities that open up when companies tap into a deeper levels of customer insight. As mentioned in Chapter 3, global hotel brands are working to personalize along almost every dimension of the customer experience, including but not limited to both simple services like reserving a room and ordering a meal (both of which can be customized to your specific preference), and more complex services like the coordination of onward travel plans and in-location experiences which are determined by marrying data from other travel providers, customer shared preferences from social media, and many other sources with the historical customer preferences and patterns that are extracted from hotel-owned and managed data sources.

Finally, while it seems everyone in the travel sector, including Nawal, is thinking about ways to re-craft their travel company in the image of the most successful retailers, we may be well served to consider some important aspects of the travel industry that even world-class retailers look at with envy. While most airlines would gladly take a page out of the Amazon playbook when it comes to applying analytics to the online customer experience, even the retail masters of customer insight recognize the unique and saleable value many airlines have developed with their loyalty programs. What is more, while opportunities abound to more effectively apply big-data and analytics to the very real operational challenges of coordinating the actions of hundreds of aircraft, thousands of flights, and millions of passengers, few industries do as much to satisfy so many each and every day with such thin margins. It is easy to focus on the many ways our industry can improve, but by seizing the opportunities that new technologies are making available each day, and by focusing on the difficult but important work of making those emerging solutions work effectively across a complex and high-pressure business, forward-thinking airlines that choose the right partners to turn their goals into reality will continue to thrive. Perhaps we can all read about their future success in Nawal's next edition.

Dallas, USA

Foreword

John Slosar

Chief Executive
Cathay Pacific Airways

It is high time that this book has been written! In *Designing Future-Oriented Airline Businesses*, Nawal Taneja builds a powerful argument that the future of aviation is going to look radically different from the past but, importantly, not in the way that most airlines and industry pundits expect.

The thrust of Taneja's argument is that the pathway to success for airlines in the future lies predominantly on the revenue side of the equation, the almost obsessive efforts on cost management having been largely successful leaving only incremental cost reduction opportunities on the table. This is "new box" thinking, especially when considered in the context of the Chapter 11 restructurings, layoffs and low-cost focus which continue to dominate the aviation news these days.

Taneja's point is not that revenue growth means more unbundling of the airline product so as to increase ancillary revenues as ticketed fares stagnate or decline. He has in mind a more complex challenge, which is that consumer perceptions of value and service are changing radically and literally at light-speed, led by the innovations of the high-tech sector. Airlines must come to terms with the fact that these new perceptions of value and service extend across all business segments and have become the new norm against which consumers judge the offerings of all businesses. Future consumers will make no allowances for aviation being a "legacy" business; they will expect all companies to connect with them and to respond to their needs in the same brilliant and innovative way that the companies of the "new" economy have done.

We are now in an era of tech-driven mass customization. Think buying running or basketball shoes is just about driving to a shop, trying them on and buying them? Think again. Today's consumers can order almost any running or basketball shoes online and at the same time customize the colour scheme and some other elements of design while purchasing. Consider the implications of this new paradigm of customer interaction for planning processes, marketing, sales, customer relations and supply chains for sport shoes manufacturers. The same mass customization is now even offered by some of the highest value fashion brands so it would be short-sighted to conclude that it is just a gimmick. Do consumers value having control over the product they will purchase? You bet they do.

This trend represents a severe challenge to today's airlines and Taneja is persuasive in stressing that the successful airlines of the future need to start measuring themselves not against other airlines but against the best of today's high-tech, online, mass customization consumer businesses. This is a big ask.

But in challenge there is also opportunity and it is here that Taneja is at his most original, arguing that those airlines that are prepared to focus on understanding the changing perceptions of value of their passengers will not find that service is irrelevant and all that matters is cost. Quite the opposite—they will find that there are a large untapped opportunities for value creation that passengers are more than willing to pay for. This is stirring stuff which should inspire passionate airline executives, planners, marketers and IT heads to do some serious thinking.

In case that is not challenge enough, Taneja also warns us of the fate awaiting those airlines that end up of step with the value and service norms of the high-tech consumer. There are increasing signs that many high-tech companies focusing on enabling flexible group contact and activity (think Facebook, WhatsApp, Google and Groupon) have their sights set on intermediating airlines, travel agents and passengers, thereby laying claim to a share of the always under-pressure airline value chain—for example, Google's purchase of ITA Software for $676 million in 2010. Pulling these strands together—for airlines, the status quo going forwards is not an option. Future fortune is going to favour the tech-savvy and customer-centric bold.

Where to start then? Taneja proposes that successful future airlines will need new and forward-looking models for understanding and segmenting customers, new skill sets for technology-based service planning and delivery, new strategies and capabilities for interfacing with customers, or perhaps more accurately, for allowing them to choose how they would like to interface with you. It is likely that these skill sets will need to be sought outside the current aviation industry.

Top all that off with plenty of capital for investment—none of this is going to come cheap.

From the perspective of the airline CEO, this all sounds disruptive to think and difficult to do. No doubt, that is true. At the same time, standing in the path of progress yelling "stop!" is not destined to produce the industry's next winners. One of my observations is that doing hard things, and doing them well, is not only what separates the winners from the losers. Mastering the ability to do hard things often is the foundation of sustainable competitive advantage.

Once again, in *Designing Future-Oriented Airline Businesses*, Taneja provides the thought leadership about the future direction of the ever-volatile aviation industry. I am confident that this book will be read far and wide in the aviation industry. Most importantly, I believe we will see many of its ideas widely adopted.

Hong Kong, China

Foreword

Jeff Smisek

Chairman of the Board, President and Chief Executive Officer
United Airlines

If there's one thing I've learned in my nearly 20 years in the airline business, it's that the most successful competitors are those most willing to constantly change and adapt—after all, this is a business that evolves at 500 miles per hour. In his newest book, *Designing Future-Oriented Airline Businesses*—Professor Nawal Taneja outlines a compelling vision for the future of our rapidly-changing industry. Prof. Taneja's book comes along at a particularly interesting time in airline industry history, as airlines are moving away from survival-mode and into a position where they can operate as stable, successful businesses for passengers, employees and shareholders.

The airline industry of today is vastly different than the one I became a part of in 1995 when I joined Continental Airlines. Since then, we have struggled through the incredible tragedy of Sept. 11. We went through a terrible global recession that impacted business travel—our bread and butter—and froze the credit markets. We've been impacted by volatile fuel prices, multiple wars and other geopolitical events, pandemics, security events and natural disasters.

The airline industry has always been highly vulnerable to exogenous shocks, but even in the best of times, our business is tremendously complex. We're governed by diverse laws and regulations in the many countries we serve, we have co-workers and customers across the globe, many of us are highly unionized, and we have a very complicated operation that is impacted by many things that are outside of our control, like the weather. In addition, our industry is ferociously competitive. We compete vigorously with network and low-cost/new entrant carriers in our domestic markets. Globally we compete against carriers like those in the Middle East that benefit from positive, rather than detrimental, national airline policies that recognize the tremendous benefits that airlines provide to their nations' economies.

Given this backdrop of challenges, I can tell you that I'm more encouraged now than I have been at any time in my two decades in this industry. As we have worked our way through decades of challenges, we've reshaped ourselves, as an industry, by adapting to the evolving, increasingly global economy in which we operate.

Among other structural changes such as industry consolidation, airlines have become intensely focused on capacity discipline. We know we bring great economic benefits to the communities we serve, and we take that responsibility seriously. We always listen to our customers when we decide when and where to fly, but as an industry, airlines have been responsible about making sure our network decisions are sustainable over the long term. Additionally, airlines have become very focused on generating sufficient, sustained profitability so that we can continue to bring benefits to our customers, employees and shareholders.

Airlines have made tremendous strides toward behaving like not only airlines, but also like businesses. While we are still a long ways away from the profitability standards of other industries, we are no longer merely struggling to stay afloat. We can now focus on things like investing in new aircraft, investing in standards-based customer service training, investing in better and more modern facilities, investing in new tools so our employees can more efficiently serve our customers, investing in better technology so we can stay in touch with our customers and customize their travel experience, and investing in a product that gives customers more choices while offering new revenue streams for airlines.

Congratulations to Prof. Taneja on this compelling look into the forces that will shape our industry in the years to come. It's an exciting time to be in the airline business, and I look forward to seeing what the future holds.

Chicago, USA

Foreword

Rob Torres

Managing Director
Google, Inc.

The core experience of travel remains the same today as it has for years; the sights and sounds of a foreign destination are powerful, bringing new perspective and understanding of the world. However, today's travel is enabled and heightened by digital connection in ways previously unimaginable, with the internet used across all stages of travel—and on nearly *every* occasion for research and planning. It is within this new context of constant and pervasive connectivity that we must evolve our understanding of the consumer's expectations of the airline industry and our potential to improve the business from within. This newest book from Nawal Taneja, "Designing Future-Oriented Airline Businesses", is rooted in the fundamental notion that, based on this elevated level of connectivity, nothing will ever be the same for travelers or marketers.

In particular, we at Google have identified and are acting upon three distinct directional shifts in the travel industry. More than just trends for 2014, these shifts are ongoing and pervasive changes shaped by increasingly connected consumer behavior, defined by technological development, and validated by marketer action.

Nawal's book features examples from airline industry leaders who are looking forward as well as proposes a challenge to those who are not quite keeping up with the exponential change being driven in our industry by digital. When it comes down to it, our solutions come from the same source as our challenges: connectivity at the core.

Firstly, connectivity is fragmenting the traveler's pathway prior to purchase. What was a multi-step journey has now splintered further, with travelers planning and researching travel across multiple screens in "micro-increments". A recent Google study with Ipsos about multi-screen behavior revealed that travelers move across screens at all stages of the travel process, with 71% demonstrating sequential screen behavior for research and 35% for booking. Winning industry players will be the early movers who demonstrate that they are in tune with the connected consumer by building product and marketing strategies that provide a consumer with one seamless experience. With 26% of air queries coming through mobile devices, a company only thinking about desktop search is missing a full quarter of moments in which travelers are actively demonstrating travel-specific intent. Connectivity both fragments the process and serves up the technological platform to weave disparate moments of brand-consumer interaction together for even greater impact. One major retailer has actually built an in-house consumer experience panel that serves as an advisor for all digital solutions the brand undertakes; in the face of so many possible paths to booking, true success will be measured through the lens of user experience. Airlines who focus intently on user experience will be able to make the best of, rather than be hindered by, the fragmentation of the pre-trip pathway.

Secondly, connectivity is driving new patterns in content consumption by the traveler. As this book alludes to in Chapter 5—*Building Stronger Brands*—there is a major directional shift toward greater consumer demand for and interaction with content. Travelers are looking for more complete, robust content at their fingertips—wherever they may be. One billion photos are uploaded to the internet monthly. If you started watching travel content on YouTube today, you wouldn't finish until the year 2282. Without a doubt, airline brands must be concerned with the *curation* of this vast amount of content; when someone searches for a flight, what other information besides price and destination might be relevant factors to influence that traveler? In the end, more complete curation of relevant content will increase the likelihood that a consumer will engage with your brand.

In today's digital video ecosystem, it is not just about one:30 spot, but about related content that will inform, inspire, and entertain. Consider how one major beverage company showed a

Super Bowl commercial that earned 11 million+ views on YouTube (beyond the views it received on TV); though the main event was certainly memorable, the "behind the scenes" content of children singing in languages around the world (which required minimal production input) earned video views of over 200,000 apiece! Air travelers, especially business travelers, are spending an increasing amount of time with digital video and savvy airline brands are starting to capture this shift with behind-the-scenes, destination-specific, and collaborative content video collections. In today's world, the power to engage with content lies with the traveler, so airlines must think strategically about how to present relevant content at each point of consumer interaction as well as how to curate video in a manner that allows for ongoing, deeper brand engagement.

Thirdly, continuous connectivity has dramatically heightened the expectations that consumers have of travel brands. As Nawal mentions, big data must be not only mined for insights, but used as a driving force for ongoing sales and customer-relations activity. Our increasingly connected traveler expects that certain information about him/her will be known, without having to be explicitly given. A simple manifestation of this would be automatically populating the origin airport for a flight search, based on a user's location. In our historically data-driven industry, it is no surprise that many airlines are already integrating data-driven improvements in the path to purchase. The airline industry has the lowest customer satisfaction of any industry, sadly, so it is our responsibility to make the travel purchase process shorter, smoother, more enjoyable.

Today's traveler, however, also expects that travel brands will use available data cues to provide a more personalized trip. KLM is using social cues to craft an on-board activity beyond just getting to your destination. Virgin Atlantic is using Google Glass to provide customized drink service and flight status information to VIP flyers. This type of 1:1 attention is a far cry from simply sending ten free drink coupons every year—and never even tracking if those coupons are used. Additionally, eMarketer reports that 39% of airline passengers globally will use mobile devices to purchase ancillary services; that is clear revenue-related opportunity that stems from using cues from the connected traveler to surface relevant offerings at the right moment. Overall, there are very high expectations of travel companies today to entertain, inform, and provide utility; to do that, we need to leverage the digitally connected world to build an advanced understanding of the end consumer.

Google's well-known mantra is "Focus on the user and all else will follow." Well, our user is a traveler increasingly informed and delighted by digital connectivity. This book serves as an actionable guide for airline companies who are excited to view the connected traveler not as an obstacle, but as an opportunity. I look forward to seeing more airlines become truly future-oriented and thank Nawal for the insights that he is bringing to our industry.

Seattle, USA

Foreword

Erik Venter

Chief Executive Officer
Comair Limited

After a meeting and discussion with Nawal on the future shocks awaiting the airline industry, I concluded that what is new is not the occurrence of shocks, but the rate of change and the impact of change across a broader spectrum of employees. The historic shocks relating to the oil price, terrorism or engineering crises used to typically impact a specialized field within an airline. The new shocks will relate to integrated data, consumer behaviour, new alliances, etcetera, and will occur faster and require further reaching solutions. The real issue is therefore as much about how to deal with change, and specifically the accelerating rate of change, as it is about what specific changes we will be facing.

In fact, identifying the future challenges that each airline will face is perhaps the more difficult part of the equation, and so I will leave this to more learned colleagues who can speak with authority on consumer power, selling intermediaries, new alliance structures, big data, etc. I will stick to the simple topic of creating capacity for change.

But, first a bit of background. Comair was founded in 1946, and started operating on the main South African routes after deregulation of the domestic skies in 1992. It signed on as a British Airways franchise in 1996, and launched the first South African low cost carrier, kulula.com, in 2001. Today it still operates as a franchise of British Airways in Southern Africa and kulula.com has become a significant on-line distributor of travel inventory. The two brands carry approximately 5 million passengers a year in Southern Africa with a fleet of 22 scheduled Boeing 737's. Comair faces competition from the state funded South African Airways and its low cost subsidiary Mango, and has survived the launch and demise of 11 private airlines in the past 20 years. Comair has a history of 68 consecutive years of operating profits.

The three internal ingredients required to operate an airline are equipment, skills and corporate culture. It is the last component—also highlighted by Nawal in Chapter 8 of his book—that seems to get the least attention within the industry, perhaps because we are so notoriously focused on operations. All of our efforts tend to be spent on the logistics of the business, and this is the environment from which most of our managers are sourced, thereby perpetuating this focus. Yet when the pumpkin really hits the fan, it is the corporate culture that will determine whether an airline has the resilience to weather a shock without degenerating into a crisis.

If management can proactively build a culture that delivers innovation, accepts constant change, builds flexibility into solutions, and aligns the interest of the individual with that of the airline, then there will be few shocks that will catch the airline unawares, and/or not be dealt with in the ordinary course of business. Such a shock-proof culture is likely to exhibit some of the following:

1. Active monitoring of consumer trends and technology, and employees who are early adopters.
2. Flexible and dynamic medium term strategies and business models.
3. Structures for the fast delivery of solutions, such as an EPMO (enterprise project management office), a research unit with business analysts, partnering with technology providers, and flat decision making structures.
4. Flexibility built into supplier contracts, alliances, IT solutions and employee contracts.
5. Functional structures rather than divisional structures in the organization, or a combination in a matrix structure.
6. Active management of the corporate culture and of employee engagement.

The shock-proof culture therefore inherently builds the structures that support the values of this culture. However many of these structures require yet other components of culture to allow them to work, such as humility, recognition, tolerance, and teamwork. Building the complete cultural solution is therefore hard work. It needs to be lived from the top down; it needs consistent and transparent communication; it needs to be integrated with performance management and all HR policies; and it needs to be regularly refreshed. Clearly more than can be dealt with in these few paragraphs.

But the results are worth the work.

1. Employees support the initiatives of the airline if their risks and rewards are aligned with those of their employer. This also contributes to a longer term focus by employees.
2. All employees contribute solutions and efficiencies within their areas of influence, and self-regulate wastage.
3. Hierarchies are broken down if all employees, including the executives, demonstrate that they live by exactly the same code. This builds trust in management and therefore less resistance to change.
4. Employees actively participate in change, and look for the opportunities coming out of change.

This might all sound very cute and flowery, but being a pragmatic and stingy practitioner, I am not about cute and flowery. I am certain that the culture that has been built at Comair over many years was critical in allowing it to rapidly implement a crisis management strategy in 2011 when the combination of the oil price shock and a 70% increase in airport charges posed a real threat to its sustainability. The same culture has assisted Comair to make the systems, process and structural changes that delivered record profits in 2013, and will continue to keep Comair at the forefront of the aviation industry for many years to come.

Bonaero Park, South Africa

Foreword

Wang Yingming

Chairman
HNA Aviation Group Company Limited

The China civil aviation industry is on a fast and steady growth track, offering a promising future. In 2013, the total passenger traffic of the China aviation industry was 354 million, an 11% increase compared with 2012 and ranked number 2 worldwide. In 2013, a total of 10 airports in China had more than 20 million passenger volumes. It is predicted by the Civil Aviation Administration of China that the passenger traffic of China will reach over 700 million in 2020.

In this growing market, we will witness the profound changes of technology-driven innovation and passenger behavior. Some creative airlines in China such as Hainan Airlines have noted this and are adapting their business models gradually to be compatible with the changes.

Firstly, big data, social media, cloud computing, and mobile technology will bring changes to the ways of doing business in China.

Hainan Airlines and some other airlines in China are using big data to collect the passenger information from touch points. Passenger segmentation, marketing and passenger service will be oriented from a better understanding of individual demand with the support of big data and analytics.

Social media has become an effective way to communicate with customers and no airlines can ignore it. Wechat, China's largest social media platform, nowadays has more than 500 million users. Hainan Airlines has created its Wechat corporate account to release the company information regularly to the followers. Microblog is another popular social media platform in China. It offers a solution for corporate users to exchange information with the public. The fans of Hainan Airlines and its sister airlines' Microblog are over 4.30 million.

Mobile applications have become a part of the life style in China. By 2013, the users who surf the Internet by mobile phone reached 500 million. In less than 2 years, downloads of Hainan Airlines APP is over 1 million.

Secondly, the Chinese flying population keeps expanding as the disposable income grows and passengers are more conscious with the 3 Cs, which are Convenience, Control and Choice.

According to the report of McKinsey Insights China, the proportion of the middle class families with annual disposable income ranging from $16,000 to $34,000 will reach 51% by 2020, and that with annual disposable income above $34,000 will reach 6%. The two groups will compose 186 million families. With this expansion, more air transportation demand will be created. The middle class will no doubt occupy the main passenger market.

The characteristics of middle class passengers' consumption behavior are diversified, personalized and value conscious. According to the data released by the China National Tourism Administration in 2013, over 90% of Chinese travelers organized their trip by themselves, not by travel agencies. China's new generation are smart consumers, expecting to be recognized and respected as individual consumers, preferring relaxed journeys with self-control and multiple choices, and pursuing simplicity and convenience.

Technology-driven innovation and passenger behavior changes urge airlines to transform from carrier to retailer. Most Chinese airlines realized this and adopted initiative action on this. The business scope of HNA Aviation Group ranges from corporate jet, full service carrier to low cost carrier, offering a full series of products to the market. We also invest in hotels, travel agents, car rental and other aviation related businesses. We are now unbundling our service package and trying to give more choices to passengers with ancillary products based on their demands.

Professor Nawal K. Taneja is a respected expert in the airline industry and we have had many in-depth discussions. His "Designing Future-Oriented Airline Businesses" gives us new thoughts and visions on ways of doing business based on future perspectives. It addresses the challenges and opportunities facing the airline industry, provides us a deep insight on how to change the mindset, apply digital technology to establish a customer-centric business and create new business. He extends his demonstration on how to share travel margins by enhancing airline responses to customer needs and expectations with the use of new technologies.

Hainan, China

Foreword

Juan Carlos Zuazua

Chief Executive Officer
VivaAerobus

According to several global market forecasts, Latin America would be the second fastest growing aviation sector in the world, after the Middle East for the next 20 to 25 years.

Latin America is one of the most urbanized regions of the world, with a growing middle class, which is key for commercial aviation. Several studies forecast that Latam's middle class will represent 55% of its total population by 2032, with some regions leading and others lagging.

Mexico is Latam's second biggest country with a population of over 112 million. Currently a third of its population is middle class and it is expected to reach 50% by 2025, with an estimated annual GDP growth of at least 3%.

Clearly the macroeconomic factors are in place for a significant boost in air travel demand. The question I constantly ask myself is: Is the Latam Aviation Sector ready for this opportunity?

History tells us the Airline Industry has been unprofitable. Many factors support this:

1. The Aviation Sector is extremely unbalanced, with some key players in the value chain like Airports having ridiculous margins, particularly in Latam & Mexico, whilst most airlines have tiny margins and just a few make good profits like Ryanair, Southwest, easyJet, Copa, Allegiant and Spirit.
2. Historically most airlines were run by governments, and there was no interest or willingness on making profits. Most of these airlines were privatized to rich business men, who inherited a bureaucratic organization with people and habits hard to change.

3. Finally, the combination in Airline owners and managers of EGO + PRIDE + MONEY is the perfect recipe to erode shareholder value and turn a billion dollars into a million dollars.

Fortunately the aviation industry is so critical for the world's and regional economies and so linked to GDP growth that all key players within the whole sector are finally getting to work together and realizing that the passenger has the right to choose. If the sector as a whole is not willing to change, become more efficient and provide affordable air travel, the industry will not be able to capture the opportunities on growing economies.

Now let's focus on Mexico and the opportunity for air travel. On 2013 nearly 30 million passengers took a domestic flight within the country, while 2,700 million passengers took a domestic bus journey within Mexico. Yes, 2.7 billion passengers traveled by bus, this is a huge number. And the reason for this huge difference is mainly related to price. We have indeed a very big market; unfortunately it is very price sensitive.

I'm a Mexican with the privilege of running one of the most efficient young airlines in the world. VivaAerobus has a fleet of nineteen 737-300s, and we are in the process or renovating our entire fleet and moving to the A320 family within the next 3 years, with a recent fleet order of fifty two A320s. We have succeeded in becoming the lowest cost operator in the Americas, and most importantly a profitable one. This is a result of running an airline with staff that believes in the low cost culture and "walk the talk". Our staff focuses in maximizing productivity and making our operation more efficient every single day, which allows us to reduce our cost. Staff who constantly says NO to "good" or "sexy" things, and most importantly that keeps in mind our most valuable stakeholders: Our passengers and our shareholders.

What I have found in this industry is that traditionally airline managers focus their time in trying to meet passengers' "Wants". At VivaAerobus we focus on trying to meet the passengers' "Basic Needs", and this is an enormous difference.

Any passenger will always have a lot and constantly changing number of "Wants", while his or her "Basic Needs" would rarely change. The need to travel from one point to another, paying an affordable price, flying safe and on time, and having an efficient travel experience which commences the day they book airline tickets and ends when baggage is delivered.

At VivaAerobus we focus on a strategy called "Easy to Buy – Easy to Fly" which centers in meeting the passenger "Basic Needs". These needs may be different according to geographical regions, and they might also evolve with new technologies in the market.

To give a couple of examples:

1. When we started our LCC in Monterrey, Mexico back in November 2006, we thought most of our reservations would be done online and paid with a credit card. However, Mexican credit card penetration is less 0.15 credit card per capita (vs 2 credit cards per capita in the US). Internet penetration is growing by double digits thanks to the world's richest man Carlos Slim, and so is the mobile penetration. So there was no doubt we needed to innovate: we became the first airline in Mexico to allow a passenger to book online with a Cash Payment option; we will hold the reservation for 24 hours while the passengers goes to a convenience store called OXXO (+10,000 stores in MEX) and pay CASH!

2. Transferring bus passengers to the air has proven to be a not easy task, but we have been succeeding. While Internet is growing in Mexico, the vast majority of transportation is happening in bus stations (2.7 billion domestic bus passengers vs 30 million domestic air passengers). Thanks to our Mexican shareholder Grupo IAMSA, the biggest bus conglomerate in Mexico, we were able to design and implement the world's only *Bus to Air Trade Up System*. By linking VivaAerobus' reservation system with the bus companies' reservation systems, we gained access to over 300 bus stations in Mexico. Therefore, we are able to trade-up the bus passenger in the same bus station and counter they purchase bus seats. It is as simple and seamless as going to McDonalds and asking for a *Super Size* option on your fries and drink! Thanks to this initiative, nearly 20% of our sales occur in bus stations. We are giving Mexicans the opportunity to fly for the very first time!

These are just some examples how we need to think not only "Outside the Box" but "In a New Box".

What I really liked about reading "Designing Future-Oriented Airline Businesses" is the approach of seeing an airline not only as a transportation company, but as an e-commerce / retailer / transportation company. This approach provides a lot of value to consumers in meeting their basic needs and other features that they might buy before or after the traditional airline booking experience.

This book will challenge airline managers like me to constantly take a deep dive in the ways we are doing things and ask ourselves whether there are new or more efficient ways of doing business. This book provides real good examples on how passengers are evolving, and so are their basic needs, for instance the need of getting efficient and timely information before, during and after his travel experience.

I would like to congratulate Mr. Nawal Taneja on this exciting new book and my sincere recognition to his endless efforts in constantly challenging this unique and passionate industry.

Mexico City, Mexico

Preface

Designing Future-Oriented Airline Businesses is the eighth book in a series that addresses the ongoing challenges and opportunities facing all generations of airlines. It challenges and encourages managements to take a deeper dive into new ways of doing business. This need for airlines to explore new ways of doing business is the result of the following five trends:

1. Customers, armed with abundant information and engaged in social media, are looking for value, increased transparency, and more personalized services.
2. Customers expect their needs and preferences to be evaluated from timely and meaningful engagements with them as well as analyses of hard data, and not from management's conventional wisdom and beliefs.
3. Customers expect companies to redesign their business systems and processes, as well as to acquire the necessary human skills to make it easy to do business with them and have a positive experience in the purchase and delivery of services.
4. Customers are comparing their experience with airlines to what other companies are providing, both established and new, such as, ALDI, Amazon, and Uber.
5. The availability of information, social media, and analytics makes it possible for (1) customer demand to be aggregated from otherwise unconnected customers, and (2) powerful information synthesizing companies to enter the distribution arena.

Designing Future-Oriented Airline Businesses shows how an airline management can respond to these trends and redesign its airline business to become a high margin and a sought-after brand. The key element is a change in focus, for example, to change from managing costs incrementally to dramatically transforming revenue streams beyond the current strategy to increase ancillary revenues through fee-based products and services. This change in focus is not to imply that costs are not important; but rather, that airlines have gained significant achievements in the cost area and that further decreases would be marginal. Dramatically transforming the revenue streams, on the other hand, is not going to be achieved simply by developing superior products with the hope that they lead to a lasting competitive advantage. Rather, the comparative advantage (as opposed to the competitive advantage) will be derived from "downstream" opportunities created through an engagement with customers using technology. As such, it provides a framework for identifying and developing strategies and capabilities, as well as executing them efficiently and effectively to change the focus from cost reduction to revenue enhancement and from competitive advantage to comparative advantage.

The main audience of this series continues to be senior-level practitioners of differing generations of airlines worldwide as well as related businesses. The material presented continues to be at a pragmatic level, not an academic exercise, to lead managements to undertake some critical thinking by asking themselves and their teams some thought provoking questions, including some questions about conventional wisdom in this industry:

1. How can managements develop strategic foresights by asking "what business are we in and what are the best ways to use our limited resources?"
2. Doesn't innovation go beyond adding incremental features to products and extending the brands, for example, to competing in new ways by not just "thinking outside the box," but, "thinking in a new box" —electronic luggage tags with intermodal transfer capabilities, end-to-end travel experience, door-to-door travel?
3. Are airlines mistakenly raising customer expectations by continuously providing higher and higher value that gets taken for granted and, therefore, not seen as value?
4. Where is mobile technology heading, and what is the implication for airline strategies, given that travel, by its nature, is mobile?

5. Is the airline industry focused more on competitors than on customers, particularly with respect to lacking knowledge of their behavior as well as their articulated and unarticulated needs?

6. Is the airline customer *focused* or customer *centric*? Where should it be on the customization spectrum given its stage of growth, resources, and value proposition(s)?

7. What do different segments of customers want, and even more important, are they willing to pay for what they say that they want?

8. How can an airline deliver, and charge for, meaningful, consistent, and predictable value?

9. What are some ways to provide customers a differentiated experience (physical and digital), not just during the travel, but also during the shopping phase—experience that relates, for example, not just to the functionality of the website, but also its design, such as the least number of clicks to find an answer?

10. How should different airlines provide their content within the travel trade, given the proliferation (and now cross over) of search engines that deliver market transparency, not just with respect to price and schedules, but also such features as the availability of Wi-Fi, USB ports, images and descriptions of meals, and videos showing the configuration of seats with respect to pitch, width, and degree of recline?

11. Are airlines providing sufficient information or do consumers want more detail that they can now get through third parties, raising the probability of new and progressive intermediaries?

12. Airlines seem to be "pushing" information, either directly or through intermediaries. Should they be focused more on the type of information that consumers want to "pull" based on their preferences, behaviors, and situations?

13. How much personal information is needed to engage with each customer individually, and at the level each desires, to provide a better experience but at the same time protect privacy and security?

14. Are airline marketing initiatives inadequate given airlines' traditional "laser-like" focus on the complexity of the airline

business, the scale of operations, and inward design thinking based on the belief that the airline industry is quite different from other business sectors?

15. Are airlines truly "earning" customer preference or are they merely "buying" customer loyalty through free tickets, upgrades, early boarding, and access to airport lounges?

16. Shouldn't airlines build stronger brands by linking better their branding and business strategies and shouldn't management have a "laser-like" focus on the relevancy feature of brands?

17. Does being a member of an alliance build brand equity? Should some airlines pay more attention to vertical alliances (possibly with technology businesses fortified with compelling information that is synthesized, and with data mining capabilities to capitalize on future opportunities), than horizontal alliances (with more airlines as partners to share codes, loyalty programs, and airport lounges)?

18. Should airlines develop the needed technologies and innovation competency internally or go outside their own organizations?

19. Is air travel perceived to be "cool" or "painful" and should airlines be working to add to the "cool experience" or providing "pain relief?"

20. If technology, particularly information technology, is growing explosively and if global markets are becoming highly diverse, then how are these two developments stretching the competitive landscape?

21. In trying to answer these questions, should leadership frame and articulate a vision in terms of a "story"—a business narrative that connects, engages, and inspires employees at all levels (through the addition of an emotional dimension), provides a clear time horizon (from start to finish), and links the past with the present and the future in a narrative form, instead of numbers?

Exploring such basic questions, merging business and brand strategies, engaging with customers and employees, collaborating with partners, and connecting the dots to explore the white spaces to design the airline business, will lead to transformative, as opposed to incremental ("me-too") changes to make "real" money.

Based on the author's own experience and ongoing work in the global airline industry, as well as through a synthesis of leading business practices, both inside and outside of the industry, this book builds upon some concepts contained in previous books in this series. These areas include business model innovation, value propositions, segmentation, pricing, distribution, branding, loyalty, and technology (in this case, big data and analytics, as well as mobile, social, and the Cloud). It builds upon these concepts by conveying contemporary thoughts on the framework in which to pursue the redesign of the business based upon relevant findings, as well as examples, including five Thought Leadership Pieces in Chapter 9.

Designing Future-Oriented Airline Businesses tries to demystify numerous concepts being discussed within the airline industry (customer centricity, personalization, big data, merchandising versus retailing, dynamic content distribution, earning versus buying loyalty, and so forth) and to facilitate managements to identify and articulate the boundaries of their business models. It provides material which managements can sort through to answer the above questions, especially with respect to strategies, capabilities, and execution. They can choose the degree and type of actions to test or redesign depending on the mandates set by leadership, the available resources such as time, money, and capability, as well as the specific situations relating to the stage of development of an airline or its base of operations. Whichever business model is selected, it must be flexible to make iterations. With respect to timeliness, airlines, in the past, have tended to wait to implement major transformations until it is almost too late — when they are literally at the verge of bankruptcy, and, in some cases, did file for bankruptcy. American Airlines and Japan Airlines are just two examples. Successful managements need to master both "fast" and "slow" thinking. Was Southwest too slow to change or has AirAsia been too fast? And, as to the viability of strategies over a longer period of time, the book suggests that managements should foster a culture of experimentation and iteration (given the increase in uncertainty), exemplified by the initiatives of jetBlue, Norwegian, Qantas, and Singapore Airlines.

The key message for airline managements is that they should consider focusing more on the revenue side ("downstream") than on the cost side ("upstream") by responding to customers through analyses of their behaviors and through interactions and engagements within an acceptable framework of consumer privacy relating to the use of personal information. If airlines do not undertake such analyses and respond, new tech-savvy intermediaries will, and they, in turn, will have the opportunity to make enormous profit margins. The question then is: What margins will be made by airlines versus new intermediaries entering the travel trade, especially the new technology companies who have enormous power to "mine and synthesize big data" and transform through the use of social technology to supply the type of information and travel-related services that airlines and existing intermediaries are not providing but that consumers are seeking? History could repeat itself with respect to the enormous disparity relating to margins earned by airlines versus other members within the travel chain.

Chapter 1
Rethinking the Airline Business: Where Do We Stand?

The Director General and CEO of IATA, Tony Tyler, described "the natural state of the airline industry as being in crisis, interrupted by brief moments of calm." Thus, while change, or even its rate, is hardly a new phenomenon within the airline industry, uncertainty, risks, a sense of urgency, and, particularly, the need to experiment and iterate are now becoming much greater for all segments within the global airline industry. From this perspective, while many airlines have been changing their business models to adapt to the marketplace, the changes, with very few exceptions, have been at the incremental level rather than at the transformative level. On the other hand, at least, the 12 challenges mentioned in this chapter are mandating airline managements to go beyond incremental changes and to rethink, realign, and, possibly even, reinvent, their businesses by gaining insights from both inside and outside the airline industry. Although growth has varied by region, the global airline industry has been, and continues to be, a high growth industry. To continue to capitalize on this growth, while facing the challenges of new entrants that are rapidly adapting to the changing landscape, the established airlines need to move at a much faster rate of transformation.

Business Model Transformation Spectrum

At what point on the business model transformation spectrum should an airline be—incremental, or transformative, or somewhere in between? Consider some examples at the two ends of the spectrum. Two examples of incremental strategies (of short term nature) are: (1) changes in capacity to match demand, and (2) some new fee-based services. Two recent examples of transformative changes (longer term strategies) are: (1) pursuit of mergers to increase economies of scale to reduce cost and economies of scope to increase market share, and (2) virtual operations. Incremental changes, while being relatively easier, are not going to address the 12 challenges (discussed below) facing the industry, other than for airlines with special circumstances, such as, government protection (for instance, Air India) and special niche markets (for instance, British Airways at Heathrow). Even the assumption of "too big to fail" has proven to be invalid. Inertia and scale alone ("too big to fail") did not prevent American Airlines and Japan Airlines from filing for bankruptcy. The other two circumstances may enable, at least in the foreseeable future, some airlines to continue to work with incremental changes.

Let us examine the need for realignments of airline businesses at the transformative level from a more fundamental perspective shown by the information in Figure 1.1. On a worldwide basis, in 2012 airlines earned a mere US$2.60 in net profit on each departing passenger on a revenue base of more than $200. How does this figure compare with the profit margins on a cup of Starbucks coffee or a bottle of Coca-Cola in a restaurant in Europe? Shouldn't airline shareholders expect a far better financial performance given the required level of investments and the level of risks? Assuming the answer to be yes, managements need to adopt a transformative vision and culture, supported by disruptive technologies (relating to information, analytics, and mobility), dramatic changes in processes and functions, as well as insights from the best practices from both inside and outside the industry to dramatically improve the margins. From this perspective, a few airlines are beginning to "see" that the future shape of the airline business is at a point of inflection—just as when American, in the very early 1980s, used the then big data and analytics to analyze the reservations and booking data to undertake what was at that time known as "yield management." It is this process that enabled airlines to match low fares offered by low cost airlines and reserve seats for high paying passengers booking closer to the flight departure times. Now, big data, analytics, and digital

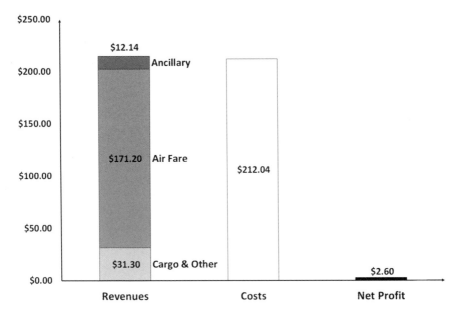

Figure 1.1   Costs, revenues, and profits on a typical flight
Source: International Air Transport Association

technology (including mobile) can be used to redesign the airline business, just as Uber transformed the traditional taxi business.

Need for Realignment

Leaving aside the historical poor margins, here are at least 12 other considerations supporting the need to redesign the airline business at various levels.

1. Competition is now no longer limited to traditional peers. New players from within the airline business are succeeding with new business models, attacking areas considered to be critical for traditional airlines—for example, (1) feeder traffic from short and medium haul markets, specifically in Europe, and (2) emerging hubs, at such alternative airports as Panama, Istanbul, Addis Ababa, Dubai, Guangzhou, and Honolulu. Moreover, there is room at the low end for competition from even newer types of airlines given that it is *relatively* easy to start an airline (with barriers to entry being *relatively* low even though they continue to exist).

2. The relatively newer generation of global airlines, such as those based in the Persian Gulf, and to some extent those based in China, are proving that they not only have staying power, but that they intend to change the historical airline industry landscape. Etihad Airways is not only growing its own capacity, but it is also implementing truly strategic relationships with existing airlines—some through codeshares (such as with Air France–KLM) and some through equity positions (such as with Aer Lingus, Air Berlin, Air Seychelles, Darwin Airline—renamed as Etihad Regional, Jat Airways, Jet Airways, and Virgin Australia).[1]

3. Investors in the airline industry are no longer mostly "day traders." Many investors now have a much longer term orientation. This change is requiring airline CEOs to focus much more on the quarterly and annual financial performance.

4. Lower cost airlines are finally finding the ingredients to succeed in intercontinental and business travel markets, validated by the operations of Jetstar and Virgin Australia. This phenomenon will proliferate as airlines get new aircraft such as the Boeing 787 and the Airbus 350 (with the right cost performance features) and as they develop new operational capability. Norwegian Air Shuttle, for example, uses a new operating certificate (Norwegian Long Haul AS), the fuel efficient Boeing 787 (with 291 seats in a two-class configuration) and non-Norwegian-based, lower cost crews working out of Bangkok to operate in such markets as Bangkok–Oslo–New York.

5. Niche airline service providers are beginning to emerge around specific segments of the market to position their products and services to match the demand. For example, the US-based Allegiant is a travel company that happens to operate an airline. In Brazil, Azul Brazilian Airlines has been extremely successful in providing service in noncompetitive markets. In Iceland, Icelandair is achieving profitable growth by using its Reykjavik hub to transport passengers between North America and Europe. In Mexico (VivaAerobus) and in Colombia (VivaColombia), are ultra low cost airlines that are competing with buses in medium and long haul markets.

6. Increasing liberalization of air transport markets, particularly in the Asia Pacific region, is enabling new-generation airlines with profoundly different business models to be serious threats to mature airlines. AirAsia Berhad, for example, has been able to find creative ways to integrate its resources to set up operations throughout Asia.

7. A shift in the economic power from the Atlantic to the Pacific is creating unprecedented opportunities for airlines. Figure 1.2 shows the expected growth in the middle classes — segments with the means to purchase tickets to fly on airplanes in Asia compared to other global regions. The actual and expected rise in lower fare travel warrants a major shift in the airline business models, especially of traditional legacy carriers. And, the proactive airlines are moving fast, exemplified by the change in strategies of Singapore Airlines (expanding its brand portfolio) and Qantas Airways, not only setting up a virtual airline operation (with Emirates Airline), but also expanding the operations of its subsidiary, Jetstar Airways.

8. Enlightened governments, for example, in Panama, Colombia, and Peru, are beginning to facilitate the development of aviation facilities, recognizing the huge contribution of the aviation sector to their local economies. The government initiatives may involve the expansion of an airport, coordination among the government, airport and airline policies (as in Panama), or the authorization to allow new entrants (as with VivaColombia).

9. Maturing low cost airlines focused on national markets, having begun to face legacy-like challenges (relative to the workforce, systems, and maturing markets), are expanding into traditional business markets and entering international markets via mergers, codeshares, and indirect networks. Examples of the first include GOL Transportes Aéreos, JetBlue Airways, and Southwest Airlines. An example of the third is WestJet Airlines, intending to fly across the Atlantic from Toronto and Ottawa, in Canada to Dublin, in Ireland with a stop in St. John's.

10. The availability of the astounding breadth and depth of information has led to significant transparency in passenger fares, leading, in turn, to heightened price competition. Since

most airlines have accepted their business to be more or less a commodity business, airlines with lower cost structures have been winning in the marketplace.

11. The emergence of external organizations providing intelligent and trusted search is leading to disintermediation of the airline to its customers, causing airlines to lose interaction with potential passengers. These businesses, armed with the capability to deploy vast quantities of information (especially unstructured data from sources such as social media) and advanced analytics show the potential to become new powerful intermediaries. These new, non-airline entrants have the competency, agility, resources, and connections to offer travel-related services and market personalized itineraries, including the support of 24/7 travel concierges.

12. The relationship between airlines and airports is changing. Some airports, for example, have begun to bid for service from airlines. At the extreme, Ryanair Ltd has a Request For Proposal website via which airports can submit bids for Ryanair to provide a scheduled service.

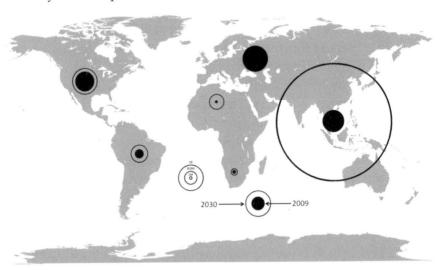

Figure 1.2   Global middle class in 2009 and prediction for 2030

Source: International Air Transport Association (the OECD, and Standard Chartered Research)

Blurring of Airline Classifications

Before discussing these points, it might be helpful to mention that the distinction between low cost airlines and full service airlines is blurring with the entrance of hybrid airlines. Initially, the low cost airlines had some or all of the following attributes:

- lower fares with simple fare structures;
- no frill service;
- one aircraft type;
- high density and single-class seating;
- point-to-point service in short and medium haul markets;
- no interline services;
- service to secondary airports;
- distribution through an airline's website;
- high fleet utilization through fast turnaround times;
- no membership with a globally branded alliance.

Then, when some full service airlines began to adopt selected features of low cost airlines and some low cost airlines began to adopt selected features of the full service airlines, the term "hybrid" appeared. For example, while low cost airlines had an excellent capability to distribute their products to price sensitive (non-business) segments in domestic markets with the use of an airline's website, the distribution process was much too complex to cater to the needs of travelers coming through the corporate departments, through travel agents, and passengers traveling in international markets. Consequently, low cost airlines needed the capability to use multiple channels to distribute their products— their own websites, call centers, mobile apps, and agents (both online and brick-and-mortar) to broaden the reach to attract higher yield passengers such as the corporate segment and to support interline connections. EasyJet Airline, for example, began to use all three of the major Global Distribution Systems (GDSs) to increase the number of corporate travelers (price sensitive but higher yield), a segment now approaching almost 25 percent of its total passengers. Air Berlin is a member of the oneworld alliance and, as such, needs, eventually, to be able to codeshare, interline, and participate in other alliance partners' loyalty programs. It is also noteworthy that the distinction between the above mentioned categories is also blurring in that a number of full service airlines have also developed their own low cost divisions.

Low cost airlines offer more than one quarter of the seats on a worldwide basis and the number could easily approach one third by the end of 2015. The percentage varies by region and by country. Within Southeast Asia, for example, low cost airlines account for more than one half of the total seats. The variation among countries, with respect to low cost airlines' penetration, is also significant. The penetration within the Philippines is about one third. However, the Philippines even has two low cost airlines that offer long haul services, Cebu Pacific Air and AirPhil Express.

Based on the aforementioned 12 considerations, airlines are beginning, albeit at different paces, to design market-oriented businesses. For their part, network airlines have already adopted many features of traditional low cost airlines such as the unbundling of the product and à la carte pricing systems. Some are also redesigning their short haul operations. Lufthansa German Airlines, for example, is strengthening and clarifying the role of its Germanwings brand. Aer Lingus not only *provides* service in short haul markets for other airlines, but also *receives* short haul service from other airlines for its own operations. Japan Airlines is outsourcing some of its short haul operations to Jetstar while All Nippon Airways is doing the same thing with Peach Aviation. Even China Airlines and Transaero have announced their decision to launch low cost subsidiaries, leading to the availability of low cost service in all ten of the top ten markets in Asia's Northeast/Southeast region.

The airline industry is also gaining insights from experimentation and iteration around the world. AirAsia and Malaysia Airlines took an equity position in each other and attempted to create a powerful alliance with government approval. The experiment failed. AirAsia also attempted to start a low cost operation in Japan in cooperation with All Nippon Airways. The concept was not readily accepted either by the general public, or by the legacy carriers. However, the experiment did provide valuable insights for future initiatives.

Some traditional low cost airlines are beginning to add features normally associated with full service network airlines, for example, service to conventional airports, multiple fleet types, interline agreements, and distribution through GDSs. JetBlue, for example, has hubs at high cost major airports such as New York Kennedy and Boston Logan, operates two types of airplanes, offers a quasi-two-class cabin, flies to destinations in the Caribbean and South America, has codeshare agreements with about 30 airlines, and offers its products through multiple channels. This convergence in market positioning is leading to the establishment of hybrid airlines, exemplified by the operations of JetBlue, Vueling Airlines, and Virgin Australia that totally rebranded itself. Virgin Australia flies large aircraft such as the Boeing 777 with a three-class configuration featuring a seat selection system, offers in-flight entertainment and in-flight connectivity, has a frequent flyer program, offers airport lounges, and has developed a partnership with major intercontinental players such as Delta Air Lines, Etihad, Singapore Airlines, Tiger Airways, and Virgin Atlantic. Consequently, while the traditional airline classification structure (legacies, low cost airlines, and ultra low cost airlines) is blurring, this book will use it because the transition is not yet complete. Carriers in each classification are adopting the best features from other classifications. For example, à la carte pricing schemes, first implemented by low cost airlines, are now being adopted by legacy carriers. Multiclass configurations used by legacy carriers are now being used by some low cost airlines.

While some airlines have made great strides, there is a tension that exists in that the changes in operations and products (introduced by all sectors of the industry, low cost, full service, and hybrids) are in the right direction and they are necessary, but they are not sufficient to meet the ever increasing demand and expectations of empowered consumers and the needs of the airlines to enhance their margins commensurate with their investments and risks relative to other businesses. The step they need to take is to move further in the direction of customer centricity (described in Chapter 3) by capitalizing on the digital and mobile spaces. This tension is not only beginning to be recognized but is also being addressed by the more innovative airlines. Consider three innovation ambitious airline examples below, JetBlue,

Qantas, and Singapore Airlines, showing how some carriers are beginning to make changes that are fundamental, structural, and of a longer term nature. While Qantas clearly falls in the category of a transformational change that is likely to be more permanent, both JetBlue and Singapore Airlines fall more in an experimental category.

Three Examples of Airline Transformation

JetBlue Airways
JetBlue's vision and strategy not only represents a "contrarian" concept but its business model has been a market disruptor from the beginning. Launched in February 2000, the founders set out to disrupt the leisure route coach concept that existed at that time. JetBlue set out to offer customers a better *experience*, a concept new at that time in the airline industry, and at a lower price. Consider just a few significantly different elements in its business model:

- It started with a base at New York's Kennedy Airport, a high cost and a congested airport, instead of a small secondary airport.
- It selected new airplanes (Airbus 320s) with leather seats, instead of 15 to 20-year-old airplanes.
- It started with a state-of-the-art in-flight entertainment system, featuring, for example, satellite television and radio offered at no charge.

This contrarian viewpoint continued as JetBlue expanded its operations. For example:

- It added a second type of aircraft (Embraer 190s) when the conventional wisdom was to stay with a single type of aircraft.
- It reduced the number of seats in the mainline fleet, enabling it to reduce the number of flight attendants required by the regulatory body and save fuel from the resulting lower aircraft weight, rather than increase the number of seats to reduce seat mile costs.

- It introduced a new product, "Even More Space."

And JetBlue's transformation, based on the contrarian vision and strategy, is continuing:

- It does not charge for the transportation of the first bag that is checked.
- It did not join a major global alliance but, instead, chose to develop more than 30, one-way interline and codeshare agreements with other airlines.
- It made significant investments in information technology that not only led to a superior product (onboard TV, for example), but also enabled the airline to develop partnerships with airlines from all over the world in order to increase the number of destinations offered worldwide.
- It is planning to introduce not only lie-flat seats, but also lie-flat suites. See Figure 2.2 in the next chapter.

Clearly, the vision and the strategy not only proved to be a success, but they led other airlines to find new ways to compete. For example, it was partially JetBlue's entry into the marketplace that led Delta to launch Song. Moreover, JetBlue's value proposition (an upscale product at a better price) also shed some light on conventional wisdom in a number of areas. For example, conventional wisdom was that the New York–Florida market had matured. JetBlue's initial growth, coupled with its subsequent development of a significant hub at Fort Lauderdale, show much room for development.

One key component of JetBlue's transformational plan is its selected position on the segmentation spectrum. In the "JetBlue Analyst Day" Presentation, management clearly outlined three pillars of their plan—"differentiated product, competitive costs, and high value geography."[2] Consider the first element. For a hybrid airline (a mid frill carrier), entering the US transcontinental market (premium and highly profitable) with a premium product (such as a uniquely designed seat accompanied by a sophisticated "Fly-Fi" in-flight connectivity system) could be a game changing development. JetBlue came up with its own approach (finding its own partner and using a Ka-band satellite-based solution), leading to a higher quality product at a lower cost. As for costs, JetBlue's unit costs lie between the low cost carriers and the network carriers. With respect to the "high value geography" element, JetBlue is concentrating on hubs at five focus airports in terms of size and location—Kennedy, Boston, Fort Lauderdale, Orlando, and San Juan—enabling penetration in the Caribbean and the northern part of South America with the existing fleet. As for the targeted segment, JetBlue sees its "sweet spot" to be the group between the "High Value Leisure" and "Mixed Wallets"— passengers who fly for business and leisure. Although this is viewed as their main focus, JetBlue is careful not to overlook the subsegment of "Road Warriors"—passengers making a couple of dozen trips per year—in selected markets, such as some in and out of Boston. See Figure 3.5 in Chapter 3. For both segments, the transformation objective reported appears to be "a preferred product in a commodity business."

Qantas Airways
Qantas, based in a country with a relatively small population and a large landmass (being an end-of-the-line carrier), facing unusually heavy competition, has had to redesign its business exploring numerous strategic alternatives. In domestic markets, Qantas was performing reasonably well in light of its four competitive advantages, namely: (1) a two-thirds of the domestic market share in terms of passengers and more in terms of revenue, (2) a lion's share of the corporate and government travel market, (3) significant influence over the distribution chain, and (4) a financially strong frequent flyer program. However, in international markets, Qantas had been performing poorly, not to mention that its dominance in regional markets was eroding.

Qantas undertook seven dramatic initiatives in order to deal with its loss making international and regional operations: (1) the development of a hub located outside its country, (2) expansion and integration within Asia, (3) the start of a dual brand with a different type of a low cost subsidiary, (4) the development of a virtual network by partnering with Emirates (the "asset light model"), (5) the grounding of the entire mainline fleet (more than 100 aircraft) in October 2011 to resolve ongoing industrial disputes and achieve a viable labor cost base and operational flexibility from staff, (6) realignment of its routes to South and North America, and (7) pointing out to the Australian Government that the playing field is uneven, given significant ownership of Virgin Australia by Etihad Airways, Singapore Airlines, and Air New Zealand. Within the entire global airline industry, these initiatives can certainly be considered to be of a transformative nature. For example, the partnership with Emirates will link Qantas's European kangaroo route services over Dubai instead of over Singapore, enabling Qantas to focus more on the traffic between Australia and Asia. For example, flights to and from Asia could be scheduled to meet the needs of the local origin and destination traffic. Moreover, Qantas could also link, to some extent, its flights to Asia with Emirates's flights to and from Asia. As for the realignment of routes to and from the Americas, the flights to Buenos Aires, Argentina were moved to Santiago, Chile where they could be codeshared with LAN (a oneworld alliance partner) and Qantas formed a joint venture with American and initiated flights to and from Dallas–Fort Worth airports.

The Jetstar initiative consisted of a group of value-based airlines based in six countries: Jetstar Airways based in Australia and New Zealand (wholly owned by the Qantas Group); Jetstar Asia based in Singapore (49 percent owned by the Qantas Group); Jetstar Pacific based in Vietnam (30 percent owned by the Qantas Group); Jetstar Japan (a joint venture with Japan Airlines); and Jetstar Hong Kong (in partnership with China Eastern Airlines and the Qantas Group). The Jetstar subsidiaries, again, of a transformative nature, provided three fundamental advantages:

- They insulated Qantas from low cost airlines competition (Virgin Blue from the year 2000 on).
- They complemented service on marginal international routes (by Jetstar Airways, for example, to Japan).
- They provided a platform for expansion into Asia (starting in Southeast Asia). As of the beginning of 2014, Jetstar is also planning to have a base in Hong Kong, Jetstar Hong Kong.

The Jetstar subsidiaries are also strategic for future growth outside of Asia. For example, Jetstar could easily start service to Europe from its base(s) in Asia using the Boeing 787–9s and

Singapore, Bangkok, and Hong Kong could become connecting hubs to compete effectively with Singapore Airlines and the Persian Gulf-based airlines. As for Hong Kong, it is a gateway to China even though it does not enable Jetstar to serve the domestic market within China (Hong Kong being a regional market that is regulated by different aviation policies than those for Mainland China). However, taking over some of the routes flown by China Eastern from Hong Kong to the Mainland will provide a good entry point into the Chinese market. Jetstar Airways could also start service to the US, either on some marginal routes or to complement routes flown by Qantas. While providing these strategic benefits for Qantas, Jetstar also benefits from the purchasing power of Qantas, codeshares with full service airlines, and participates in Qantas's powerful frequent flyer program that includes numerous arrangements with a wide array of retailers.

Singapore Airlines
Singapore Airlines had been facing challenges on all fronts since the beginning of this century—a lower level of growth, loss of market share to budget airlines growing in the region, rapid rise of carriers based in the Persian Gulf (and, more recently, some based in China, such as China Southern) engaging in the carriage of the kangaroo traffic, and a reduction in profits. Low fare traffic in and out of Changi Airport began to increase (now approaching 30 percent compared to zero in 2003 and compared to less than 10 percent at Hong Kong). To deal with these challenges, the airline decided to balance its portfolio by (1) rebranding the two existing subsidiaries and adding a new subsidiary to compete in the rapidly growing budget and regional markets, and (2) rationalizing its global network.

Singapore Airlines already owned a full service subsidiary, SilkAir (Singapore) Private Limited, that operated in short and medium haul markets to serve the higher end of the budget market (two-class cabins, power outlets, drop down screens, downloadable wireless in-flight entertainment), and fed the long haul operations of Singapore Airlines that operated only wide body aircraft. SilkAir—celebrating its twenty-fifth anniversary in February 2014, was neither a low cost carrier nor even a hybrid carrier. It was simply a short haul operator with lower operating costs than its parent. Even with a fleet of almost 50 aircraft (Airbus 319/320 and Boeing 737s), it is a relatively small subsidiary, accounting for about 6 percent of Singapore Airlines Group's revenues. Within the rebranded initiative, Singapore Airlines decided to grow SilkAir within Asia and, in the case of India, for example, have it either replace Singapore Airlines's routes in India, or supplement them, or serve routes that were not served by Singapore Airlines. There are huge growth opportunities for SilkAir to serve the fast growing secondary markets in countries such as China, India, and Indonesia, both as point-to-point services as well as connecting services for Singapore Airlines, especially in the future with the new-generation aircraft, such as the 31 slightly longer range Boeing 737 MAX8s on order. In January 2014, SilkAir served 45 destinations across 12 countries, with Singapore–Kathmandu as the longest route (about five hours). In future it could serve routes as long as eight hours. Recently, SilkAir formed a joint venture with Nok Air, a low cost airline based in Thailand.

Singapore Airlines also had an interest in Tiger Airways (launched in 2004) that operated within Asia (offering services on a point-to-point basis at the lower end of the market) as well as in domestic markets within Australia. Tiger already has affiliates in Australia, Indonesia, the Philippines, and Singapore and could have new opportunities for affiliates in other countries such as China, Korea, and Myanmar. Tiger Airways represents an important subsidiary as its passengers are allowed to land in Singapore and connect with other flights without having to clear immigrations—the "tigerconnect" product. Recently, Tiger Airways itself announced the formation of a joint venture, Tigerair Taiwan, with Taiwan's China Airlines.

Scoot Pte Ltd, launched in June 2012, is a wholly owned subsidiary of Singapore Airlines, offering services in medium and long haul secondary markets at budget fares and competing with the likes of AirAsia X and Jetstar. Scoot initially started operations with the Boeing 777–200ERs with 402 seats in a two-class configuration to compete in the long haul low cost sector with Jetstar and AirAsia X. The plan is to provide Scoot with ten Boeing 787–8s, followed by ten Boeing 787–9s to compete more effectively. The Boeing 787s are planned to have a two-class configuration with premium economy and economy class seats. The premium economy seats are expected to be offered at fares that legacy carriers charge for economy class seats.[3]

The Singapore Airlines group is trying to develop a clear distinction among the value propositions offered by the different brands within the portfolio. This distinction is partly for the benefit of travelers and partly to minimize cannibalization. Scoot is branded to provide "affordable, budget travel," whereas SilkAir and Singapore Airlines are branded as "premier service" airlines. Scoot is to partner with Tiger Airways and its subsidiaries in Australia, Indonesia, and the Philippines to supplement its point-to-point services. Initially, the idea for Scoot was not to partner with Singapore Airlines or SilkAir but that decision was changed in early 2013 to partner on a limited basis. The partnership details are complicated as to which partner can connect with which other partner and for what type of services.

SilkAir is a premium short haul operator compared to Tiger (both Singapore-based and Australia-based). SilkAir's yield is about 10 cents compared to about 6 cents for Tiger. Tiger and SilkAir provide about the same amount of capacity at Changi Airport (7–8 percent) compared to Singapore Airlines at more than 30 percent and Scoot at about 2 percent. SilkAir now operates many point-to-point routes (with less than 50 percent of the traffic being connecting), attracts the higher paying traffic, and does not match fares offered by low cost carriers. It is able to compete quite effectively with other low cost carriers as a result of its stronger business model (feeder traffic from Singapore Airlines and a better brand that is not only tied to the parent company, but also offers frequent flyer miles). There is a close relationship between the two budget carriers (Tiger and Scoot) and between the two full service carriers (SilkAir and Singapore Airlines) but not between the budget and the full service carriers. This aspect is different from the one at Qantas where there is a relationship between the budget and full service carrier (Jetstar and Qantas).

On the route rationalization side, Singapore Airlines cut out the unprofitable flights to the US, rationalized services to Europe (for example, eliminated Greece, but added Scandinavia), and increased the regional markets in Asia. To compete more effectively with the Qantas–Emirates partnership (the two operating 14 flights daily between Australia and Dubai), Singapore Airlines has been increasing its capacity from Singapore to Europe on the one side and to Australia on the other side. For example, Singapore Airlines operates four daily flights to London, Heathrow alone (three with the Airbus 380 and one with the Boeing 777–300R). Singapore Airlines canceled the flights to Athens and the nonstop flight between Newark, New Jersey in the US and Singapore (the longest long haul flight launched in 2004). The latter decision means that there is no longer a need for five Airbus 340–500s, all-premium-class configured aircraft with about 100 seats. This was a high profile product but very expensive as it required a special fleet as well as a special operating framework due to the extra long range (approaching 16–18 hours).

Singapore Airlines has accepted the fact that almost all growth will be achieved through the operations of its subsidiaries, primarily SilkAir and Scoot. In addition, Singapore Airlines is focused on developing partnerships (including with low cost carriers) inside and outside the Star Alliance to achieve expansion. Examples include GOL, JetBlue, SAS, Transaero, Virgin America, and Virgin Australia. Of particular interest are the partnership with Tata Sons in India and the potential partnerships in China, in light of the forthcoming changes in the regulatory policies of the Chinese Government relating to services offered by low cost carriers. Some partnerships include interline agreements, some codeshares, some equity investments, and some joint ventures (as in the case of SAS) that involve antitrust immunity and could involve metal neutrality if the partner were to start flying to Singapore. In June 2013, Singapore Airlines sold its 49 percent equity in Virgin Atlantic to Delta Air Lines.

Based on the discussion above, although airlines such as JetBlue, Qantas, and Singapore have begun to redesign their businesses at the transformative level, other airlines are still continuing to explore the traditional areas in order to improve their business models, develop areas that relate to networks, fleet, operations, and various types of partnerships, enhance their revenues and decrease their costs as they still see some development opportunities in these areas.

Value Derived from Innovation

Airline Sector

Let us put the aforementioned strategies in a past–present–future perspective. Figure 1.3 provides this perspective in the context of history and a forecast of the Relative Revenue Contribution Impact. One line shows an index of the value of network/fleet-related innovations, and the second line shows the value of product/service-related innovations in driving airline revenue contribution (revenue minus directly attributable costs), over and above the impact of changes in the economies (measured by GDPs).

From such a higher level perspective, Figure 1.3a shows that the relative contribution to revenue by product/service and pricing innovation seems to have exceeded the innovation from networks/fleet and airport facilities. In recent years, airlines have clearly made significant progress in exploiting the non-traditional area of ancillary revenues. Airlines based in North America have led the charge in this area with over $15 billion revenues generated in 2012 from ancillary revenues. There is still room for growth, not only on the network/fleet side (for example, in light of the growth in emerging markets) but also on the product/services side (from further exploitation of fee-based products and services). This belief is displayed by the two dotted lines beyond the point of intersection. See Figure 1.3a. However, Figure 1.3b puts forward another perspective that there are *many more* opportunities for achieving growth in revenue and margins from innovation in products/services, other than from fee-based products and services. Examples include providing value-based options (through airlines or through new proactive intermediaries) that improve and offer customized products and services, door-to-door services, and an end-to-end experience.

Customers do not want to be owned. They want to be served. And it is the information-rich and tech-savvy companies that will serve them by knowing them better (who they are, where they are, where they are heading, what their preferences are, and what challenges they are facing at the time). Information and its use yield both opportunities and challenges. Consumers may enjoy

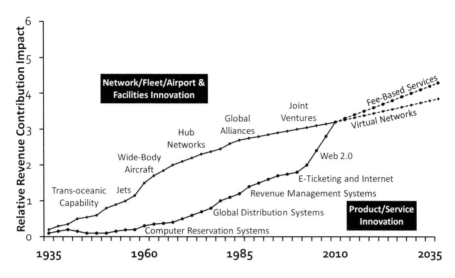

Figure 1.3a   Value derived from two areas of innovation

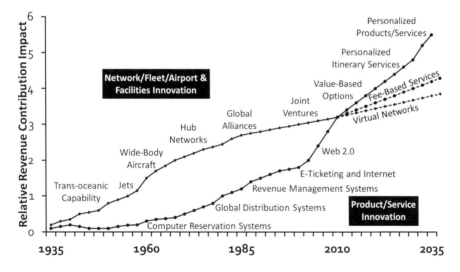

Figure 1.3b   An increasing consumer-centric world

the relevant and personalized products and services that may be derived from data and analytics but, at the same time, they may be concerned with their privacy—a "double-edged sword" situation. The greatest difficulty being that this balance between the two can vary not only from person to person, but also by situation.

From the opportunity perspective, airlines could serve travelers better not only by knowing them better but also by offering them everything from everyone that is necessary from the start to the finish of their journeys. They could work with suppliers or simply buy part of their inventory such as X percent of airline seats and Y percent of hotel rooms. To this inventory they would add their own product/service features relating to upgrades, cancelation charges, and so forth, as well as add features such as 24/7 concierge service around the world. What they would be known for is offering the context-based content conveniently and in a customized manner.

Other Business Sectors

To envision the kind of opportunities shown in Figure 1.3b, airline managements need to review the experience of a few non-airline businesses to see how they began to look at their businesses from much broader perspectives. Think about how IBM and Apple forced themselves to "imagine" new ways of doing their businesses that met customer needs while overcoming their internal business hurdles and finding new areas of profit. In the case of IBM, to deal with strong competition in all of its segments, not to mention a shift to smaller and open systems, the company transformed itself from a business selling mainframe computers (product focus) to a business that provided information technology solutions (customer focus).

Apple, facing significant losses as a result of competition from Microsoft's cheaper Windows-based systems (not to mention the depth and breadth of available applications), totally changed its business to design and manufacture consumer electronics. It is noteworthy that Apple's management was not only able to overcome an almost insurmountable constraint in its industry, the existence of copyrighted music, but also at the same time develop an entire system of products, applications, and partnerships. Even more important than its solid balance sheet, Apple deployed its well aligned leadership to accomplish this feat. Sony, on the other hand, struggled, and Nokia and Research in Motion missed the tide altogether in spite of their once dominant market share.

Take another company, BIC. For over two decades after its founding, the company thought about innovation within the "low-cost plastic disposable writing implements" box. While the business was successful, it was looking to grow. When the idea of making lighters was suggested, a shift in thinking placed the emphasis on "disposable" rather than "writing." This shift in thinking "in a new box" enabled BIC to "see" other disposable products developed around this framework — lighters and razors — offering them in 1973 and 1975, respectively. The company also forayed into other areas — experimenting in a variety of products including perfumes, surfboards, and inexpensive pre-charged mobile phones. While the company achieved success in some areas more than others, the creation of "the new box" with new perceptions and strategies has undoubtedly helped maintain its status as a market leader.[4]

Rosetta Stone, a language learning company based in the US, began a business transformation in 2008. The initial business model involved selling software CDs to teach users languages. However, over time, to grow the business, the company needed to add an online component to enable learners to (1) get coaching and (2) interact with other "learners." The problem was that they did not know how to engage customers in these endeavors. The underlying problem was that the company did not have much knowledge with respect to how consumers used their products that in turn could be attributed to fragmented sources of customer understanding and measurement. Data, which was mostly sales related, was reported to separate individuals rather than a centralized entity. The result: "no one assembled the data into a coherent picture of what mattered to customers, or reported their findings back to the business as actionable insights."[5] Moreover, even when a customer experience issue was detected, it was not clear who was responsible for correcting it. Emphasis was placed on abandonment of customer service calls. It was recognized that all post-sales customer contact needed to be centralized so that the company could channel its entire customer data, glean insights, and assign responsibility in terms of addressing customer experience issues. The results include (1) the launch of online product components such as chat sessions and games, and (2) the monitoring and management of 13 customer conversion points, with the majority linked to engagement but not directly to sales.[6]

Airline managements can also look to the pharmaceutical, communications, and retail (brick-and-mortar and online) industries for some insights. Just like the airline industry, the pharmaceutical industry, too, is extremely complex and risky. It must meet large volumes of tremendously strict requirements set by regulators. It can take years to bring approved products to market. And the cost to get a drug through the approval process and into the market can be up to a billion dollars. The failure rate in bringing out a successful medicine, even after clearing many hurdles, can be 30 to one.[7] Yet, despite the existence of complexity, uncertainty, and high costs, the pharmaceutical industry, reported to be a $325 billion a year business, is "America's toughest and one of the most profitable" businesses.[8] Moreover, companies such as Novartis have differentiated their business practices, for example, in their segmentation process—committing the R&D budgets to potential blockbuster drugs or targeted drugs. In the case of Merck, the company obtained higher volume through higher non-price value, not lower prices.[9] Within the communications sector, CNN, the cable channel owned by Time Warner, thinks it cannot support itself by the delivery of just the news. It is transforming itself to lift ratings and increase its audience by distinguishing itself by airing "original films and television series," recognizing the trend that today viewers can get news elsewhere and want to be entertained.[10]

Within the retail industry, consider the ultra discount retailer, ALDI, which has strived for simplicity—focusing on the basics and doing what is necessary rather than doing everything possible. As a result, ALDI achieves three times the margin of the average business in Germany! Consider also the specialty retailer, Trader Joe's (acquired by ALDI) that appears to have successfully implemented some of the best aspects from the retail sector, such as high end customer service, but combined with a relatively low cost structure to keep prices reasonable. Imagine a global airline redesigning its business to achieve such a feat. As for an online retailer, consider Amazon.com. This business has been truly focused right from the beginning on (1) getting the basics right, and (2) designing the business and its strategies to meet customer needs. Consider Amazon's customer focus initiatives relating to not just *what* it sells, but also *how* it sells. There is "1-Click Ordering" on Amazon's mobile app. Next is the "Subscribe & Save" feature that enables customers to schedule replacements of items purchased on a regular basis. Then there is the "Lockers" program that enables customers to pick up their orders at certain stores in certain cities to ensure security and receipt of the package. Finally, there is Amazon's comparative advantage of exceptional speed.[11] It was the feedback from customers that led Amazon to sell more than just books. It was the customers' desires to get faster delivery that prompted Amazon to establish increasing numbers of distribution centers at strategic locations to speed up delivery. Now it is reported that Amazon is transforming itself again to not just increase the number of products available for sale, but also make the delivery the same day.[12]

Rethinking Airline Revenue Streams

With insights from the best global business practices, how could a progressive airline think differently about the revenue side to bring about the kind of revenue growth envisioned in Figure 1.3b? As the competitive landscape is changing dramatically, and as many airlines try to penetrate the revenue side, one way of staying ahead of the competition could be to leverage innovation that can be identified from the intersection of marketing and the deployment of technology. For example: Since the well branded airlines know that a disproportionately high percentage of the revenue comes from frequent flyers and other loyal members, the redesign can involve the improvement of customer experience through customization using technology not only to maintain their loyalty, but to increase it.

The innovation that can result will have a dramatic effect on airline competitiveness just as the introduction of American Airlines's AAdvantage frequent flyer program did in disrupting the new low cost-based competition. While unlike the low cost carriers that emerged in the late 1970s and early 1980s, Internet "pure play" businesses (such as Amazon, eBay, Facebook, and Google) are not likely to fly airplanes, they do have the power to disrupt airline profits by leveraging the behavioral data available for the creation of direct and customized itineraries and offers that are timely, relevant, and significant—a redesign, for example, through the "uberization" of the airline business. Smaller intermediaries are already serving as leaders in providing information to travelers, as illustrated by examples in the previous book in the series and also in Chapter 3 of this book. Consequently, regardless of what the digital companies are doing, progressive airlines worldwide must develop plans of their own to adapt to the marketplace. Otherwise, revenue will be generated through innovation in this area, but the lion's share of the new revenue will be passed to other businesses and not to the airlines. And, as in the past, airlines will point to the fact that everyone in the air travel chain has made money but the airlines.

What can airlines, even those at the cutting edge of innovation, do? First, all airlines can address the tension mentioned above. The airline business continues to be heavily focused on three elements of the product—network, fleet, and schedules. However, while not forgetting about these three critical elements of the product, not to mention the importance of operations, some airlines can consider the customer centricity aspect. Even a shallow analysis of the area of the intersection of marketing and technology shows two immediate areas for airlines to innovate dramatically—revenue management and customization. Revenue management that has progressed from segment-based to O&D-based to network-based to alliance partner-based, can now move to an individual basis (a particular individual within a particular bucket, *including forecasts of expenditures on ancillary products and services*). In the second area, innovation lies in the ability for an airline to go direct, not just to reduce distribution costs, but to provide customized and situation-based offers resulting from knowledge and a two-way dialogue, within the acceptable framework of the information provided by customers.

For the innovation ambitious airlines, the key to an increase in the movement toward customization is not just the acquisition and deployment of new data, but the creative use of the data that airlines already have, to do things differently. To an extent, a few airlines have begun to move in this direction, some on the operations side and some on the commercial side. For example, rather than flying their own aircraft, they are beginning to set up virtual airlines, as in the case of Qantas, as previously discussed. On the commercial side, some have begun to sell seats differently, as in the bidding process to buy upgrades. A few have started to generate ancillary revenues beyond the fee-based processes, instead focusing on value-based strategies. On the commercial side, the process is first to integrate the data that already exists internally and then complement it with additional data from internal and external sources to understand and anticipate customer behavior so as to be proactive in meeting customers' perceived needs. The data can be used to generate new revenue streams such as through selling a much wider array of products and services to captive audiences than just the very limited number of items on the duty free cart for a few minutes during very long haul flights—thinking, not just "out of the box," but also "in a new box," as BIC did in the above example. The threat is that if airlines do not become proactive in this area, other customer-centric and information-savvy companies (Amazon.com, Apple, eBay, Facebook, Google, to name just five) could and would step in, perhaps even in alliances with airports, to capture traveler value through leveraging situation-based behavior to offer such high margin services.

To accomplish innovation in these two areas alone, an airline would need both an expanded capability to leverage the behavioral data available, as well as a robust environment for measuring the impact of innovation as it tests and learns iteratively. As pointed out throughout this book, the behavioral data is often unstructured, coming from sources such as web analytics and social media. However, data can also come from conventional sources never "mined" in detail before (such as from call centers and kiosks) and integrated with other existing data (usually transactional and located in disparate functions and silos). All this data can then be used, keeping in mind privacy issues, to perform advanced "predictive" or "behavioral" analytics that facilitate innovation in two simple ways. First, an airline can "predict" the purchase of new ancillary products by type and value within each bucket in the revenue management system. Second, the airline can "predict" individual customer behavior for revenue management purposes, including, for example, the likelihood of being a *"no-show" by individual* but also further out, more innovative characteristics such as "willingness to give up the seat" that can be useful for not only denied boarding but all kinds of seat management innovations.

The critical success factor for innovation just in these two revenue-focused areas alone is the management of the constantly changing passenger behavior. Airlines that are interested in moving up on the customization spectrum (a topic discussed at length in Chapter 3) must be willing to transform even just the existing revenue management and reservation *processes* to facilitate the creation of customized offers based on the information provided through two-way communications during the shopping and purchase processes. Management must then be willing to transform the processes involved to go direct by *enhancing* existing mobile capabilities to help travelers do everything (all components of travel including shopping, purchase, and two-way communications while traveling), *with ease*. Finally, management must be willing to change the process to facilitate the integration of existing data, the collection of behavioral data, and the deployment of analytics and the supporting technology and systems. It is the transformation of such processes that will place a global carrier at the cutting edge of *differentiated* revenue-focused strategies in order to achieve profitable and sustainable growth while creating a differentiated product and digital experience, leading to a price commanding brand that would be difficult to copy by competitors.

Book Outline

This chapter has provided a framework that shows how different generations of airlines can realign, redesign, and perhaps even reinvent, their own businesses through the evaluation and implementation of different value propositions and through different strategies (based on sustainable competitive advantages) to increase the value provided to passengers and margins for themselves. Particularly important is the point that although the recent trend has been for airlines to focus on the 25 percent of the passengers who travel on various types of premium fares, in delivering their value propositions airlines cannot ignore the other 75 percent.

Recognizing that a few airlines around the world are still operating in pure "survival" mode, many have been implementing incremental changes discussed early in this chapter. One can easily see the diversity of strategies being followed in different regions of the world from the viewpoint of structures, operations, networks, and fleet—Azul, Delta, easyJet, Ethiopian Airlines, Etihad, Hawaiian Airlines, Norwegian, Qantas, Singapore, and Turkish Airlines, are just some examples. Constant iteration (an emerging corporate culture) is becoming the new norm for the development and execution of strategy as exemplified by JetBlue, discussed above. Such a change in culture and the metamorphosis of business models is evident from the strategic and tactical movements at other airlines also—AirAsia and Virgin Australia, for example. Moreover, just the three airlines discussed earlier in this chapter show a clear and compelling need to recognize the cyclical nature of the industry, the necessity of continuing evolution of the operating model, and the imperative of modulating risk.

Next, Chapter 2 addresses the need to recalibrate passenger value systems. Are the *reported wants* in alignment with the *actual buying* behavior of passengers, especially in terms of willingness to pay? This chapter discusses the need to reexamine and reset passenger expectations with respect to the core product offering as the essence of the core product has changed over time. For dramatic changes in the way the airline business is conducted, airlines can look at consumers not just as passengers (old box), but as travelers (new box). With white spaces in mind, they can develop business models to meet the needs of travelers through more innovative ways of integrating strategic resources and select not only the orientation, operations versus product, versus customers, but in the case of customers, the position on the customization spectrum. This is the subject of Chapter 3 which contains an explanation of the differences between customer focus, customer centricity, and personalization—all positions on the customization spectrum.

The sustainability of, and the dependence on, the current ancillary revenue streams are beginning to be questioned. Instead, airlines need to look deeper into the whole area of merchandising and, ultimately, retailing that encompasses customer acquisition, conversion, service, and measurement. Pricing and distribution play particularly important roles. With respect to distribution, the New Distribution Capability (NDC) initiated by IATA is discussed at some length. From this perspective, airlines can draw on the experience of the retail industry, capitalizing on the captive audience and providing a "flying bazaar." As such, retailing, particularly pricing and distribution, are the subjects of Chapter 4. Related closely to products, pricing, and distribution are the topics of loyalty and branding.

Chapter 5 identifies the challenges that airlines have faced in terms of branding, especially in the case of legacy carriers relative to low cost carriers. This chapter recognizes that the branding element has become further complicated due to subsidiaries, alliances, and mergers & acquisitions. Particularly important is the need to distinguish between brand *awareness* and brand *appreciation*. This chapter addresses a number of important aspects of branding such as design thinking, co-creation, and branding in the digital era. Again, airlines can look at the experience of other industries (including travel-related businesses such as hotels and also the retail sector) to gain relevant and strategic insights, especially in terms of differentiating factors such as design and customer experience. Chapter 6, Addressing the Role of Loyalty, follows the chapter on branding as branding and loyalty are very closely linked—strong brands retain loyal followers. However, most airline loyalty programs as they are designed today leave a lot to be desired, both on the side of the airline and the side of the traveler, as outlined in the chapter, which calls for the reexamination and redesign of these programs to promote relevancy and meaningfulness.

Throughout this book, the emphasis is on the value of information. Chapter 7 highlights the possibilities available to create data-driven airlines through search, big data and analytics, along with leveraging mobile, especially with respect to understanding customer and competitor behavior. For those selecting to move up in the customization spectrum, the ease of research, shopping, and actual travel need to be customized to the individual traveler. Consider, for example, semantic search, in which the search engine is able to understand the *intent* of the searcher and the *contextual meaning* of the terms and the language to generate relevant search. Big data and analytics can be leveraged to gain a complete view of the customer that, in turn, can be used by all employees to serve the customer in real time. Serving the customer involves face-to-face situations as well as through the mobile channel—en route to the airport, within the airport, even while in the air as cabin crews utilize mobile tablets to serve passengers' needs. Other organizations in the travel industry have made mobile the heart of their business; airlines should look to do the same as travel is inherently mobile.

Could a transformative vision and culture lead to the successful redesign of airline business models to provide returns, on a consistent basis, that exceed the average weighted cost of capital for airlines and meet the changing demands of customers? As pointed out in Chapter 8, the answer is yes if managements can meet the needs of tomorrow's passengers—especially the Millennials—along the lines discussed in this book.

Chapter 9, Attaining Market Leadership, provides five extensive practical examples of business transformations, written by five Thought Leaders. These businesses represent a full spectrum of industries, including airlines. They are ALDI, Hertz, PricewaterhouseCoopers, Qantas, and Sabre Airline Solutions.

Takeaways

- Airlines make miniscule margins compared to numerous other businesses, given their investments and risks. The marketplace is changing structurally and fundamentally, creating both challenges and opportunities to rethink, redesign, and possibly, reinvent the airline business.
- Airlines should focus on transforming their revenue streams (more than reducing their costs incrementally) by leveraging the value of information and emerging technologies—mobile, social, data, and analytics.
- If airlines do not transform themselves, innovative technology companies circling the airline industry (and armed with data and analytics) will provide value-adding services to customers, repeating history, namely, that everyone in the air travel chain has made money, but the airlines.

- For a description of some megatrends, transforming the business landscape, see the Thought Leadership Piece by PricewaterhouseCoopers in Chapter 9.

Notes

1   As of the beginning of 2014, the press reported the possibility of Etihad taking an equity position in Alitalia.

2   Dave Barger, President and Chief Executive Officer, "JetBlue Analyst Day" Presentation, March 20, 2013.

3   "Scoot Outlook Improves as Singapore Airlines Long-haul LCC Subsidiary Prepares for 375-seat 787–9," *CAPA-Centre for Aviation Analysis*, February 11, 2014.

4   Luc de Brabandere and Alan Iny, *Thinking in New Boxes: A New Paradigm for Business Creativity* (NY: Random House, 2013), pp. 22–3.

5   Harley Manning and Kerry Bodine, *Outside In: The Power of Putting Customers at the Center of Your Business* (NY: Houghton Mifflin Harcourt, 2012), p. 189.

6   Ibid., pp. 189–90.

7   Barry Werth, *The Antidote: Inside the World of New Pharma* (NY: Simon & Schuster, 2014), p. 6.

8   Ibid., front jacket flap.

9   Michael E. Raynor and Mumtaz Ahmed, *The Three Rules: How Exceptional Companies Think* (NY: Penguin Group, 2013), p. 19.

10   "News You Can Lose: CNN's Transformation Says a Lot about What is Working Today in Television," *The Economist*, February 8, 2014, p. 65.

11   J.J. McCorvey, "The Race Has Just Begun," *Fast Company*, September 2013, Issue 178, p. 70.

12   Gary Shapiro, *Ninja Innovation: The Ten Killer Strategies of the World's Most Successful Businesses* (NY: HarperCollins, 2013), pp. 97–9, and 190.

Chapter 2
Recalibrating Passenger Value Requirements

Based on the results of surveys reported in the media, there appears to be a disconnect between passengers and airlines in terms of the value provided and value received. Passengers feel that they are paying high fares for marginal and commoditized service, especially when they encounter hassle at various touchpoints of the travel cycle.

Airlines feel that they are not making enough money, at least on a consistent basis, as illustrated by Figure 1.1 in Chapter 1. The result is total frustration all around. One answer to overcoming this disconnect is to recognize that the value system needs to be recalibrated on both sides.

Consider some potential underlying reasons that may be fueling this frustration:

- Full service airlines have tried to cater to the needs of a far too wide array of customer segments while satisfying only a small percentage of passengers in each segment.
- With the exception of a few airlines, most have set expectations that are too high.
- Most airlines think that all passengers want more choices, but in some cases, at least those traveling infrequently, travelers feel inundated with information and offers that may be confusing.
- Airlines have not fully leveraged data to gain insights into passengers' behavior (by segment) to know their needs, desires, and expectations, and even more importantly, their willingness to pay for these three elements, respectively.

- Airlines, in general, have not effectively illustrated the value of the core product offered—for example, the capability for a person to make a same day return trip involving a 1,500 mile sector length.

These issues can begin to be addressed by taking a deeper dive into the areas of customer needs, the reported wants versus actual buying behavior, the core product offering and resetting expectations around it, customer segmentation including segmentation profitability, and determining the willingness to pay.

Customer Needs

The primary need of passengers is to get to their desired destinations (for a business, personal, or leisure reason) on time, with their baggage, and, hopefully, at a reasonable fare. If a passenger living in Austin, Texas wants to fly to Kathmandu, Nepal and her preferred airline (say, American Airlines) does not fly there, then even the first component of the primary need is not met. To fulfill the network needs of passengers, airlines— being restricted with respect to bilateral as well as ownership and control rules—have developed extensive strategic alliances to fulfill the primary, network-related, needs of passengers. However, while airline alliance partnerships have broadened the individual networks of airlines, passengers continue to be frustrated by the inconsistency in the quality of service advertised and provided by various members in alliance partnerships. The core of the problem lies in the selection of partners in an alliance. Until now, the criteria have been based primarily on a carrier's ability and desire to extend the network reach as opposed to an evaluation of the "strategic" fit of the brand based on criteria such as the quality of service, consistency of the product and service, and trust, not to mention corporate culture.

Next, consider the second component of the primary need, namely, the need to arrive on time. Not only are statistics such as 80, or even 90 percent on-time arrival and or departure not sufficient, but also they refer to aircraft operations and not passengers getting to their destinations. Even if those statistics were acceptable, what lengths and hoops did passengers go through to achieve those results—passengers who took much earlier flights than needed to ensure they would make their connections or passengers who flew the night before to ensure being at a business meeting or a family gathering the following morning. In how many other businesses would an 80, or even a 90, percent performance be acceptable in today's environment? Leaving aside other attributes of the primary need, let us turn to the secondary need.

The secondary need is to fly to the desired destination with minimal hassle and have a pleasant experience. However, while alliances do enable member airlines to fulfill their passengers' primary needs, at least relating to networks, most passengers find the experience to be inconsistent, as mentioned above, due to a wide difference in the quality of services offered by alliance partners. The experience element also relates to the hassle of travel, even in the markets served by a single airline. Travelers continue to be frustrated with several areas within the travel chain—starting with the shopping phase (such as navigating through awkward airline websites to find answers relating to the service or to understand the differences in services and fares) and during the actual travel itself (such as dealing with boarding lines at the gates, especially during times of irregular operations). Even experienced business travelers in the West have been reported to spend as much as two hours in the shopping and purchasing process while some leisure travelers have been known to spend as long as five hours.

Consider the following illustration of this challenge. A person is interested in flying from Tampa, Florida, in the US to London in the UK. The person goes to the website of an Online Travel Agent (say, Travelocity) on November 9 to book for an outward journey on December 8 and return on December 14. Travelocity shows well over a hundred flights with fares ranging from $1,096 to $5,318. British Airways offers nonstop service but all other airlines provide service with one or more connections.

The problem: There is no information that explains the wide variation in the fare. British Airways offers the lowest fare even though it is the only carrier that offers a nonstop flight from Tampa to London, Gatwick (taking eight hours and 15 minutes).

Finnair offers service on a codeshare flight on British Airways from Washington, Dulles, with a connection on United from Tampa to Washington, Dulles. Other airlines offering service at the higher end in terms of fare include Iberia (on codeshared flights with American and British Airways, $3,807) and Virgin Atlantic (with a codeshare flight on Delta, $3,757). In between are airlines such as US Airways offering connecting service on their own flights (Charlotte, $2,173).

Let us assume that the passenger decides to take the lowest fare offered by British Airways ($1,096.30). Selecting that flight option shows that the outbound flight is on a nonstop aircraft but the return flight has two options. One option is on American with two connections, one in Manchester and a second connection in Chicago (the trip taking 30 hours and 45 minutes) and the second option also involves two connections, one in Paris and the second in Miami (the trip taking 28 hours and 50 minutes). There is no choice that contains a return flight that is nonstop. How is the passenger going to decide which flight to take? Going a little further on the Online Travel Agent's website provides information on departure and arrival times and the type of aircraft, with information available regarding on-time performance and seat maps for some of the flights shown. There is no information on such product features as baggage allowance, check-in options (online, airport, mobile) and costs, seat legroom, and the associated costs, if any, of meals, in-flight entertainment, and bookings using credit or debit cards.

Out of curiosity, the passenger decided to log on to the British Airways website. This site showed clearly the availability of nonstop service in both directions. The outbound flight, in fact, was the same as the one shown by the Online Travel Agent. However, the fares shown were higher—$1,474 for the flight to London and $1,611 for the return flight. In addition, the website showed different fares for different days of travel and on nonstop flights versus flights making connections. For example, on the outbound flight on the day selected, the fare could be as low as $569 for a flight with a connection or as high as $1,474 for a nonstop flight. The airline website also provided much more detailed information on fare conditions (such as change fees) and information on product features (such as the weight of baggage allowance and seat pitch). Moreover, the airline provided options for different classes of service (Economy, Premium Economy, and Business Class) each with its own fare ($1,474, $2,003, and $4,863, respectively). Finally, the airline provided information on upgrades and the features of the service in the upgraded class, for example, seven inches more legroom in the Premium Economy Class.

The frustration experienced by the traveler in the above example is only at the beginning stage—the search and shopping phases. The problem has many elements—relatively poor websites, proliferation of intermediaries and social advisories, and a large amount of mistrust of the information provided and received. It is ironic to hear some passengers who state that they spent as much time on the search, shopping, and purchasing of the flight as on the actual flight itself. This frustration relates not only to the search, shopping, and purchase phases but continues through all phases—check in, boarding, onboard, deplaning, baggage claim, and problem resolution. In a nutshell, customers are feeling that they are not getting value in travel. Customers place high importance on value. It is ironic that in some other sectors, such as retail, customers actually enjoy the shopping phase, whereas in the travel industry it is considered to be a hassle.

Reported Wants versus Actual Buying Behavior

There are two parts to the root of the problem of reported wants versus actual buying behavior. First, as stated earlier, airlines have raised the expectations of customers, expectations that cannot be met in cost effective ways. Second, while passengers complain about their unmet needs, a precious few are willing to pay for such services. Hence the extra services often get eliminated. For example, some airlines have tried to offer concierge service— being greeted and met at the curbside and escorted from the curbside to check in, through security, to boarding, including a visit to the airport lounge until the boarding time. Airlines tried to provide such a service for around $200 at selected airports in the US and about 200 euros in Europe, but some had to discontinue this service due to a lack of sufficient number of passengers.

As a result, even the passengers who are willing to pay for the desired service often cannot receive it as the provider finds it cost ineffective for the few passengers who do want it and will pay for it. For example, a study conducted by PricewaterhouseCoopers (PwC) shows that only one in ten Chinese, American, and British business travelers are interested in concierge services. This result could be explainable in that business travelers may feel that they know their way around airports. Keeping this in mind, the same study also indicated that 25 percent of Brazilian leisure travelers would be interested in concierge service; a number that is 3.7 times higher than the US leisure travelers.[1]

However, technology can now be leveraged by airlines to obtain better insights (at the segment level) with respect to *the reported wants* versus *the actual buying* behavior of passengers to improve the travel experience for passengers and increase profitability for airlines. In one survey, passengers were asked if they would be willing to purchase onboard Wi-Fi connectivity. In this survey, conducted by PwC, 25 percent indicated an interest in purchasing this service. On the other hand, a much smaller percentage (about 5 percent) actually made the purchase. Answers given for not making the purchase included lack of awareness of the service available onboard, other competing activities, and the price.[2]

Of course many airlines have strived to meet their top-level passengers' needs, both primary and secondary. At the top of the spectrum, Singapore Airlines has partnered with JetSuite to offer twin-engine, four-passenger jets to connect with Singapore's international flights from US gateways for passengers traveling in suites, first class, or business class cabins (branded "Suite-to-Suite" program). Such an offering helps alleviate such concerns as missed connections, as the airline provides a personalized service such as a dedicated number for Singapore Airlines's passengers to contact JetSuite and also a car service between Singapore's terminals and private jet terminals. Lufthansa also offers a similar program with partner NetJets. Such programs, however, come with a substantial price tag. A premium class passenger flying Singapore Airlines will be charged about $2,500 one way to connect with a JetSuite flight.[3] Even at such rates, commercial airlines pick up part of the cost of transportation provided by the private jet airlines.

At the lower end of the spectrum, as mentioned above, some airlines have continued their concierge programs to help alleviate some of the stress incurred during travel, such as American and Lufthansa, by assisting travelers in getting through the airport. However, these services are considered to be expensive by the majority of passengers traveling in Economy Class, even with costs ranging from $125–$300. Consequently, while many airlines have offered concierge services, some have had to discontinue the offering due to lack of sufficient business, possibly due to lack of willingness to pay, as previously stated. The disconnect between the "wanting" and the "willing to pay for" is not just related to the secondary need. Relating to the primary need, passengers may want a nonstop flight, but is there a sufficient number that are willing to pay for such a service in many markets? Air Canada tried to offer nonstop service between Toronto and Delhi, India, but only a few passengers were willing to patronize such a service, making it cost ineffective for Air Canada to continue the offering. Instead, most passengers would sooner make connections (such as through Europe) and pay a lower fare. Some travelers accepted even more inconvenient connections at other points along the route if it meant getting an even lower fare. Singapore Airlines purchased a special aircraft, the Airbus 340–500, that could fly nonstop between Newark, New Jersey in the US and Singapore. However, insufficient demand led to the cessation of the service.

The previous discussion involves willingness to pay for specific items or product features. At a higher level, however, surveys show that people are willing to pay around 5 percent more for simpler experiences and interactions. Figure 2.1 shows the results reported by Siegel+Gale of people's willingness to pay higher amounts in different industries. For the travel industry as a whole, people are willing to pay anywhere between 4.5 and 4.7 percent more.[4] These numbers relate to survey results at the global level. There are slight differences at the regional level.

Getting Back to the Basics—Resetting Expectations

Somewhere along the way, the value of the core product— the ability to get a passenger from A to B, a distance of 500 miles, for a lunch meeting and be back the same workday—has

Global
Simplicity premium

Depending on the industry, up to 41% of people are willing to pay more for simpler experiences and interactions. The amount they are willing to pay varies by industry but is significant.

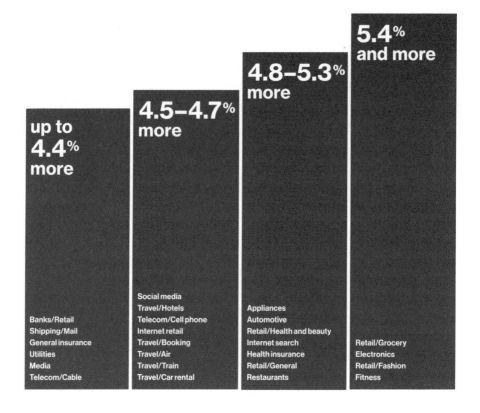

up to
4.4%
more

Banks/Retail
Shipping/Mail
General insurance
Utilities
Media
Telecom/Cable

4.5–4.7%
more

Social media
Travel/Hotels
Telecom/Cell phone
Internet retail
Travel/Booking
Travel/Air
Travel/Train
Travel/Car rental

4.8–5.3%
more

Appliances
Automotive
Retail/Health and beauty
Internet search
Health insurance
Retail/General
Restaurants

5.4%
and more

Retail/Grocery
Electronics
Retail/Fashion
Fitness

Figure 2.1   For simpler experiences, people would pay
Source: Siegel+Gale

been lost. Airlines seem, instead, focused on promoting the non-core attributes of travel, in-flight entertainment systems for example. As for travelers, they seem to be taking the core product for granted and appear to want more and more and for less and less. This is not necessarily the case in other related industries. For example, some customers will literally spend hours searching to save a few dollars on an airline fare, but then turn around and spend a considerable amount of money on food, beverages, and other items while at various points in the airport. Similarly, some customers will literally spend hours searching to save a few dollars on an airline fare, but then not blink an eye at spending an exorbitant amount of money on a taxi to get from the airport to the desired destination or not blink an eye at spending an exorbitant amount of money for a bottle of water in the hotel room. Why are the value systems so different in these situations? One explanation could be the difference in time—fares are often booked several days, weeks, and even months in advance, while getting to a destination on ground is a current need or purchasing a beverage or food item at a hotel is a current desire at the time. As some executives have suggested, customers tend to be in a different mindset at these different points in time.

One way of looking at value is to either look "upstream" or "downstream."[5] Downstream sources of value are not created at the place of production and included physically in the product itself. Instead, they are created through activities such as the place where the product is sold, the manner in which it is sold, and the manner in which it is consumed. Airlines have, in general, looked upstream to create value with respect to their products. They are just now beginning to look downstream where they can augment the sale of the product with value derived from components such as service, trust, and experience. Think about why some people would pay $4 for a bottle of water in a hotel room when they can get it for 25 cents in a grocery store.

A few airlines have discovered that more passengers will buy ancillary products and services during the day of travel, particularly while in the airport, such as access to the lounge, a better seat, Wi-Fi, and so forth. Passengers are even more likely to make such purchases if they can find the availability of such products and services on their mobile devices. The challenge for airlines, however, is how to push such products and services via mobile devices just prior to the flights and how to charge for them easily on mobile devices.

So, what is the basic product and how should its value be promoted? Getting back to customer needs, the basic product would be the schedule and its on-time performance. This means for the complete trip, not just on a per segment basis. Along the lines of a discussion earlier in the chapter, are airlines keeping statistics on travelers who are ignoring multiple short but legal connections and booking on connecting flights with lengthy layovers to ensure that they make their connecting international flight? Similarly, are carriers keeping statistics on passengers who are traveling the night before, even though there is an appropriate flight on the day, just to ensure timely arrival at the next day's meeting? From passengers' perspective, are airlines keeping track of the cost of the extra time spent making connections or paying for hotels, and would passengers trade off the total costs for better and more reliable schedules?

Based on the aforementioned points, customers' expectations need to be reset with respect to what comprises the core product versus what make up the "frills" around the core product. Specifically, not having charged for bags, meals, and in-flight entertainment in the past, airlines now need to reset customers' expectations as to what now comprises a basic product and a basic travel experience. Furthermore, the mindset needs to be shifted from looking at ancillaries as fees to viewing and promoting them as value-based options. This subject will be addressed further in Chapter 4, Progressing to Become Genuine Retailers.

Segmentation

Segmentation is hardly a new subject and has been reviewed many times. The big opportunity now, for a tremendous improvement in segmentation, is the availability of more comprehensive information and analytics to better understand and predict customer behavior. The data could be provided by third parties who may be using cookies and device location addresses. These third parties can provide not only vital information about the behavior of customers within finer segments, but also about individuals within segments. The data is based on analyses of customer purchase behavior across channels and brands.

Airlines could start segmenting passengers into, for example, two different groups, namely (1) those travelers *only* concerned with price, and (2) those concerned with price, but who are willing to consider other factors as well. This is a different strategy from the traditional business/leisure segmentation. It is this second group (and its subgroups) that airlines can capitalize on and spend far more of their resources on understanding customer behavior. Two business writers on market segmentation have distinguished between "price chasers" and "value chasers." Specifically, they note that it is rare to have more than approximately 10 percent of customers (in most markets) having price as their top priority, therefore representing the "price chasers." It is members of this group that are willing to forgo "key discriminating features" to get the cheapest price, whereas "value chasers" search for the best price for their "key discriminating features." They go on to state that in those markets where it is claimed that there is a much larger amount of customers emphasizing price, it often suggests that "the supply side have not taken the time to understand customers and their needs." The result: consumers are really only left with the price consideration.[6]

To airlines' credit, a few have made an attempt to learn what passengers want. Take, for example, the decision by Lufthansa to rebrand the services of its subsidiary, Germanwings. The three segments targeted consist of customers seeking full service, customers seeking comfort, and price conscious customers. The first group gets a different product–price option. The "Best" fare is targeted at the segment seeking full service and receiving such product features as upgraded seating configuration and location, reserved space in overhead bins, generous free baggage allowance, priority check in and boarding, access to lounges and fast lane for security, and higher mileage credit in the loyalty program. The "Smart" fare is targeted at the comfort seeking segment with less product features than provided with the "Best" fare. The "Basic" fare is targeted at the extremely price conscious segment, offering nothing more than a seat.

However, it is now possible to leverage information (coming from structured and unstructured data, both from within the airline and external sources) and analytics to gain a much deeper understanding of the behavior of customers. As such, airlines can now identify subsegments within segments (for example, not just those traveling on premium fares), then maintain a relationship with these passengers as their travel needs evolve, and then, in turn, design appropriate products and services to meet the evolving needs (and willingness to pay) of these travelers.

As an example of segmentation, PwC surveyed 2,000 business and leisure flyers across Brazil, China, the UK, and the US (a representative mix of each country's adult flyers with respect to frequency, spend, and preferences). Within the US, the business and the leisure segments were subsegmented into multiple personas based on value and behavior. See Tables 2.1 and 2.2 relating to two typical personas. Table 2.1 shows a typical business travel persona: his demographics, travel profile, top purchase drivers, top preferences, top add-ons, top experience themes, sharing behaviors, and channel usage. Similar information is provided in Table 2.2 for a typical leisure travel persona.[7]

Table 2.1   Snapshot of US business, elite segment

Source: PricewaterhouseCoopers 2013

Key[1]: ▢ Very High   ▦ High   ▨ Moderate   ▧ Low   ▪ Very Low

Demographics			Top purchase drivers		Top experience themes	
Age	Generation X and baby boomer		Routes/times	51%	Friendly staff	#1
			Ticket price	49%	Helpful staff	#2
Gender	Equal		Loyalty/reward programs	40%	Upgrades and freebies	#3
Annual household income	> $150K		**Top preferences**		**Sharing behaviors**	
Marital status	Married					
Company type	Large corporation		Extended recline/wide seat space	62%	Recommends airline	83%
Position type	VP/Sr. VP level, CEO		Priority security line and lounge access	75%	Repurchases after bad experience	75%
Minority presence	35%		Wi-Fi for 1 personal device	63%	Discourages after bad experience	61%
Travel profile			**Top add-ons**		**Channel usage**	
Purpose for travel	Mostly business		Likelihood of purchasing any add-ons	68%	Research	Smartphone
					Purchase	Laptop
Avg. business travel frequency	27 RT per year		Food/beverage at the airport	25%	Check-in	Smartphone
Annual business travel spend	> $24K				Boarding	Smartphone
			Checked baggage at the airport	31%	Issue resolution	Smartphone
Highest status	Elite					
Haul type	Long/overnight		Seat location	34%		
Cabin class	Business					
Time of purchase	Within a week					

Table 2.2   Snapshot of US leisure, experience-seeking traveler
Source: PricewaterhouseCoopers 2013

Key: Very High | High | Moderate | Low | Very Low

Demographics		Top purchase drivers		Top experience themes	
Age	Generation X	Ticket price	60%	Upgrades and freebies	#1
		Routes/times	44%	Helpful staff	#2
Gender	Equal	Loyalty/reward programs	29%	Seat comfort	#3
Annual household income	>$150K				
Marital status	Married	**Top preferences**		**Sharing behaviors**	
Employment status	Employed full-time	Extended recline/wide seat space	51%	Recommends airline	88%
Travel companions	Dependents and partner			Repurchases after bad experience	61%
Minority presence	39%	Priority security line and lounge access	66%	Discourages after bad experience	58%
		Most flexible flight change policy	42%		
Travel profile		**Top add-ons**		**Channel usage**	
Purpose for travel	Equal for business and leisure	Likelihood of purchasing any add-ons	84%	Research	Smartphone/tablet
				Purchase	Laptop
Avg. leisure travel frequency	6-7 RT per year	Food/beverage at the airport	43%	Check-in	Smartphone
				Boarding	Smartphone
Annual leisure travel spend	>$10K	Food/beverage in flight	40%	Issue resolution	Call airline representative
Highest status	Elite	Seat type	34%		
Haul type	Long/overnight				
Cabin class	Above coach				
Time of purchase	Within 1-3 months				

Consider the results of another recent online survey of 8,000 consumers flying Economy Class in Asia (China, India, Indonesia, Japan, Malaysia, Singapore, Thailand, and Vietnam). In a report, published by Airbus with the research conducted by the consultancy, *The Future Laboratory*, the survey showed that consumers (1) do extensive research before flying, (2) demand greater wellbeing when they fly, and (3) look for superior seats in terms of comfort (not just leg room, but also seat width). They value, "relaxation, productivity, and wellbeing." In fact, according to this survey, Asian consumers ranked seat comfort higher in importance than in-flight entertainment, meals, and duty free sales.[8]

Airlines are, albeit slowly, beginning to refine their customer segmentation processes. The US-based Spirit Airlines and Allegiant Air, for instance, target extremely price sensitive travelers in US domestic and regional markets. These passengers are willing to trade off lower fares for less frequent service, in the case of Allegiant Air, or more densely configured aircraft, in the case of Spirit Airlines (178 seats in an Airbus 320 versus 150 for a typical legacy airline). At the other end of the spectrum, JetBlue has announced its plans to penetrate the high end of the market with lie-flat seats and in-flight private suites on its transcontinental flights, as highlighted in Chapter 1. See Figures 2.2a and 2.2b. Figure 2.3 shows a different perspective of JetBlue's planned segmentation, a plot of Passenger Revenue per Available Seat Mile (PRASM) as a percent of industry average and the Net Promoter Score (NPS) for different subsegments. JetBlue's PRASM is about 98 percent of the number for the industry average. Its NPS is high, about 65 percent, close to Southwest on one side and Apple on the other side, but much higher than many legacy airlines. This chart also shows the potential value of business markets, core leisure markets, and Visiting Friends and

Figure 2.2a   JetBlue's planned lie-flat seats
Source: JetBlue Airways

Figure 2.2b   JetBlue's planned lie-flat suites
Source: JetBlue Airways

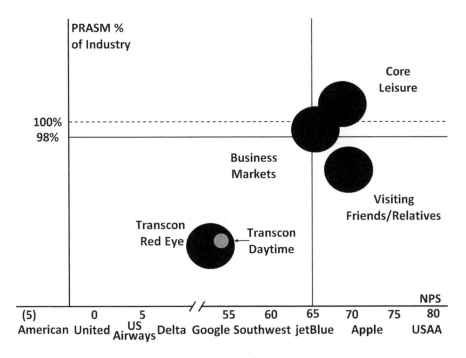

Figure 2.3   Why Net Promoter Score (NPS) matters
Source: JetBlue Airways

Relatives (VFR) markets. It is based on this information, PRASM as a percentage of industry average and the NPS, that JetBlue is planning to penetrate the "sweet spot" between "High Value Leisure" and "Mixed Wallets," discussed in Chapter 1.

Norwegian Air Shuttle is clearly targeting the lower fare travelers in selected intercontinental markets, primarily between Thailand and Europe (mainly, Scandinavia) and between Europe and the US. Norwegian already provides service between Scandinavia (Copenhagen, Oslo, and Stockholm) and the US. It has now announced a service between London, Gatwick and the US beginning in the summer of 2014, by which time there will be 14 routes to the US: six from Oslo, three from Copenhagen, three from London, Gatwick, and two from Stockholm. Destinations in the US will include John F Kennedy, New York, Fort Lauderdale, Orlando, Los Angeles, and Oakland. See Figure 2.4. Although the capacity planned to be offered between London and the US will be minute compared with the competition (that includes airlines from New Zealand, the UK, and the US), Norwegian plans to target the price sensitive travelers and capitalize on the power of social media. Based on schedules and fares announced at the end of October 2013, Norwegian will offer fares in Economy Class that are almost 40 percent less than competitors. At this level of

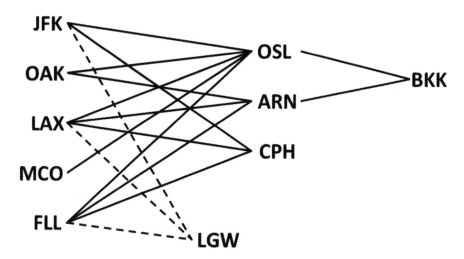

Figure 2.4   Norwegian Air Shuttle's planned intercontinental network: Summer 2014

discount, Norwegian should fill its planes with both local traffic as well as connecting traffic coming from about a dozen markets already served by Norwegian and another dozen that the airline plans to serve by the time service begins across the North Atlantic from London, Gatwick.

Some full service network airlines, such as Lufthansa and Cathay Pacific, are targeting higher fare passengers traveling in intercontinental markets. In the case of Lufthansa, one can look at the number of seats allocated in premium class cabins when it first acquired the Boeing 787–8 Intercontinental, Boeing's largest airplane (with over 90 fully lie-flat seats in Business Class as well as eight seats in the spacious First Class). In Lufthansa's configuration, this aircraft started flying with 360 seats compared to its capacity of around 470 seats in a standard configuration. In the case of Cathay, the airline is not only improving its premium class products (both Business and Premium Economy), but also going for more frequency and more destinations in intercontinental markets rather than the benefits of very large aircraft. These targets relate to the general category of premium fare travelers. Singapore Airlines, on the other hand, has decided to meet the needs of different segments through four distinct subsidiaries: Singapore for long haul premium service, Silk for medium haul premium service for the higher end of budget travelers, Scoot for long haul budget service, and Tiger for budget service in medium haul markets. The Singapore Airlines brand itself continues to target the very high end of the premium segment through product innovation—the 30-inch width of the seat in Business Class and the Airbus 380 First Class that not only has "suites," but also can provide "double beds."

Some airlines are in a niche business and they stick to that niche market, such as Allegiant. Others try to expand outside of their niche market and get into trouble. The niche can be small (as in the case of Allegiant), or large (as in the case of AirAsia), but in any case, they must stick to the niche. Those that have stayed in their niche have succeeded while those that have strayed have tended to get into trouble. For example: A typical global airline goes after multiple types of segments, but is not able to deliver effectively to all of those segments. Singapore Airlines is attempting to face this challenge by establishing four brands, each targeting a different segment of the market. Singapore Airlines itself is targeting, in its premium cabins, the segment that values and is willing to pay for higher levels of in-flight products and services—starting with its trademark, the Singapore Girl (that promoted the recognition of Asian hospitality), seat comfort, international cuisine, and in-flight entertainment systems.

The key decision on segmentation relates, of course, to the profitability of the segment. From this perspective, one place to start is by calculating the profitability of each segment, with the ultimate goal being on understanding the profitability of each individual. It is not merely just miles flown or revenue generated. Consider also the behavior of a customer. In the banking industry, for example, it could be an individual who comes into the bank frequently to conduct small transactions. In the airline industry, it could be someone who contacts the call center frequently with numerous questions on a low fare ticket. In both cases, the behavior is a strain on resources given the low return to the company from the customer. However, it is important to recognize that customer profitability is just one metric that should be considered. Another element could be the influential capacity (such as social influence) of an individual, or the overall lifetime customer value.

Determining Willingness to Pay

As mentioned numerous times in this book, passengers, particularly those traveling on low fares, continue to expect more and more services for less and less money. Many are even complaining about having to pay for features that were previously provided for free. This expectation needs to be corrected. Consider the information portrayed in Figure 2.5. While airlines have achieved tremendous reductions in their operating costs, the savings have not gone into the profits. Instead, due to the hyper level of competition in this industry, airlines have used the savings in costs to reduce fares for passengers. Consequently, the options are either to raise fares in general or through an à la carte system to provide a reasonable return on investment for airlines. However, these strategies cannot be implemented without successfully differentiating the product.

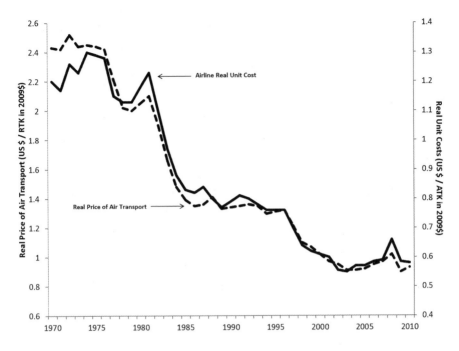

Figure 2.5   Real price of air transport and real unit costs

Source: International Air Transport Association

Consequently, there is a need for a deeper dive into the willingness to pay for the level of services desired. While this need has always been there, now airlines have access to data as well as analytics capabilities to explore this aspect of research. Take, for example, the upgrade process. Now, an airline can take silent bids for upgrades via mobile devices, prior to boarding. Similarly, airlines can now take silent bids for the willingness of a passenger to give up his reservation and to take a later flight. Another example would be a traveler choosing (via "clicking") a feature that interests him, then observing whether or not he still chose the feature once the price of the feature was revealed. What about passengers arriving at airports and wanting to get on earlier flights that are still at their gates but not willing to pay the fees to change their flight? Could experiments be conducted on passengers' willingness to pay based on numerous factors such as the time to the next flight, the possibility of a delay on the next flight, and so forth? An analysis of this level of behavior (not just if the traveler purchased the feature, but also the differentiation between did the passenger want it but did not want it at the price offered) could be one way in which airlines can better determine each customer's value system. The goal would be to determine how different passengers plan their travel in different situations — how and what passengers are searching.

Customers have the ability to pay for what they *want*, as discussed earlier with respect to taxi fares and hotel amenities. Consider another scenario: if a leisure traveler is given the choice of two legacy airlines flying a similar schedule for the same city pair, and one is a few dollars more than the other, will that traveler pay the extra few dollars? Perhaps no, because she does not see the value. Yet, at the same time, the same passenger will likely pay the same $4 for a cup of coffee at the airport. As one executive pointed out, it is ironic that airlines have a captive audience, namely the passengers, yet the airlines themselves capture very little, in this case with respect to insights relating to (1) what customers truly want, and (2) what they are willing to pay for, both in terms of products and services. Consider the case of Condor Airlines that allows passengers to upgrade their service to the premium economy cabin for $180 each way on its long flights, for example, to Vancouver, Canada. Passengers get 15 cm more leg room, premium menu, free alcoholic drinks, free headsets, and a blanket with an extra-wide pillow. The fee reflects the additional costs of removing a row of seats — a mutually beneficial marketing initiative.

The key is to engage with passengers with respect to what they are willing to pay for certain travel services, and, in turn, offer cafeteria-style programs (or bundles) based on what a passenger is willing to pay for travel services at various touchpoints. Airlines already provide such services for the higher fare paying segments, but they can now develop business cases to penetrate the middle segments with a greater array of choices (that is, in a cafeteria-style manner or in bundles), especially by leveraging the emerging mobile channel. Some airlines have already begun to develop and market bundles; however, such products can be enhanced and developed specifically for certain segments (not just business versus leisure, but different subsegments within each). Surveys already exist showing not only the willingness to pay for different bundles but also a significant variation by ethnicity. For example, returning to the study conducted by PwC, passengers from Brazil and the UK are more likely to pay a much higher premium for packaged bundles than travelers in the US, 6.7 times more in the case of Brazil and 5.0 times more in the case of the UK. On the other hand, travelers based in China are likely to pay a lot less than travelers in the US.[9]

Takeaways

- The redesign of an airline's business to attract the targeted segments and maintain their loyalty can only come after gaining knowledge of a customer's stated or implied primary and secondary needs, as well as their willingness to pay for the desired travel services.
- While airlines have focused on deriving value from "upstream" products, they need to focus on potential "downstream" revenue-generating activities.
- The value of the basic product needs to be revisited and promoted.
- The mindset needs to be shifted from looking at ancillaries as fees to viewing and promoting ancillary products and services as value-based options.

Notes

1   "Experience Radar 2013: Lessons Learned from the Airline Industry," Volume 5, October 2013, PricewaterhouseCoopers, p. 38.

2   Jonathan Kletzel and Jon Glick, "A Strong Signal," *Airlines International: Technology Supplement*, August–September 2013.

3   Kathryn Creedy, "Flexible Flyers," *Businesstravelerusa.com*, May 2012; Singapore Airlines's website.

4   "Global Brand Simplicity Index 2013: Demonstrating the Impact of Simplicity on Revenue, Loyalty, and Innovation," Siegel+Gale, New York, 2013, p. 25.

5   Niraj Dawar, *Tilt: Shifting Your Strategy from Products to Customers* (Boston, MA: Harvard Business Review Press, 2013).

6   Malcolm McDonald and Ian Dunbar, *Market Segmentation: How to Do It and How to Profit from It* (West Sussex, United Kingdom: John Wiley, 2012), p. 149.

7   "Experience Radar 2013: Lessons Learned from the Airline Industry," Volume 5, October 2013, PricewaterhouseCoopers, pp. 2, 48, and 58.

8   Martin Raymond, "The Future of Comfort: Asia," *The Future Laboratory*, London, UK, February 2014.

9   "Experience Radar 2013: Lessons Learned from the Airline Industry," Volume 5, October 2013, PricewaterhouseCoopers, p. 39.

Chapter 3
Positioning on the Customization Spectrum

It seems that these days more and more airlines are trying to become "customer centric." Since customer centricity is hardly a new topic, why is it still being discussed? In the case of airlines, answers may vary from the desire to move away from being in a commodity business to increasing margins, market share, and or loyalty. Another reason might be that load factors are relatively high and there is not a lot of room for growth in terms of products (networks, cabin configurations, in-flight entertainment systems, and so forth).

What does being "customer centric" really mean anyway? There appears to be some confusion in the airline industry. First, some airlines claim to be "customer centric," but it is important to distinguish between being customer *focused* (providing generally good, courteous, knowledgeable, and professional service *to all passengers*) and truly being customer *centric*, referring to focusing on particular segments of the marketplace. Second, there appears to be some confusion between customer centricity and personalization. Customer centricity means being focused on a specific set of segments and their needs, and then meeting the needs of all the customers in those segments using the same strategy and tactics for all persons within a given segment. This process is customization at the segment level. Personalization, on the other hand, means identifying the needs of each and every individual in a given segment and then meeting those needs on a one-to-one basis.

A Historical Perspective

Stepping back for a moment to review a little history, the airline industry began with an operations-centric focus and moved to product centricity. Operations centricity does not just include on-time performance, but also includes choosing hubs, aircraft routings, crew bases, airport operations, and so forth. In the beginning, operations centricity was needed to coordinate various elements in the aviation chain—airports, aircraft, air traffic control systems, and bilateral agreements. Product centricity came next and led to such innovations as the hub-and-spoke system, premium cabins, in-flight entertainment, alliances, e-ticketing, and lie-flat beds. Product centricity occurs when the focus is on a specific area or a department, leading to both a challenge and an opportunity. Take the case of missed connections. The challenge is that different departments have different perspectives with respect to their understanding, measurement, and corrective action. From this perspective, an airline may be looking at itself as a collection of different departments and different functions—network, operations, sales, loyalty, and so forth. However, a customer may look at an airline differently, as an organization that sells seats from A to B, or an organization that provides travel, or an organization that provides solutions to travel-related problems. The opportunity is, of course, to realign the understanding of the customer to develop a unified understanding of the issue from the customer's point of view and, in turn, a unified strategy to handle the problem. Another example would be a cabin class, such as Premium Economy. Different departments (say loyalty, marketing, operations, pricing, and revenue management) tend to have different perspectives with respect to what this cabin class means to *them*. In both cases, there is no comprehensive or integrated view of the product, let alone the customer. Are the pricing, the loyalty, and the finance departments looking at Premium Economy in the same way, let alone from the viewpoint of customers? Who gets upgraded to a seat in Premium Economy—under what situation and at what price, if any? How does an airline compute the "cost" of a missed connection, by passenger and by situation?

Next on the spectrum (although not highlighted in Figure 3.2) is market centricity where an airline can look at the market from the viewpoint of developments relating to geography, competitors, and collaborators (as in Figure 3.1). With respect to geography, clearly passenger traffic in some regions is growing faster than in other regions—North America and Europe compared to Asia and Latin America, for example. How can an airline based in one region participate in the traffic growth of another region? Some have purchased equity in airlines based in growing regions, Delta, for example, in GOL and AeroMexico. As for competitors, the developments relate more to new players than existing players, especially those in the distribution sector. These players are integrating information whereas the conventional players are integrating physical assets. Then there are collaborators leading to such developments as crowd-sourcing, crowd-funding, and consumer co-creation (co-production). Furthermore, there is also the new trend that is developing known as "socialstructing."[1] It relates to people coming together to engage in collective action to change people's lives, say, in the area of healthcare. At a lower level, in the case of travel, collaborative consumption may also come under the category of "socialstructing," as in the launch of Airbnb (discussed later in this chapter and also in Chapter 8). Next is customer centricity as described at the beginning of this chapter. The key success factor is the ability to integrate— physical assets in the case of operations centricity and information assets in the case of customer centricity. See Figure 3.1. Customer centricity has a major impact on product development and the establishment of operational priorities.

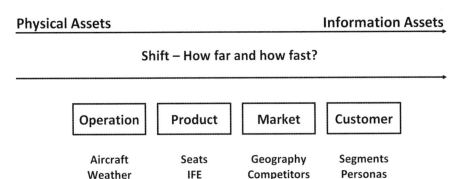

Physical Assets   **Information Assets**

Shift – How far and how fast?

Operation	Product	Market	Customer
Aircraft	Seats	Geography	Segments
Weather	IFE	Competitors	Personas
Airports	Lounges	Collaborators	Individuals

Figure 3.1   Value adding centricity

Current Landscape

Some airlines that are growing rapidly are naturally focusing on the product (network, fleet, and cabin configurations). They are customer focused in the sense that they are looking at the concerns of customers, but not necessarily at a detailed segment level or at a personalization level with various segments, except for the very, very top layer of frequent travelers in their loyalty programs.

Consider some examples of relatively new low cost airlines that are focused heavily on growth and Initial Public Offerings (IPOs) — Interjet based in Mexico, Azul based in Brazil, and VivaColombia based in Colombia. In the case of Interjet (launched in 2005) the airline is focused on right sizing the fleet (adding the 93-seat Sukoi Superjet 100s to the 150-seat Airbus 320–200s) to penetrate smaller markets, to divert passengers from buses, to transform itself into a hybrid carrier that can gain access to business traffic through relevant product attributes, to gain market share, and to position itself for a successful IPO during 2014. In the case of Azul (launched in 2008) the object was initially to penetrate the regional markets with the Embraer 190/195s, then even smaller markets with the smaller ATR turboprops, to increase market share by acquiring TRIP, and to position itself for a successful IPO in 2014 through its strength in domestic markets and its competitive differences with GOL. VivaColombia (launched in 2012) is clearly strategizing to obtain a significant size of the domestic market and start services in international markets. Clearly, the goals of these carriers are very different in terms of positioning on the customization spectrum to the legacy carriers.

Turkish Airlines, for example, is expanding its network at incredible rates. As of November 2013, Turkish Airlines offered service to 104 countries, more than any other airline, 197 international destinations from a single hub, more than any other airline, and served 239 destinations, making it the fourth largest in terms of network size.[2] In terms of traffic growth, the airline has experienced a compound average growth rate of about 15 percent for ten years (2003 to 2013). It is noteworthy that since 2009, according to one analysis, Istanbul has experienced the largest increase in connectivity, higher than Dubai, Singapore, and Hong Kong, as reflected in Table 3.1.[3]

Table 3.1   Air travel connectivity changes: 2009–2013

	Cities	Increase in Index Value of Air Travel (5)
1	Istanbul	15.0
2	Dubai	13.3
3	Singapore	11.2
4	Seoul	9.5
5	Bangkok	9.0
6	Kuala Lumpur	8.4
7	Hong Kong	8.1
8	Moscow	7.8
9	Taipei	6.2
10	Shanghai	5.8

Source: CAPA–Centre for Aviation, and Turkish Airlines from MasterCard Worldwide Insights

The focus on global growth and the enhancement of the brand is evident from the airline's announced communication plan with its advertising agency to promote the quality of its service, in general, as one of the top global airlines. See the commercials on YouTube entitled, "Kobe vs. Messi: Shootout" and "Kobe vs. Messi: Legends on Board," that became immediate hits. The second version (Legends on Board) follows the first version of the commercial last year (Shootout) that launched the positioning of the brand of Turkish Airlines. The motto was "Globally Yours" and is now changing to "Widen Your World." The enhancement of the product is not just limited to the expansion of the network but also an improvement in customer service in such areas as meal service (with "samovar, candle light, and Flying Chefs") features.

Consider another example, the International Airlines Group (IAG). To become more competitive with Air France-KLM and the Lufthansa Group, British Airways merged with Iberia (within the framework of a multinational airline holding company), acquired British Midland from Lufthansa (BMI), launched Iberia Express (a low cost airline to feed IAG's Madrid hub), and acquired Vueling (a low cost airline based in Barcelona, Spain). The restructuring of IAG's network, particularly the Heathrow and Madrid hubs, will go on for years—for example, by making Iberia a more effective competitor in the Europe–Latin America market and by making Vueling a more effective feeder for British Airways. Furthermore, Iberia's and British Airways's networks will be enhanced by having Vueling reduce its Spain-based capacity and increase its non-Spain-based capacity.

Customization Spectrum

Nevertheless, leading airlines, while remaining product focused, have begun to think about customer centricity with initiatives such as British Airways's "Know Me" program. Similarly, some other airlines are also showing an interest in moving from product centricity to customer centricity, in varying degrees. One example is the use of a Google Glass headset to obtain information on an individual customer to engage in a relevant and situation-based manner. Assuming that customer centricity means dividing the total marketplace into segments and then meeting the needs of each segment with a different product or service, then the question relates to what level of customization should be offered *within* each segment. In this case, the question is: Where does an airline want to be on the customization spectrum? In other words, how many segments does an airline want to serve, how are these segments to be established, and what are the different levels of customization within each segment? Some airlines are marketing at a "one-size-fits-all" level (one large segment), whereas others are at a level of having multiple and more defined segments, and some are even trying to provide individualized service within one or more segments, thus approaching the personalization level. Not all airlines have the need or the resources to offer *customized* products and services (by segment), let alone offer *personalized* products and services within even one segment, and certainly not within multiple segments. Figure 3.2 illustrates these different levels of centricity (operation, product, and customer) and it should be noted that the element of customer focus spans

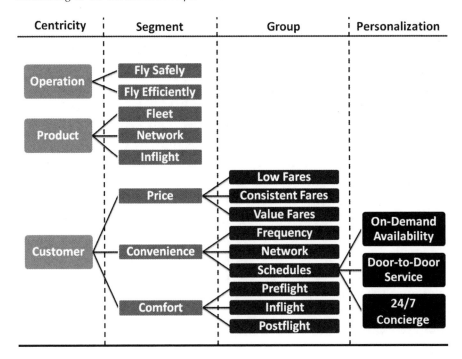

Figure 3.2   The customization spectrum

the entire spectrum. Consider the following airline example in relation to the spectrum.

Ryanair, up until now, has been offering a very clear value proposition—taking passengers from A to B at a rock bottom price and with absolutely no frills. Its customers have understood that and did not expect to build a relationship. The focus in this case has been on basic transportation. Customization has not been needed and, consequently, the strategy has been to remain operations centric (for example, minimum turnaround times and optimal location of crew bases) and product centric (for example, its passenger network). This positioning represents one end of the customization spectrum, the "one-size-fits-all" level, characterized by one large segment seeking this value proposition.

However, until recently, Ryanair could actually be categorized as being at the far end of the spectrum as it has just begun to be customer focused. Recent reports have indicated that Ryanair is trying to implement a more customer-focused approach, improving the ways it interacts with customers and working to temper its image. Some initiatives include improving its website (recognizing that it can be cumbersome and frustrating to navigate), especially in terms of redesigning the booking flow and removing the "Recaptcha" security feature, as well as eliminating the charge to download the airline's mobile app. Another augmentation to the carrier's digital marketing strategy includes launching an official Twitter account. In addition to these customer-focused initiatives, the carrier is also moving further along the customization spectrum as a result of its recent efforts to cater to the business segment, thus moving away from the previous "one-size-fits-all" segmentation strategy. Specifically, some elements that the airline has already changed that suit business travelers are priority boarding and reserved seating. Further changes include accepting the American Express card for payment as well as the possibility of mobile boarding passes and fast track security in the future.[4] Returning to the topics of customer service and experience, Ryanair's new Chief Marketing Officer, Kenny Jacobs's focus is to "improve brand perceptions using data, digital, CRM and, for the first time, TV advertising."[5]

However, in other cases, such as more traditional airlines, moving further along the customization spectrum is needed as airlines are struggling to develop distinguishable brands. Each airline could decide, based on its resources and vision, the number of segments to serve and the type of customization within each segment. For its very top segment, for example, a globally recognized brand could even try to offer personalized service. For this segment, the customization could be developed around a framework in which the airline becomes a solution provider, understanding what the specific needs of each customer are and taking appropriate action—not the *general* needs of passengers within this top segment, but the *specific* needs of every individual passenger within this given segment. Suppose an airline offers a service to travelers in its top segment—meet and escort if, and only if, they have a tight connection. Instead, the following service could be provided—meet, greet, and escort each and every traveler who desires such service, regardless of the connection time. This would represent progress at the personalization level.

As shown in Figure 3.3, developed by PwC, personalization is comprised of three elements (experience, communication,

Components of Personalization

Communication

Brands are increasing the relevance and visibility of customer communications by engaging members via alternate channels and personalizing content based on preferences, contextual information, behavioral data, and channel specific insights

Experience

Customers send signals when they engage with the brand in physical and digital forums. Customer Experience is the art and science of reading those signals from insights and interactions and turning them into personalized products, services and experiences that provide relevance and repeat engagement

Analytics

Marketing is shifting from an art to a science based on the new abilities to collect information and drive relevance through data driven insights and targeting to personalize communications and experiences

Operations

Strong operational capabilities are at the core of personalization and are necessary to support optimized customer communications, experience, and analytics

Figure 3.3   Components of personalization

Source: PricewaterhouseCoopers

and analytics), supported by reliable operations. This chart clearly shows that while experience and analytics lead to insights, experience and communication lead to interaction, and communication and analytics lead to targeting. It is the intersection of these three results (insights, interaction, and targeting) that ultimately lead to personalization.

For airlines that want to proceed to the personalization level, there are three aspects to consider in terms of the degree to which personalization can be leveraged. The first level, which is the most common form of personalization, involves leveraging information about a customer to create specific offers. This form of personalization is widely used in the retail industry. For example, knowing that a customer always books a business class seat when flying across the Atlantic but, as a result of a lack of available seats, has been forced to book an economy seat on a particular flight, an airline could offer to provide a limo service at both ends and a business class meal either for free or for a nominal price, depending on the value of the customer. The second level of personalization would be dynamic pricing, based in real time. For instance, in a two-way dialogue with a traveler as he is booking a flight, an airline could create a personalized price based on the information that the passenger is providing to the airline. For example, a passenger making the reservation could be willing to sell back the reservation to the airline for an incentive and a guaranteed reservation on the next flight, a freed reservation that the airline could provide to another passenger who needs the seat and is willing to pay the necessary additional fare, an example of on-demand seat availability as depicted in Figure 3.2. The third level, or degree of personalization, would be an airline piecing together all the events that a passenger has experienced (for instance, his luggage had been lost twice or he incurred a misconnection during the last trip) and leveraging that information to extend a personal acknowledgement to the traveler (such as entry to the lounge, an upgrade for the traveler being inconvenienced, a fare discount, or making available a seat in a closed fare bucket). If personalization is carried out well, it can lead to not only a greater share of wallet, but also an increase in loyalty. However, if carried out poorly, it can backfire. Examples include using personal data inappropriately and bombarding customers with irrelevant offers.

Where an airline is on the customization spectrum is also dependent upon the value proposition (as in the Ryanair example) and the stage in growth, such as Air Berlin and Garuda Indonesia, carriers who are focusing on expanding their routes and are therefore focused on the operation and or product end of the spectrum at this point. Air Berlin, for example, has been focused on a dramatic restructuring of its network and fleet, having joined the oneworld alliance and formed an equity partnership with Etihad. The focus is therefore on product centricity. Garuda Indonesia has a focus on both operation centricity and product centricity. Garuda does not fly to the US. Garuda hopes to codeshare with Skyteam member Delta in Tokyo but cannot do so until Indonesia gets upgraded to Category One operations within the US Federal Aviation Administration's safety assessment framework. This explains the need for the operations centricity. As for its product centricity, Garuda has concentrated on growing its domestic markets in the past and is now just beginning to focus on international markets. Operations-centric and product-centric airlines should, of course, be customer focused, but do not necessarily need to achieve higher levels of customization.

On the other hand, airlines such as British Airways, Cathay, Lufthansa, Qantas, and Singapore Airlines are at a more mature point in their life cycle and are therefore at a point where they can pursue higher levels of customization. Airlines that are striving to be more customized, up to and including personalization, can start by getting different departments within an airline to integrate their perspectives to at least agree on single views of different personas, for example, those discussed in the previous chapter. However, while a single view is essential in terms of getting all departments on the same page with respect to the point of view of the customer, it is only the first step in the process if striving for personalization. The next step is obtaining the *complete* view of each customer within the particular segment—that includes getting the missing information that relates to different personalities of a customer or customer behavior, even relating to a given personality, such as why he did chose or did not choose to travel in a particular cabin. Did he not want it, was he not willing to pay for it, or was it not even available?

Consider the multiple possible personalities of a single passenger. Let us assume that an airline does have a single view of a customer, the "globetrotting" Ms Johnson. In other words, all departments within the airline have the same information on her— the loyalty group, the sales group, the revenue management group, customer service, airport operations, and so forth. She is a high level executive with a global consulting firm. She values schedule, priority treatment, comfort, experience, and status recognition. Fare is never an issue given that she is allowed to travel in Business Class to meet her last-minute schedule needs, regardless of the fare level or the service provider. Let us also assume that she is in the very, very top status of an airline's frequent flyer program. While the airline may have a *single* view of Ms Johnson, it is highly unlikely that the airline has a *complete* view of Ms Johnson with respect to her multiple travel personalities: She is a very different person when she is traveling to participate in a convention, versus when she is traveling on vacation. She also operates a small private business. When traveling for her private business, she will travel in Economy Class but will pay for upgrades and add-ons that increase her efficiency and productivity—far from the white-glove treatment she is expecting when traveling on business for her global consulting company. Furthermore, Ms Johnson, the vacationer, is a price conscious traveler but is willing to pay for convenience, for example, opting to purchase bundled services, particularly the bundle that allows rebooking to provide flexibility. True personalization implies accessibility to information on at least these three of the many personalities of Ms Johnson.

Since airlines do not have access to the detailed information mentioned above, some airlines have begun to position themselves on the customization spectrum in terms of focusing on the needs of particular segments, not individuals. Singapore Airlines, for example, has decided to focus on four segments illustrated in Figure 3.4. The segments are based on sector length and the level of services, ranging from no frills to full service, as outlined in the previous chapter. Each of the four segments is to be served by a different brand within the Singapore Airlines Group. The idea behind the four brands is to minimize the degree of cannibalization.

Within the segment served by Singapore Airlines itself (medium to long haul travelers looking for full service), presumably, the airline will subsegment the travelers. For example, the airline could

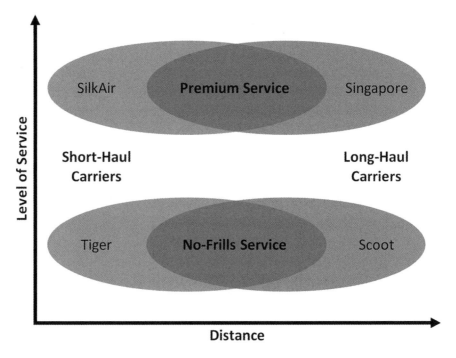

**Figure 3.4   Singapore Airlines Group: Four-brand, portfolio
                strategy**

Source: Based on Singapore Airlines's Figure in the CAPA–Centre for Aviation Analysis

build upon its current three subsegments based on the frequent flyer status in its KrisFlyer programs: KrisFlyer, Elite Silver, and Elite Gold. Next, the Elite Gold could itself be segmented into Elite Gold and Elite Platinum. The latter category, Elite Platinum could represent, for example, the top 10 percent (or even the top 5 or top 2 percent) of the flyers in the Elite Gold category. This subsegment could then be served on a one-to-one, personalized basis. Of course, the airline needs to be sure that segmentation based on frequent flyer status is a reasonable measurement of segment value, profitability (current or future), NPS, and so forth.

JetBlue has announced its plan to serve the "underserved" markets. Figure 3.5 shows a plot of Trip Purpose versus Customer Spend. Whereas the ultra low cost carriers seem to be focused on the segments in the lower left hand corner and the major network carriers seem to be focused on the segments in the upper right hand corner, JetBlue is planning to capitalize on the middle segments, especially the group between the "High Value Leisure" and the "Mixed Wallets." This segment represents JetBlue's "sweet spot."

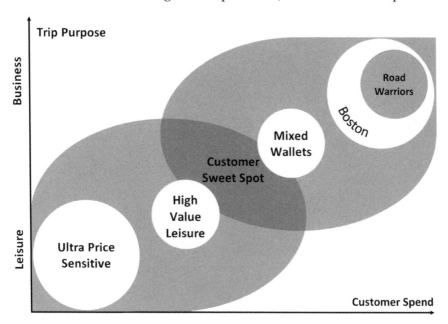

Figure 3.5   JetBlue Airways's Strategy: Serving the underserved markets

Source: JetBlue

What each airline needs to do is to revisit *how* the segments are to be determined. For the most part, airlines have been segmenting based upon frequent flier status. The obvious challenge in doing so is that a person who is traveling on business once a month within the US, say at an average fare of $300 each trip, is valued more than a business traveler who makes a trip once a year from the US to Asia at a fare of $10,000. Factors that could be considered in the resegmentation process are lifetime value and profitability that can be calculated on many different components, not just revenue or even frequency, but also other factors such as social influence. Also, it is important for an airline to not just discard its existing segmentation and select a new one, but rather to transition from the existing one to the new one.

Furthermore, many of the global traditional airlines have been focusing on the business travel segment given that this segment provides a disproportionately higher percentage of the total revenue, a disproportionately higher percentage of the total travel, a much higher yield, and, possibly, a higher profit margin. However, first, the business travel segment is decreasing as the other segments of travel are increasing (leisure, VFR, and so on). Second, the competitive pressure is increasing to divert the business travel segment over to newer generation global airlines (such as those based in the Persian Gulf and China). Third, the lower cost airlines have not only diverted a large percentage of the short and medium haul travel to themselves, but also many are now trying to penetrate the business segment within these sector lengths, exemplified by the recent initiatives of EasyJet, JetBlue, and Southwest. Even Ryanair is starting to fly to and from major conventional airports such as Brussels and Rome Fiumicino. Moreover, the lower cost airlines are also beginning to redesign their fleet-network plans to develop cost effective service in intercontinental markets, exemplified by the announcements of Norwegian Air Shuttle based in Scandinavia and WestJet, based in Canada.

Some large traditional global airlines, however, have begun to revisit their strategy relating to the non-business segments. Lufthansa, for example, having sold its financial stake in its charter subsidiary (Condor) and the tour operator subsidiary (Thomas

Cook), not to mention reducing its network relating to leisure destinations, must now redesign its strategy to cater to the needs of the non-business segments. Air Canada has launched Rouge. However, focusing on the non-business segments means more than simply viewing it as "filler" traffic. It means identifying the segments (for example, not only the Millennials and seniors, but also their subdivisions, based on ethnicity and culture), their needs, and clear value propositions that encompass the entire spectrum from product, to distribution channels, to loyalty programs. Given the very different needs of some emerging segments (again, say the Millennials that place a high value on the digital experience), it may make sense for an airline to develop strategic partnerships with newer generation members in the value chain. These new players could include, for example, technology firms that specialize in the deployment of information and communications technologies as well as analytics to conduct semantic search and develop dynamic packaging based on access to the real time availability of inventory in all components of the journey.

If customers are looking for experience, then why not consider segmenting customers by the level and type of experience desired. An airline could start by listing some product and service features that customers would value and then segment passengers by the features desired. The features could include, for example, on-time performance, seat comfort, meal service, problem resolution, airport check in, smartphone booking and check-in capability as well as bag labeling and tracking, loyalty rewards (earning and burning), and so on. Then, even within each feature type, there could be subsegments, or groupings, of different features as there are customers who value experience from different angles. One may want seat comfort and on-time performance. Another one might value on-time performance and meals. Yet another may prefer total mobile capability—shopping, booking, check in, and baggage labeling and tracking. Based on the airline's experience, these segments will undoubtedly show significant variation based on ethnicity and culture. For example, the British customers may have a very different preference for mobile capability than the Brazilians. However, it is important to note that the idea is not to get back to categorizing customers in the traditional way (by purpose of travel—for example, business travelers ranking on-time performance much higher than leisure travelers) but to categorize by those that rank it higher regardless of the purpose of the trip.

Furthermore, for each segment selected on the spectrum, an airline could provide more information and the type of information that passengers in the designated customer segment are likely to desire. In my last book, *The Passenger Has Gone Digital and Mobile,* several third party intermediaries were discussed in terms of providing much desired information to travelers. This trend seems to be continuing as a number of other intermediaries have launched, many in an effort to provide information to travelers that they are not receiving from traditional suppliers. For example, Routehappy's "Happiness Scores" indicate shorter flights with better planes, seats, amenities and flyer ratings, as described on their website, which highlights that their mission is to help users easily find and purchase the "happiest" flights for the lowest price.[6] Other intermediaries are providing information to travelers in the hotel sector. Room 77 strives to save travelers "countless hours" searching for the best deal in terms of hotel rooms,[7] while the premise of HotelTonight is to provide easy mobile booking of deeply discounted last minute available rooms.[8]

The question is, where do airlines want to be in terms of being information providers? Do they want to continue to let intermediaries be the primary source of information to travelers? As it stands, there are three possible scenarios with respect to the role of airlines as providers of information. First, carriers could invest in the technology and resources to be the primary provider. This could help to change the perception of airlines in the eyes of customers as airlines become viewed more as value providers in terms of information, thus providing airlines an opportunity to encourage and drive loyalty. However, this comes at a cost— both financially and in terms of resources. A second option is to purchase third party software that will conduct information-providing operations for the airline in a way that is seamless to the traveler navigating the airline's website. This scenario still, of course, involves a financial investment, but alleviates the resources needed to conduct the operations. Finally, the third option is to leave it as is, with third party intermediaries servicing as the primary information providers.[9]

Insights from Other Industries

It appears that some members of the hotel industry are "walking in the shoes" of their customers to understand some of the "pain points" customers incur when consuming hotel products and services. Consider some of the bold moves that members in this sector of the travel chain have implemented. Starwood has dramatically changed the traditional hotel business model with respect to check-in/check-out times. Specifically, the hotelier's "Your24" program allows its top members (those who stay at Starwood hotels 75 or more nights per year) to choose their own check-in time, a system that works on a rolling 24-hour basis. Therefore, if a member does not check in until late one evening, then he will not have to check out until that same time the day when he is leaving. Starwood also goes out of its way to cater to the needs of its 2 percent of guests who generate about 30 percent of profitability.[10] About 50 percent of Starwood's guests are in their loyalty programs. However, Starwood hotels appear to be identifying and engaging not only a subsegment of the other 48 percent already in the loyalty program but also a subsegment of the 50 percent not within the program.

While Starwood's "Your24" program appears to target top tier travelers in terms of frequency (those who stay at Starwood hotels 75 or more nights per year) and therefore represents a more customer-centric initiative, consider some other programs that have been implemented that appear to span greater segments of travelers, and therefore have a more customer-focused approach. Westin Hotels & Resorts, a member of Starwood, is also featuring a weekend program—"Make Monday Better"—in which travelers may extend their check out on Sundays to 3pm for free in order to enjoy a longer weekend.

Hyatt has distinguished itself in terms of a different "pain point" of travel—forgotten items. Specifically, Hyatt advertises that they offer items from "chargers to curling irons to yoga mats" to borrow—items that travelers may have forgotten to pack or need while they are away from home. Another area that Hyatt is addressing is food options. Specifically, Hyatt advertises that they are rethinking menus in terms of offering smaller portions and "create your own" dishes in an attempt to recognize that travelers may have different needs at different times of the day— giving the example that what someone may eat at noon, they may not want to eat at midnight. It is interesting to note that both advertisements stress that these offerings have put the traveler in control—the first stating "It's hospitality with you in charge," and the second stating, "They're designed with you in charge."

Another example of an hotelier that is looking toward reinvention is Marriott. Marriott launched a new global marketing campaign, "Travel Brilliantly" emphasizing "the lifestyle of the next generation of travelers, who seamlessly blend work and play in a mobile and global world." In conjunction with this new campaign, Marriott has introduced an innovation website that illustrates their current ideas in terms of reinventing travel, the ideas that others have submitted, and invites users to share their ideas.[11]

Airlines can also look to some non-traditional companies in travel-related industries. Consider a different type of hotel service, discussed further in Chapter 8, Airbnb, which serves more as a "community marketplace"[12] for accommodations— anything from a room, to an apartment, to a house, even a castle! Consumers are able to list, search, or book short term rooms to rent via mobile or online. It appears that Airbnb goes way beyond simply providing a rather generic product, that is a hotel room, rather it offers travelers the specific, personalized experience they may be searching for while at their destination, for example, in residential neighborhoods. Airbnb reportedly develops user profiles and reviews to identify compatible renters and clients.

Consider a company that has leveraged mobile to make the process of getting and using a taxi service much more customer centric and even personalized. Uber, also discussed further in Chapter 8, leverages mobile to connect customers and car service providers of varying levels of service. The central nervous system of the business is mobile—leveraged to determine the location of the customer, the location of the driver, the times between the two parties, even to make payment. Mobile is truly at the heart of the operation.

Takeaways

- All airlines do not have the need or the resources to offer customized products and services (by segment), let alone offer personalized products and services within even one segment, and certainly not within multiple segments.
- Regardless of the type of segmentation and the level of personalization, airlines need to address all areas of customer concerns to succeed at being customer focused — professionalism, knowledge, friendliness, and ease of doing business, especially with respect to the ease of buying.
- The three main components of personalization are experience, communication, and analytics, all supported by reliable operations.
- Airlines need to make mobile the heart of their system as travel is mobile by nature. Airlines' top customers as well as up-and-coming customers (such as the Millennials) are most likely to be mobile centric, leading to a need for a redesign of the business to make it easier to research, buy, and experience travel.
- Airlines need to determine where they want to be in terms of being information providers. If they do not provide the information sought by travelers, other third party intermediaries can and will, thus earning the loyalty of consumers.

Notes

1 Howard Rheingold, "Three Harbingers of Change," *strategy+business*, Winter 2013, p. 74.

2 "Turkish Airlines Reiterates Growth Opportunities and a More Profitable Outlook for SunExpress," *CAPA–Centre for Aviation Analysis*, November 23, 2013.

3 Ibid.

4 "Ryanair's New Customer-Friendly Approach. Really?," *CAPA–Centre for Aviation Analysis*, October 3, 2013.

5 Sarah Vizard, "Ryanair's CMO on how the airline is communicating the 'new' Ryanair," *MarketingWeek*, published on March 27, 2014 (accessed April 2, 2014 online).

6   https://www.routehappy.com/about (accessed April 3, 2014 online).

7   https://www.room77.com/about.html?pid=QYaZxi&id=a0vOXJ (accessed April 3, 2014 online).

8   http://www.hoteltonight.com/ (accessed April 3, 2014 online).

9   Based upon a presentation given by Adam Goldstein, Co-Founder & CEO, Hipmunk, at the International Airline Symposium in October, 2013.

10   http://www.starwoodhotels.com/fourpoints/about/news/news_release_detail.html?Id=StarwoodReinventHotel (accessed April 3, 2014 online).

11   Marriott News Center, June 17, 2013 and www.travelbrilliantly.com (accessed April 3, 2014 online).

12   https://www.airbnb.com/about/about-us (accessed April 3, 2014 online).

Chapter 4
Progressing to Become Genuine Retailers

One critical area in the transformation and the redesign of the airline business is retailing. It is an essential requirement for customer centricity described in the previous chapter. An airline really does need to know how to sell to targeted segments before it can create customized service to avoid selling primarily on price. Retailing has the potential to make an airline a higher margin business by creating better experiences for the targeted passengers, leading to a differentiation of brands—a mutually beneficial situation for both airlines and passengers. Airlines are clearly embracing the *merchandising* concept, a first step to retailing, having unbundled the product and having started to market ancillary products and services—again, mutually beneficial for both passengers and airlines. Having made significant progress in the areas of product enhancement and pricing with respect to "seat managing *the values*," they are still struggling in the area of "romancing" the customer so as to be able to make a particular airline the preferred airline of the customer rather than the customer feeling forced to choose a particular airline. To become dynamic *retailers* of services, however, they need to comprehensively address such matters as customer acquisition, conversion, service, and measurement. This chapter discusses retailing with respect to some of these phases within the context of products, pricing, and distribution, relating to the decision on not just what products to make, but how to deliver them.

Retailing

Within the global airline industry, the importance of retailing is escalating due to the following factors:

- customers are becoming increasingly empowered, increasingly demanding, and are seeking seamless, consistent, and differentiated brand experiences;
- many customers are seeking personalized services and travel experiences at various touchpoints;
- the marketplace is becoming much more competitive with ultra low cost airlines and hybrid airlines adding to the list of low cost and full service airlines;
- the number of channels is increasing with the growing use of the Internet (meta-search sites such as Kayak, online consolidators such as Vayama International, and content aggregators such as TravelFusion);
- pricing strategies relating to the use of intermediaries may need to change;
- sophisticated technology companies (Amazon, Concur, and Google, for example), armed with vast quantities of information on customer behaviors and attitudes as well as analytics, could become significant players as new kinds of distributors; and
- enhanced retailing, through customer engagement and dynamic offers on the one hand and sophisticated merchandising technology on the other hand, can lead to higher margins and brand differentiation.

Customers are now constantly connected and tech-savvy (shopping, planning, buying, and sharing online), have specific needs, and increasing numbers are expecting to receive personalized services. Airlines face an even greater challenge with respect to segmentation as airlines tend to deal with a much broader customer base versus traditional retailers, for example. Persons shopping at high end stores and those shopping at ultra discount stores could be on the same flight. Meeting these needs raises two basic questions: (1) are the demanding customers willing to pay for services expected, and (2) how can airlines evolve from selling ancillary services to becoming effective retailers for different segments, such as the two distinct groups outlined above?

The airline industry has already undertaken the first step to retailing—namely, merchandising—an initiative that has produced significant revenues and, in turn, net profits, as the additional costs to generate these revenues were minimal. These ancillary revenues achieved through the sale of complementary products and services not only improved the financial performance of the industry, but also led the airlines on a path of trying to match the availability of products and services to the needs of customers from the viewpoint of value. The process of unbundling the core product should be in favor of customers in that it provides consumers greater choice of the features they value and desire to purchase. It also improved the quality of service provided in some areas. For example, it has been reported that less bags were mishandled after the introduction of fees.[1] On the other hand, the process also led to an increase in complexity in the purchase process, not to mention raising the question of price transparency. In fact, many "ancillary" revenues simply originated in the form of collections for "fees" for fuel surcharges, credit card handling, boarding card printing, rebooking, and so forth, resulting in customer frustration. Airlines can now become genuine retailers by:

- identifying customer profiles and segmenting product/ service features by value to those customer segments;
- making search and shopping easier and transparent, regardless of the channel (including mobile);
- offering only relevant products and services, keeping in mind the location and situation of the customer, not to mention the customer's profile;
- optimizing, analytically, the sale of ancillary products and services, just as they did with inventory and fare buckets using revenue management techniques;
- optimizing distribution by channel; and
- capitalizing on mobile technology to make timely offers, including day of travel, and charge for such services on mobile devices.

In light of these considerations, the retailing cycle has to be rethought. First, there are phases of the retailing cycle that have not been addressed adequately, for example, the inspiration phase. Second, it is not fully understood that true retailing impacts multiple departments, processes, and systems. The central one is, of course, revenue management. However, there are many other functions that are impacted—loyalty, products, passenger service systems, third party content and availability, branded fares, service recovery, channel management and Internet booking, just to name a few. And even within one phase, there are subphases. Take, for example, passenger service systems that deal with such functions as reservations, inventory, and departure control that, in turn, deal with check in and load control. Third, the purchasing process is changing due to an increase in the use of mobile and social technologies. For example, the post-trip phase includes sharing that, in turn, relates back to experience. Similarly, inspiration and shopping can relate back to the sharing part of the post-trip phase. Finally, the average travel search is well researched and is conducted across multiple channels. It involves users seeking, providing, and sharing content. In addition to using multiple channels, travelers are also leveraging the omnichannel experience, namely, using multiple channels simultaneously. They are always "on," with mobile in hand.

Becoming genuine retailers requires a focus on five phases and subphases of the retailing cycle shown in Figure 4.1. Until recently the focus has been on the purchase phase. Customer acquisition, that relates to two phases, inspiration and shopping, has not been adequately addressed. The important part here is to identify potential customers and to engage with them to determine their needs and preferences. The idea is to explore how an airline can help customers make the purchase decision and how likely various customers are to spend money in different phases of the retail cycle—inspiration versus shopping, for example. They will spend more if they are given information, options, and ideas that may lead them to be inspired and shop. Think about the following statistic. Google research shows that 70 percent of people do not know where they want to go when first thinking about booking a trip.[2] Admittedly, this segment represents the leisure group,

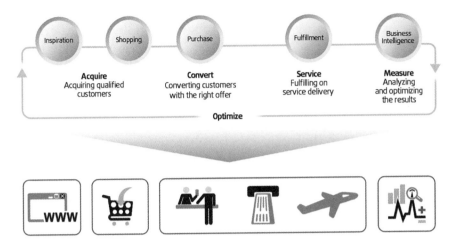

Figure 4.1   Adapting retailing to the airline business model
Source: Sabre Airline Solutions

but the potential is enormous given the forecasted increase in the middle classes in emerging markets (see Figure 1.2 in Chapter 1).

The next phase is the purchase phase. The idea here is to win (convert) the desired customers with the right offers and at the right time. The next phase, fulfillment, relates to the provision of the actual service itself, consisting of numerous subphases, actual check in, services onboard during the flight, and fulfillment aspects of the experience. The idea here is to provide a high level of customer experience at each touchpoint.

The final phase, business intelligence, relates not only to the gathering and analysis of information after the flight but, even more important, to enabling travelers to share their experience, recommendations, and photos after the trip. This last element is particularly important given that social media has become an integral part of travel, starting with the pre-planning phase and ending with post-trip phase. Consequently, enhanced retailing relates not only to the development of new products and services, but also to new ways to acquire and retain customers relating to loyalty, offering consistent content and experience (physical and digital) with respect to the use of multichannels (leveraging the omnichannel experience), and fully deploying social media.

In recent years, most of the attention has been focused on the ancillary products and services provided by airlines themselves, such as early boarding and access to lounges. However, there are also opportunities for selling ancillary services provided by third parties. Traditionally, the third party services have included cars, hotels, travel insurance, and sightseeing tours. However, there are also services such as 24/7 digital travel concierges, services that enhance traveler productivity, and airport transfers — ancillary services that passengers desire and for which airlines could collect commissions. Moreover, the sale and seamless delivery of such services, particularly those that enhance the total travel experience and lead to personalization, could enhance an airline's brand as well as competitive differentiation. See Figure 4.2. The sale of third party ancillary services can enable an airline to keep its basic fares even lower, just as sales of its own ancillary services do. Passengers will pay for services they feel they need.

The keys to the capitalization of this source are: (1) knowledge of customer profiles, and (2) technology — smartphones and mobile payment methods to make the right offer to the right person at the right time (at various touchpoints and various phases of the journey). As for data, in the early days of travel, airlines obtained data on customers from sources such as reservations, check in, and surveys. Next came such sources of data as the loyalty programs. Now, the sources include the Internet and social media. Passengers clearly want information. Consider the success of businesses such as Hipmunk, SeatGuru, and TripAdvisor. Consider also the value that can be delivered by emerging technology companies that enable airlines to provide upgrade capabilities on a silent bid basis or for airlines to purchase back non-refundable tickets that have already been sold and will not be used by their purchasers.

While others have piggy-backed on the basic transportation service provided by airlines, similarly, now airlines must look to other business opportunities on which they, in turn, can piggy-back. Airlines can, for example, look at potential opportunities for selling and advertising in the "flying bazaar" given that the "captive" travelers pass, not once, but twice, through an airline's "flying bazaar." Travelers are also a captive audience for several hours at the gate area. Airlines, in turn, can target high end retailers. During the holiday season of 2013, it was predicted that "one in four" travelers in the US was likely to purchase a gift at an airport.[3] The same report highlights that some airports are transforming themselves as high end shopping malls. Could it be that some malls will become "shopping malls with runways?" Some airports are also offering different levels of VIP services for different prices.[4]

Airlines can also offer business centers, much like hotels do, enabling passengers to conduct business while flying. Let us also not forget the subsegment of business travelers that want to remain productive during the flight, a particularly difficult task in Economy Classes on long haul flights. Other examples include casinos onboard, and investment in social and mobile technologies. These initiatives require a different mindset. Since airlines have not made money selling seats (as illustrated in Chapter 1), they must find other opportunities, especially relating to customer marketing opportunities. Think about ways to enhance the shopping experience or reduce stress. With respect to the development of new streams of revenue, think of the potential opportunity that an airline has with its airline.com website, "its global storefront."

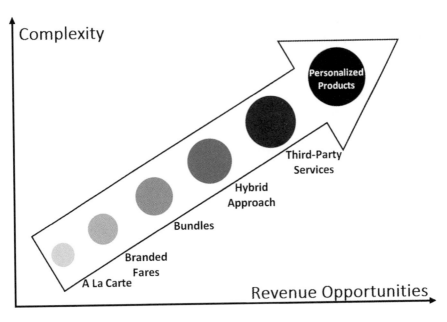

Figure 4.2   Revenue opportunities

Products

In recent years, the focus in innovation has been on seats, first, in Business Class and, second, in Premium Class, in long haul intercontinental markets. A few, such as Singapore Airlines and Emirates Airline, have also put resources into first class cabins (suites), and some others, such as Air New Zealand, have attempted to innovate in the economy class cabins (the Cuddle Seat). The rationale is clearly based on profitability. For the industry as a whole, while premium travelers may only account for about 10 percent of total travelers, the revenue generated from this segment (those traveling in Business and First Class) is approaching almost one-third of the total revenue. In light of the importance of premium travelers, Singapore Airlines has always been at the cutting edge of the in-flight product, seats, in-flight entertainment, cabin attendants, and so forth.

While the business class product in intercontinental markets is acknowledged to be profitable, there is, however, an ongoing debate on the profitability of the first class product that is still offered by some airlines in intercontinental markets. On the "for" side, arguments go along the following lines: We must provide a full breadth of products. First Class is our flagship. Some passengers buy our business class product hoping that they would get upgraded to First Class, a purchase that would not be made if we did not offer a first class product. On the "against" side, arguments go along the following lines: The real cost of the first class product is actually higher than the fare even with the fare being a large multiple of the economy fare. Costs must be assigned not just to the additional space, but also to lower load factors based on paying passengers, greater number of flight attendants, higher costs of food and beverages, access to special areas of lounges, separate check-in facilities and staff, and so forth. The evidence seems to weigh in on the "against" side except for a few unique carriers such as British Airways operating in the exceptionally high density and high premium markets (New York, John F Kennedy–London, Heathrow, for example) or operating unique aircraft (the high capacity Airbus 380 operating in high premium markets such as Dubai–Heathrow). The upgrade argument is weak given the high ratio of business class seats to first class seats. The flagship argument is also weak based on the experience of other businesses. Volkswagen could not sell enough Phaetons and Mercedes-Benz could not sell enough Maybachs!

The business class product and the premium economy product are clearly hits. Now even low cost airlines are beginning to offer some degrees of premium products. AirAsia offers, for example, not only dedicated check-in counters, priority boarding, access to an airport lounge (at selected airports), fast track through immigration and security, and priority baggage service, but also, for some passengers, golf cart service to the aircraft.

As the recent online survey discussed in Chapter 2 indicated, the new emerging affluent travelers in Asia are looking for more comfort (sleep, wellbeing, and relaxation) when flying Economy Class. According to the results of the survey, these passengers are willing to pay more money for more seat space (not just leg room, but also seat width). One section of the study reporting the survey divides the customers into two groups, NEATS (New Emerging Affluent Travellers—first-time careerists) and HIFTs (High-Income Frequent Travellers—higher earners). According to the survey, for the NEATS "a wider seat means they can store more personal items and socialise more." For the HIFTS, "a wider seat means they can relax, sleep and work more."[5] According to Airbus, the report also identified three other trends for comfort demanded by customers traveling in Asia. These are: (1) the Wi-Fi enabled "always-on cabin", (2) 3-D technology enabling high quality film viewing and shopping experience, and (3) energizing cabin in terms of air quality, noise, mood lighting, and cabin configuration.[6]

As with seats, airlines have also focused on in-flight entertainment systems. However, this product is now raising some questions. On the one hand, the old system with screens embedded in the seats carry higher costs in terms of the initial investment (as much as $15,000 per seat), maintenance, and higher fuel costs due to the extra weight. On the other hand, they can provide higher quality programming such as high definition screens and large screens. And, they do not interfere with the use of table space at meal times. The use of the tablets, a second option, means lower costs in terms of investment (around $600 per unit), but requires some work on the part of the flight attendants in terms of loading and updating the content as well as charging the systems. The third option is for passengers to use their own mobile devices and stream the content using the airline-provided Wi-Fi services. This method can be slow depending on the availability of broadband and the capability of the devices used by passengers. It is more cost effective and airlines could charge for the streaming services used. The jury, however, is still out as to whether airlines can make money selling onboard access to the Internet. Although the initiative is a recent phenomenon, according to a few airlines, less than 10 percent of passengers have been willing to pay for such a service. On long haul intercontinental flights the percentage also may not be higher for full service airlines as they offer high value content (first run movies, for example) for free on their own traditional in-flight entertainment systems and, as such, could hardly charge passengers who use their own devices. Tablet usage by crew will be discussed in Chapter 7.

Specifically with respect to the availability of Internet access onboard, a couple of questions are raised. First, some really old aircraft would need significant modifications to provide connectivity onboard. Second, airlines would need to decide on the charge for such services and the options packages such as fixed costs or costs based on usage as well as bundling options. Next, could the charges, regardless of the method, be eventually competed away? On the other hand, even if the Wi-Fi access is given away for free, there are other benefits such as the marketing value of information available through the usage of this service, not just by airlines, but also by potential partners, airports and other retailers, worldwide.

Service recovery is another component of the product that has been receiving significant attention from leading airlines. On the negative side, the problems causing disruptions are increasing, relating not just to weather, mechanical systems, insufficient capacity of the infrastructure, and labor actions, but also as a result of staff limitations, numbers, and skills. On the positive side, however, information and technology are enabling airlines to increase the speed of service recovery by not only reaccommodating passengers quickly, but also by providing passengers with options to meet their situations in real time. For example, airlines can not only push more information through self-service kiosks, but also enhance the functionality of these kiosks to enable passengers to reaccommodate themselves in almost any situation. Mobile, with its superior capabilities, represents another area of technology that can not only help passengers reaccommodate themselves, but also assist in the recovery of bags, not to mention coordinating crews. The great challenge in service recovery is that flights are so full. The opportunity, therefore, is in the introduction of more sophisticated tools so that travelers can find "the needle in the haystack."

Clearly, most airlines have been focusing on seats, in-flight entertainment services and systems, and service recovery in terms of product innovation. What is next? If we assume that product components can be divided into those that enhance the physical experience and those that enhance the digital experience, then it is the second group that shows enormous opportunity, especially with digital natives. One possible area, as mentioned earlier in the chapter, is collaborating with third party providers, such as 24/7 digital travel concierges. In a time when consumers are always "on" and "connected," such a service would appear to generate value, particularly with the proliferation of mobile devices and social media.

There is one other aspect of the product that could be pursued through the use of digitization—reducing the stress associated with travel. Stress is caused in different phases of travel— shopping, check in, getting through security, flight delays and cancelations as well as subcomponents of a particular phase. Stress relating to delays and cancellations can be further separated into stress from getting information about rebooking and waiting in lines to actually getting rebooked and resolving problems relating to rebookings. This stress could be eased if the passenger was simply able to get the information from an agent on the phone about the options available—with the passenger selecting the desired option, the agent making the rebooking, and the agent providing information on price changes to be debited or credited to the passenger's charge card, all while the passenger is still on the phone.

Pricing

Airlines have clearly not made a reasonably consistent profit, as illustrated in Figure 1.1 in Chapter 1, and as mentioned earlier in this chapter. Yet they have had difficulty in increasing the average basic price based on the unwillingness of passengers to pay higher fares. Within US domestic markets, airlines were only able to raise the average fare by about 3 percent (after adjusting for inflation) in the past ten years compared to the price of fuel that increased by a factor of three. Therefore, instead of increasing fares across the board, airlines adopted the merchandising concept. Simply stated, while they can continue to compete on the price of the core seat based on marginal costs, airlines can classify and market ancillary services around the core product (for example, seat location and lounge access) at prices well above their variable costs. The incremental revenues generated from the sale of ancillary products and services have generated almost all of the profit in the past few years. Two key aspects of marketing ancillary products and services have been that the prices charged for these services have varied by (1) passenger, and (2) flight, resulting in the "management of seat *by value*." This concept, while new to airlines, has been used by other retailers. Sellers of books online, for example, have varied the charges to customers by offering some customers free services, such as shipping and gift wrapping.

Although passengers have started to accept some fees for ancillary services, there is a limit on how much more they can be increased. One alternative is to segment passengers based on value desired and provided and charge accordingly. For example, customized pricing, based upon information given (two-way dialogue—through a call center or website), can shift the concept from fee-based pricing to value-based options. Even though the passenger makes a reservation for a specific flight, if the passenger has flexibility, would the passenger be willing to sell back the reservation for a discount and a guaranteed later departure at an agreed time? The passenger gets a discount; the airline can sell the reservation to another passenger for a higher fare and build loyalty with both passengers. Knowledge of the customer is instrumental to success and it goes well beyond the standard demographic characteristics. In the two-way dialogue the airline needs to become a solution provider and offer the right product at the right time at the right touchpoint. Consider the following statistic. According to Michelle Fischer, Vice President of Strategy & Marketing for NCR Travel, "Approximately 53% of shoppers want unique pricing, deals and discounts based on loyalty and purchase history."[7]

One key area that is still an issue is trust. Passengers are concerned about when to book—if they book at a certain point is the fare going to be less later, if they book too late it could go even higher. This issue can be addressed in part by the fact that the average traveler does not have a clear understanding of revenue management. It can also be attributed to the fact that on any given plane there will be people seated near each other who paid vastly different fares for the same product—a seat in the same cabin on the same flight. Contrast this to a movie theater experience, where, for the most part, people in a particular movie theater at a particular time have most likely all paid the same ticket price to attend the same show. This leads to the inadequacy of communications on the part of airlines about the time value of some features—different seats have different values on different flights on different days and based on the dates and conditions under which they were purchased.

Low cost carriers started with the basic idea of à la carte pricing. Some full service carriers, led by Air Canada, began to offer branded fares. Next, carriers started to offer bundled packages. In the future, airlines can start to offer customized products and services using customer insights and offer dynamically packaged ancillaries. If airlines do not do so, third party intermediaries are likely to enter the marketplace. See Figure 4.2. As such, airlines no longer need to just be sellers of seats from A to B. They can be retailers by understanding a customer's needs and desires and offer a meaningful product at the right time and at the right point of sale.

The historical revenue management systems were based on a forecast of passenger demand within each fare bucket and an allocation of the number of seats in each fare bucket. With the introduction of ancillary fees, pricing has become much more complex, in terms of both challenges and opportunities. On the challenge side is the need to forecast the sale of ancillary products and services and passengers' willingness to pay, a concept explored earlier in the book. For example, would a passenger choosing a low fare pay a fee for a better seat location and leg room, or early boarding or prepaid baggage? It is possible to answer this question by having access to historical data on the sale of ancillary products. Most airlines have not been warehousing such data in detail such as by route, by flight, by fare bucket, let alone by specific customer. On the opportunity side is the value of keeping the basic fares low and making the margins through ancillary revenues. Consequently, there is now a need to balance the reduction in the basic price of the ticket and the increase in the ancillary revenue, especially through effective retailing (not aggressive marketing or distractive marketing campaigns such as charitable donations, including for carbon offset). Additional complexities do arise as currently some ancillary products cannot be distributed through indirect channels, Global Distribution Systems (GDSs), and travel agencies (online and brick-and-mortar), as well as codeshare partners.

Another example of an opportunity is the potential value of increased revenues through the sale of bundled fares (also known as family fares and branded fares, a topic that will be discussed further in Chapter 5) that include defined amenities and restrictions and reduce, but not eliminate entirely, the need to purchase individual "add-ons" for additional comfort and convenience features. It is important to note that there are some differences between the terms "fare families" and "branded fares." For example, while they may be sold out, branded fares are always offered on each flight. Second, the amounts to upgrade between different branded fares are well defined. In the case of American Airlines there are three branded fares, Choice, Choice Essential, and Choice Plus. To upgrade to the fare, Choice Essential, the additional fare is $34 in each direction and $44 to upgrade to the fare, Choice Plus, in each direction. For example, suppose a passenger purchased an individual roundtrip fare for $200. The fee to change the reservation would be $150, the fee to check a bag would be $50, and the fee for early boarding would be $18. On the other hand, an upgrade to the fare, Choice Essential, would be $68 (for a roundtrip) that would enable the passenger to change the reservation, check a bag, and board early. It is interesting to note that the savings of $150 represents the fee for making the change to the reservation. Those passengers taking advantage of all three features do save $150; those taking advantage of just the checked bag and early boarding come out even.

Technology is now available to optimize revenue in real time through the use of dynamic packaging, mobile devices, e-commerce, and social media. For example, customers tend to buy more ancillary products on the day of travel through the use of their mobile devices. Take e-commerce, for example: retail-savvy airlines are just learning to market the appropriate products and services on the day of travel, leveraging the timing element, through the mobile channel. This is in alignment with the discussion in Chapter 2 regarding the fact that customers tend to be in a different mindset at different points in time, perhaps more price conscious when buying plane tickets months in advance versus buying a cup of coffee at the airport or a bottle of water in the hotel room. Furthermore, such personalized marketing (at the right time, at the right place) can help airlines achieve "the top of the arrow" highlighted in Figure 4.2. Consequently, airlines are starting to sell ancillary products and services at the time of booking, continuing the process using emails after the booking, at the airport during the check-in process (for preferred seats, for example), after passing security (for airport lounge access, for example), just prior to boarding (for early boarding, for example), and during the flight (for upgrades, for example).

The idea of attracting passengers using low fares and then persuading them to buy extras is not new. Auto dealers have been practicing this marketing technique for a long time. Neither is the concept of bundling new. Again, the auto dealers have been marketing such packages as Winter, Sports, and Luxury for decades. Disney also sells a product called "Magic Morning" that allows early admission to the park, similar to early boarding for an airline. Disney also sells discounted tickets for entry to multiple parks. Cruise lines now charge fees for early boarding and various dining options, for example, at different times and in different locations, as well as priority reservations. Despite the difference in price, a significant percentage of passengers do buy the higher priced bundled fares.

Charging fees for ancillary products and services are reasonable up to a point, especially for product features that were free initially, but the practice can be carried too far when it begins to affect the brand. There are two possibilities. The first is to charge for products and services that enhance the experience in different phases of travel. Examples of initiatives already taken include (besides preferred seats, early boarding, and lounge access) tablets with pre-loaded entertainment, empty seats next to the seats reserved, premium class meals served in the economy class cabin, and baggage delivery to the final destination.

The second option relates to fare packages. An all-inclusive fare can also have value in the long term with respect to branding—making it easier to purchase and travel, reducing complexity and stress. Bundled fares could be the answer; in between à la carte fares at one end and all-inclusive fares at the other end. Clearly there are passengers who prefer one type over another type. The answer is to segment customers by preference, à la carte, versus bundled, versus all-inclusive. Airlines have already benefitted significantly from the early stages of unbundling and rebundling the product and capitalizing on the higher margins achieved than on the sale of seats. Now, they can analyze customer behavior and attitudes to better define passenger value systems, and then engage with customers appropriately to optimize revenue from each customer in the short and long term. New generations of consumers are much more willing to shop (browse) and buy online and take advantage of different price–service options, not to mention convenience. In fact, according to an IBM survey, a significant percentage of shoppers surveyed are willing to spend 20 minutes on average to help a retailer understand the shopper's desires so as to be able to provide the shopper with more meaningful promotions and offers.[8] Consider the value Amazon derives from getting customers to provide more data on themselves to enable Amazon to build better customer profiles to make relevant recommendations on products, including complementary products.

Distribution

Distribution within the airline industry has been evolving for decades. First, the product was distributed directly by airlines through the reservation systems that they built themselves. Then, airlines enabled agents to distribute products by giving agents the content from the airlines' reservation systems. Next, GDSs enabled Online Travel Agents (OTAs) to expand the distribution landscape. Currently, there are three broad types of distribution channels. There are the traditional brick-and-mortar and online agents working with GDSs. Second, there are the direct connect organizations such as Kayak, Priceline, and Farelogix. Some of these represent "meta-search" sites that advise the customer by browsing various OTAs and other "distribution" websites and then send the customer to an airline's website to perform the actual booking and the payment process. And, there are the airline websites. On the horizon are also new intermediaries, technology companies (including GDSs) with vast amounts of information on customer profiles and buying attitudes and behaviors—the likes of Amazon, Apple, Concur, Facebook, and Google.

Airlines feel the need to take greater control of their destiny in distribution. The desire to go direct is based on the desire to: (1) reduce distribution costs, (2) enhance revenues by developing direct relationships with customers, leading to the potential sale of more personalized products and services, especially, a better experience, (3) increase transparency, and (4) overcome commoditization to develop strong brands. All three existing channels (and the new powerful technology companies) will, however, co-exist, with the distribution mix decision customized to each market and with the intervention depending on the degree of personalization, customer value provided, and the available technology. Airline websites have already been providing greater personalization and greater customer value and as such have been gaining higher revenues, for example, through the sale of ancillary products and services. Airline websites have also been able to attract direct corporate travel by providing corporate discounts to travelers making their own reservations as well as integrating some discounts into their merchandising offers.

While some airlines have tried to increase the amount of traffic coming through the direct channel, they have faced three significant challenges. First, there is the entrenched relationship between the travel management companies and the GDSs (both relating to finances and processes). Second, there is clearly a large market worldwide where an individual airline's reach is limited, warranting a need to use the services of agents. Currently, about 60 percent of the business continues to come from indirect channels, the percentage varying by region and by airline. A typical global airline could be making about 50 percent of its sales direct (say 35 percent through its website and 15 percent through its call centers and ticket offices) and about 50 percent indirect (say 35 percent through offline travel agents and 15 percent through online travel agents). And, in any case, even if an airline were to be able to reach some travelers in locations outside the network of an airline, these passengers may choose not to go direct for comparative reasons. It is reported that for low cost airlines the percentage of reservations derived through their websites is about double the percentage derived by full service airlines, and the full service airlines derive about double the percentage of reservations through GDSs than for low cost airlines. One reason could have been that the fares charged by low cost airlines were easier to explain and understand so that passengers did not require assistance from agents. However, some low cost airlines have begun to participate in the GDSs, for example, JetBlue and WestJet. Third, GDSs can deliver more of the sought-after business travelers to airlines.

Like airlines, distributors have also been adapting to the dramatically changing landscape with respect to travelers, agents, and airlines. In the early days, the role of GDSs was simply to show availability, fares, and enable bookings. Next, they began to provide pre-departure services such as check in and departure control. In recent times, the forward thinking GDSs have been updating their technology (for example, XML[9]) to accommodate the needs of both airlines and travelers to provide for more detailed information on products—the kind of seat, meals, entertainment—and to be able to sell on a personalized basis. Going forward, the distributors are likely to be called upon to provide even more information, such as the communication of the brand, features that differentiate one airline from another, the speed and the ease with which the information is synthesized and delivered—for example, price changes in real time. And, there will be ever increasing pressure by airlines to reduce the costs of distribution, particularly from the use of GDSs, now that airlines have reduced the costs of distribution through the agents.

The main point, however, is that airlines are trying to become sophisticated retailers and they need to offer a differentiated and personalized product not only through their own direct channels (call centers, websites, kiosks, and mobile apps) but also through third parties to offer and price content dynamically and through customer engagement. Consequently, distributors (agents— both online and brick-and-mortar working with GDSs) will need to provide even more enhanced and cost effective retailing capabilities to remain viable. For example, there will be a need for recognition of the customer so that personalized service can be provided, such as no charge for baggage given the status of the traveler with a particular airline or the way a corporate traveler is treated if he or she were traveling outside of the corporate agreed working framework with the airline. However, airlines will need to establish business rules for this level of personalization and to establish new processes to fulfill personalized services. Consequently, the function of the third party is to provide the content in the way the customer wants to receive it and in the way the provider wants to send it, customized from both sides.

The airline business requires enormous investments and the risks involved in running an airline business are huge compared to the minuscule returns generated relative to returns achieved by consumer packaged goods companies, not to mention companies selling beverages, such as Starbucks and Coca-Cola. One difference in these other businesses is the amount of attention devoted by them to analyzing customer behavior and attitude by segment and by sales channel. Airlines still continue to sell more than half of their products through channels that have, until now, been running on older generation technology. Consumers cannot see, let alone appreciate, many features of products offered by airlines. Agents, brick-and-mortar and online, using traditional GDSs, for example, could only show, until recently, their clients information such as destinations served, schedules available, and fares available, making the airline product virtually commoditized. They can now show, for example, at least a photo (if not the quality) of the Skycouch seat in the Economy Class of Air New Zealand.

Passengers are looking for all relevant information with respect to product options to plan their trips. Consider the statistic available from the following Google analysis: Typical travelers shop 22 websites before booking.[10] No longer is it sufficient to just have information on the schedule and the fare. Consumers also want information on such product features as seat configuration, in-flight meals, entertainment, Wi-Fi, and access to airport lounges. Airline websites provide information on product attributes. However, passengers shopping through travel agents (brick-and-mortar or online), accounting for 60 percent of the total on a worldwide basis, may not be able to see some of this information. The problem, as mentioned, is related to technology. The current distribution systems were developed with standards established by the industry that included airlines, agents, and technology companies, resulting in a capability that could not provide information at a very detailed level. Recall the survey of Asian "Emerging Flyers" who are now searching for all kinds of information from the seat width to the "always-on cabins." The technology constraints relating to the distribution channels used by agents limited the information available to passengers and, possibly, the revenue generated for airlines. Now customers can not only see such features as seat comfort based on location in the cabin but also the ability of a shopper to purchase such a product feature.

Given the perceived limitations in technology—for example, for distributors to sell à la carte products and services—IATA initiated its NDC to introduce some data transmission standards to connect airlines with distributors. The standards refer to passenger reservations, fare filing organizations, interline messages and airline–agent communications, and can stimulate innovation. Ultimately, customers will benefit in terms of an increase in transparency and consumer choice, not to mention customer recognition and customer preferences. One advantage of the NDC is that while passengers may be willing to share their personal information with airlines to obtain customized offers, the current systems used by agents do not easily provide the capability to obtain and transfer such information from the buyer to the seller. The airline will clearly benefit by being able to differentiate its products and services from its competitors. The idea is to provide transparency and a seamless purchase experience across all channels of distribution through the adoption of some standards in the Internet era:

1. If a product is available through an airline's website, it should also be available through agents and travel management companies (all schedules and availability, all fares, and all ancillaries), generically or on a customized basis.
2. Customers need to receive a "dynamic and personalized" response to an inquiry based on the "who, when, what, and how" aspects of the inquiry to provide, possibly, better discounts, better rewards, as well as better terms and conditions.
3. As the content (product components) is made up by airlines they must remain in control of the process and they must provide the response back to booking requests based on the individual making the request.
4. It is important not only to have all products available, but also to consider the manner in which they are presented, for example, Singapore Airlines's "Suite-to-Suite" service or Air New Zealand's "Skycouch" seat, or AirAsia's "Red Carpet" Service.
5. In distribution, or selling, partners must be able to show product differentiation, the value of product features, and unique airline brand attributes to facilitate comparison shopping using easy to search displays.
6. Customers must have timely information to look at any product attribute (given the dynamic airline shopping environment) and know how they can access additional information not just to be able to purchase an airline ticket, with flexibility, from one city to another, but also to be able to purchase product features that provide the desired experience.
7. Distributors, or third party sellers, should be able to deliver a captivating user experience. Again, Singapore Airlines's "Suite-to-Suite" service would be an example or even a simple value-adding feature such as extra legroom, the availability of Wi-Fi, on-demand audio and video entertainment, fewer restrictions on fares, or many aspects of the cabin ambience.

8. All information should be available through a customer's mobile device, such as a smartphone. Is the business class seat a lie-flat seat, a seat that just reclines a certain amount, or an economy seat with an empty seat next to it?

Although GDSs have been addressing these concerns and desires on the part of airlines and travel agents, the speed at which progress is being made may need to increase to keep up with airlines that are introducing, at an ever increasing speed, new ancillary products and services, particularly those on an à la carte basis or in terms of bundled fares to provide increasingly clear value propositions, as well as flexibility and choice. However, to speed up the compatibility aspect may require more than an adoption of cutting edge technology. Incentives, for example, may also need to be addressed, not to mention "who pays what to whom." Although airlines are focused on reducing their costs, including the cost of distribution, would they be willing to pay higher commissions for higher levels of revenues generated by indirect channels? Moreover, it is clear that if customers wish to provide personal information to obtain a more personalized offer, they can do so, but they are not required to provide any information considered to be sensitive, affecting privacy and security.

The standards being discussed are hardly going to reduce the need for third party distributors. However, their roles, capabilities, and pricing structures could change. To start with, is the word distribution still valid in the airline industry? Should it be replaced by the word shopping? In the old days, it was the paper ticket that was physically distributed. Now, what is being distributed physically? With respect to roles, the "distributors" may need, with some cooperation from airlines, to become experts on destinations and advice that enhances the experience. With respect to capabilities, they may need to become more tech-savvy. While customers could do the search online for a destination or a price as well as make the actual reservations, some may prefer not to do so, as it may involve tiresome search and frustration, including contradictory reviews. Typical search for air travel and accommodations, including the making of reservations, can take between two and five hours, as stated in Chapter 2. The problem is multifaceted. On the one hand, the issue may not be the lack of information; rather, it could be the availability of too much information. On the other hand, agents can only sell based on the products and information that are available to them.

With respect to pricing structures, airlines could explore alternative methods of payments for future third party intermediaries. Airlines could, for example, sell at wholesale prices and let the intermediaries set the final sale price. They could renegotiate a different commission structure and incentives relative to past practices. Consequently, retailing is likely to make the jobs of agents more complex, leading to a sales functionality. Such a change raises the question of agent productivity (the number of tickets sold) and economics ("who pays whom what"). What about GDS booking incentives? What if an airline were to respond to a request with an offer that includes no charge for a better seat, for expedited boarding, and for access to the airport lounge? What would be the commission for the agent for the value of these features? One option might be for specialist agents to charge a planning fee, ranging from $50–$500, depending on the complexity of the trip. And the fee could be applied toward the cost of the trip. Agents could also charge an hourly fee for travel consultancy concierge services.

Evolution to Retailing

The evolution to retailing begins with an integrated solution that comprises five fundamental areas. First is the merchandising platform that relates to merchandising, packaging, and personalization. Second is customer acquisition that involves acquisition and conversion of prospects. Third is consumer e-commerce and self service that involves product content across all channels. Fourth is the analytics piece that involves measurement and conversion. Finally, there is revenue optimization related to trip and customer-centric optimization, taking into consideration the purchase of ancillary services. See Figure 4.3. Airlines need an integrated solution that is designed specifically for the airline industry, enabling airlines to manage the complete retail life cycle to increase conversions and share of wallet. Such a solution will enable airlines to manage the complete retail life cycle from acquisition to conversion, fulfilment, measurement, and revenue optimization.

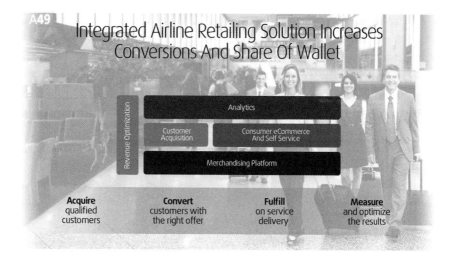

Figure 4.3   Integrated airline retailing solution

Source: Sabre Airline Solutions

A Best Practice Example—Disney

Since its beginning in 1955, the Disney organization has focused on innovation and creativity to improve guest experience, for example, the "FastPass" (now upgraded to "FastPass+"), "My Disney Experience," "MyMagic+," and the "MagicBand." The key aspect of innovation has been to take a holistic view of the guest to provide a seamless and stress-free experience—from vacation planning to purchasing, to visiting theme parks, to sharing memories afterwards with family and friends:

- "FastPass+" service (included in the price of admission) allows guests to skip lines for rides and shows and reserve areas to view fireworks and parades, as well as meet Disney characters. Guests can reserve up to three attractions daily for up to 60 days prior to entry to the resort.
- "My Disney Experience" is a website and a mobile app for all-inclusive online planning and booking—dining reservations, entertainment times, information on FastPass+, and so forth.

- "MyMagic+" is a technology advancement that enables guests to customize their entire visit by connecting almost all aspects of the experience (at no charge), for example, booking guaranteed ride times for guests' chosen shows and attractions even before arriving in the park and enabling families and friends to connect and coordinate plans and share photos.
- "MagicBand" is a colorful, reusable, wristband embedded with Radio-Frequency Identification (RFID) technology enabling a guest to just "tap" the band against shining Mickey Mouse heads located throughout the theme parks and hotels to activate a wide array of functions. These wristbands can enable guests to, almost effortlessly, enter theme parks (without having to wait to go through turnstiles), enter their Disney Resort hotel rooms, and make purchases (food and merchandise)—guests can "tap" to pay if they have connected their MagicBands to their credit cards. Even the FastPass+ and the PhotoPass systems can be accessed via the MagicBand.

Disney is using technology to provide a more "immersive, more seamless and more personal experience" for every guest vacationing at a Disney resort. The technology enables guests to make the most of their limited times, enjoy the rides and shows instead of waiting in lines, and for Disney to have their guests spend more money in the stores and restaurants. Interactivity and engagement are important features of the use of technology. Interactivity allows Disney to: (1) manage lines in which guests are kept engaged in the story before they even get into the attraction, making the time waiting in line pass quickly, and (2) enable guests to have a personalized experience with selected characters. Since Disney is able to gather lot of information on guests through their online sessions, email addresses, and their wristbands, the company recognizes the guests' concerns for security and privacy of information linked, for example, to the MagicBands. Disney is actively addressing these concerns. For example, guests can choose the information they are willing to share with Disney, for instance, through the "opt-in" features.

Takeaways

- Retailing in the airline industry in the past was limited to a discussion on pricing and distribution, particularly with respect to price transparency and proliferation of channels (including, the matter of direct versus indirect).
- As for the product, while the focus has been mostly on the physical attributes (such as the seat and even that mostly in premium class cabins), airlines now need to explore the potential digital aspects of products and experience.
- As for digital experience, focus should be on the inspiration, shopping, and purchase phases to "reduce the clutter," so that passengers can "experience" the physical products before the travel phase.
- There is a potential new group of third party distributors that airlines must deal with, given their information and analytics capabilities.
- IATA's NDC will change the way consumers buy and airlines sell air travel through the availability of relevant information about the products and services offered by competing airlines, enabling product differentiation and price comparison.
- Control regarding airline choice will be in the hands of digital passengers with their smartphones, laptops, tablets, and e-Readers, not to mention passengers' access to social networks where they can get all sorts of inspiration and advice from their peers.
- The Thought Leadership Piece by ALDI in Chapter 9 provides substantial insights for airlines, for example, the need to make it easy to shop.

Notes

1   Jay Sorensen and Eric Lucas, "Shocking News: A la Carte Shopping is Good for Consumers," An *IdeaWorks* Report sponsored by Amadeus, April 30, 2012, p. 12.

2   Jonathan Crocker, "Going Places with DoubleTree by Hilton: Digital Engagement in the Travel Market," *Google/Think Insight*, August 2013.

3   Michelle Fischer, "Easier Holiday Shopping? 1 in 4 Travelers Will Buy Gifts at Airports," *NCR Travel*, December 13, 2013.

4   Jay Sorensen and Eric Lucas, "VIP for a Fee: Airport Services Designed for High Value Customers," *IdeaWorks*, February 4, 2014.

5   Martin Raymond, "The Future of Comfort: Asia," *The Future Laboratory*, London, UK, February 2014, p. 11.

6   "Airbus Group: Asian Passengers Shaping Long Haul Economy Air Travel," Airbus Group, Press Release reported by *Air Transport News*, February 13, 2014.

7   Michelle Fischer, "Best Practices for Creating an Exceptional Passenger Experience Part 3: Easy Merchandising," *NCR Travel*, September 25, 2013.

8   Kali Klena and Jill Puleri, "From Transactions to Relationships: Connecting with a Transitioning Shopper," *IBM Institute for Business Value*, Executive Report, May 2013, p. 3.

9   Airlines have used the Internet programming language (XML) on their websites to try to provide the shopping experience that consumers get when shopping for other goods and services. Some GDSs, on the other hand, use older-generation messaging infrastructure to develop offers based on fares and schedules, with the customer remaining anonymous to an airline until after the transaction is completed. This process was less flexible for supporting contemporary retailing business practices, for example, the ability for airlines to sell a wide array of ancillary products and services and to make customized offers via the indirect channel. However, with the adoption of new technology, this process has now been changing.

10   Henry H. Harteveldt, "The Future of Airline Distribution: A Look Ahead to 2017," A Special Report Commissioned by IATA, December 5, 2012, p. 3.

Chapter 5
Building Stronger Brands

The hallmarks of branding are well known—choice, consistency, differentiation, experience, relevance, trust, and delivering on the brand promise. Within the airline industry, there are a few airlines that have focused on at least some of these attributes to build a strong brand. Building a strong brand involves aligning the branding and business strategies of a company. Singapore Airlines and Southwest Airlines are two examples that have succeeded in doing so. In the case of legacy carriers, however, most have struggled in their ability to clearly highlight what they stand for, and therefore have had difficulty in differentiating themselves, keeping them in a commodity trap in spite of the ambition of many carriers to position themselves as "premium" or "5 Star" airlines. Many low cost carriers, on the other hand, have been successful in conveying clearer value propositions, not only between themselves and legacy carriers, but also among themselves. Examples include Southwest and JetBlue in the US, Ryanair and easyJet in Europe, and AirAsia and Jetstar in the Asia–Pacific region. Ryanair, for example, differentiates itself not only from British Airways, but also from easyJet. Similarly, JetBlue differentiates itself not only from American Airlines, but also from Southwest. In the case of Ryanair, even though it is strategizing to attract some business travelers with added product features, many people patronize the Ryanair product for the low fares and on-time performance.

While most airlines, both legacies and low cost carriers, have fairly strong brand *awareness*, legacy carriers, in general, struggle to identify what is it that they stand for, and therefore, in turn, suffer from a lack of brand *appreciation* in terms of value. For example, while British Airways has a very strong brand awareness, would a passenger traveling between, say London, Heathrow and St. Petersburg, have enough of a brand appreciation to stay with

British Airways, or choose another carrier, such as Transaero Airlines? As such, low cost carriers, as a group, have been the "big winners" in terms of branding.

Brand Messages

Companies use messages and visuals to convey how they want consumers to view their brands, but this is not always how it is received. Many brands struggle to tie their views of themselves with their customers' views of the brand.[1] Some examples of brands that have succeeded in matching the way they view themselves with the way their consumers view them include ALDI, Apple, Coca-Cola, Disney, and Starbucks. While legacy carriers have tried to get across what they stand for through different campaigns, in many cases the message was not clear, not measurable, and or the promise was not delivered. As such, in most cases, the campaigns have faded. One exception would be Singapore, as noted above, that has built a strong brand having clearly linked its branding and business strategies. While some others have tried to follow this strategy, Singapore has been able to deliver consistently and throughout most touchpoints because of (1) management's commitment to the brand, (2) integration of brand and business strategies, (3) allocation of resources, and (4) the monitoring of the execution.

This commitment at the very top was also illustrated by the initial success of Virgin Atlantic and the turnaround of Continental Airlines. Virgin Atlantic, under the leadership of Sir Richard Branson, developed a brand emphasizing high levels of customer service and value for money through such innovations as individual TV screens, in-flight beauty therapists, complimentary limo service to and from airports, and a "Drive Thru Check In" at London Heathrow Airport. In a somewhat different way, Continental Airlines, under the leadership of Gordon Bethune, set the goal of moving "From Worst to First," and later the carrier's initiative to move from "First to Favorite."[2] He achieved incredible success by (1) aligning Continental's business and brand strategies, (2) framing and articulating Continental's business strategy in terms of a "story" — a business narrative that connected, engaged, and inspired employees, and

(3) incentivizing employees to provide higher levels of customer service. The "story" line was communicated to the employees in the form of a pyramid in four layers (Enterprise Customer Relationship Management—CRM). The lowest layer emphasized the need for safety, cleanliness, and reliability. The second layer emphasized the need for product differentiation that is visible to customers. The third layer emphasized the need for focus on recovery during irregular operations. The top layer emphasized the need for, and the value of, building relationships with customers. The success of this vision, its communication, and its implementation is very clear. In the mid-1990s, Continental's revenue per seat mile was 10 percent *below* the industry level. In the mid-2000s, it was 10 percent *above* the industry level.

Ryanair, in some ways, also makes it clear what it stands for—no frills, ultra low cost—much like retailer ALDI. The critical success factor in both cases has been the linkage of the brand and business strategy. Other airline examples in the US include JetBlue and Virgin America (two carriers of different ages) that have achieved varying degrees of success in creating differentiated brands. While these two are very strong brands, they are relatively small and or regional airlines, and as such some consumers in the US (even though they recognize the brands) do not have access to these brands, for example, those traveling nationwide within the US or in long haul intercontinental markets.

Examples of full service airlines now focusing more on their brands include the three Persian Gulf-based carriers, Emirates Airline, Etihad Airways, and Qatar Airways. Emirates is a global airline that is reported to be targeting "international travelers who care about schedule convenience embodied in accessibility and availability, and who seek service rather than price."[3] According to Brand Finance, a brand valuation consultancy, Emirates ranked number one in the 2013 list of the top 20 most valuable airline brands in the world.[4] Emirates's brand attributes include a superior product, a lower price, and a recognizable brand. The airline is growing rapidly its network, fleet, and capacity while very carefully managing its brand. One distinguishing element of the carrier is its young fleet. It is interesting to note that Emirates will be replacing, in a few years, its "old" Airbus 380s with "new" Airbus 380s when many major players would not be operating any Airbus 380s. Adding to its reputation as a global brand is the fact that, according to its website, Emirates has over 15,000 cabin crew of more than 135 nationalities who speak over 55 different languages.[5] Another distinguishing element of promoting its branding strategy is its focus on the sponsorship of sports events. Sponsorships include soccer, rugby, tennis, motorsports, horse racing, golf, cricket, sailing, and Australian Rules football. These sponsorships have been a high contributor to the recognition and development of a premium brand around the world. Emirates also provides arts and culture sponsorships. Such sponsorships are a way to connect and build relationships with its customers.[6]

What factors are behind a strong brand *message*? As pointed out by Jim Stengel, former global marketing officer of Procter & Gamble, the concept of a "brand ideal," a shared goal of improving people's lives, is a critical success factor for branding. Stengel notes that brand ideals are not tied to specific business models, but rather are adaptive and flexible. Brand ideals actually yield new business models and strategies, thus keeping brands fresh. He stresses the importance of brand ideals to give leadership the ability to drive results by being clear about what is valued through a simple message that can be carried across all members of an organization.[7] This is what global airlines need to do to transform them and what Singapore has been doing. As for improving people's lives, along the lines of Jim Stengel, consider some of Southwest's advertisements: "You're Now Free to Move About the Country," "Grab your bag. It's On!," "If it Matters to You, It Matters to Us."

One way for airlines to differentiate themselves is through simplicity. Let us examine ten global brands that have succeeded in differentiating themselves through simplicity from Siegel+Gale's Global Brand Simplicity Index, a research report that demonstrates the impact of simplicity on revenue, loyalty, and innovation. More than 10,000 consumers rated brands on the perceived points of simplicity—or complexity—across touchpoints. The top ten global list includes, in order, ALDI, Amazon, Google, McDonald's, Kentucky Fried Chicken, Carrefour, C&A, Samsung, IKEA, and Pizza Hut. Going around the world, Germany-based ALDI is viewed as a discount store providing good value for money; US-based Amazon is seen as easy to do business with its simple click-through purchase process; France-based Carrefour is recognized as a store that carries a wide array of inventory in individual stores to match local tastes; Korea-based Samsung is viewed as a company offering products that show creativity, modernism, and accessible technology; and Sweden-based IKEA is recognized for its easy to assemble products at low prices and easy to navigate stores.[8] The common denominator in people's evaluation of the top ten brands is the ease of doing business with them, also known as simplicity.

Within the airline industry, Southwest would serve as a good example of simplicity in terms of its value proposition. Southwest's value proposition is very clear to understand and to remember: free bags (for the first two checked bags), no change fees, and a straight forward loyalty program with respect to unlimited reward seats, and no blackout dates. The key characteristic is simplicity, which is highlighted on the carrier's website in the excerpt from the message contained in "The Southwest Experience:" "We pride ourselves on making it both simple and fun to fly to 97 destinations in the United States, Mexico, and the Caribbean."[9] Simplicity is a remarkably important component of branding. However, according to one writer, a business should not confuse simplification with being simplistic, giving the following example of being simplistic: thinking that one can create incremental customer value by changing a name or a logo. Simplification can create "stronger associations between a brand and its real benefits."[10] In the case of Southwest, the carrier now needs to maintain its simplicity element in its branding strategy while its business becomes more complex from its strategies to penetrate the business segment and to fly to "near" international destinations.

Southwest is likely to succeed because of its laser-like focus on how customers view the company in terms of meeting their needs, the ease of doing business, and making it fun to do business with, according to Jason Cieslak, Siegel+Gale's President, Pacific Rim. Manning and Bodine of Forrester Research show this in a pyramid where the base layer reflects strategies to meet customer needs, the second layer reflects strategies to make it easier for customers to do business with the company, and the top layer reflects strategies for customers to enjoy doing business with the company. They point out that while the focus on customer experience is powerful, it is a misunderstood element of corporate strategy.[11] In a similar way, Dixon, Freeman, and Toman point out, in a *Harvard Business Review* article, that companies should stop trying to delight their customers. Instead, they should focus on simply solving their problems in satisfactory ways. It is the implementation of such strategies that will increase loyalty.[12]

Branded Fares and Branded Products/Services

Two areas of branding in which airlines have made some progress are branded fares (including the similar, family fares), a topic introduced in Chapter 4, and branded products/services. Air Canada introduced the concept of family fares. It offers multiple fare categories to meet travelers' needs. It clearly outlines the different features associated with each fare type, thus providing transparency to the customer between Tango, Flex, Latitude, and Business Class. On some routes there is even a fare for Premium Economy and the Business Class is divided into two separate fares, Business Lowest and Business Flexible. Each category above Tango provides an increasing amount of amenities representing comfort and conveniences at increasing prices. On the positive side, customers can get extensive information on the features included in the bundled fares. On the negative side, the process can become complex and confusing for some customers. On top of this, the difference between the lowest fare (Tango) and the highest fare in Economy Class (Latitude) can represent a factor of two or three.

Compare Air Canada's strategy with Southwest's strategy. Southwest came out with its three families–Wanna Get Away, Anytime, and Business Select. The first implies that there are restrictions and the second implies that there are no restrictions. The third has no restrictions and provides extra benefits such as early boarding, a free drink, and much higher mileage credit. There is no need to look up information using drop-down menus. As with Air Canada and Southwest, the family fares are capacity controlled. When the lowest fare sells out, the customer needs to buy the higher fare.

American introduced the concept of fare brands, surrounding different bundles of base fares (Choice, Choice Essential, and Choice Plus), with different combinations of ancillary services such as same-day standby, same-day flight change, early boarding, access to extra legroom seats, in-flight Wi-Fi, advanced seat assignment, and checked baggage. As with cars and cable services, customers wanting additional product features or services will need to buy the higher fare brands or, possibly, pay separately for the feature desired. The idea is to encourage buyers to move upwards making them feel that they are getting better value. As with Air Canada, the names of American's branded fares do not convey a simple explanation of their meaning. Again, compare the names selected by Southwest.

Some carriers have also strived to differentiate themselves through branded products/services—United with its Economy Plus and Air New Zealand with its "cuddle class" seating in Economy Class, Emirates offering showers in First Class, and Singapore offering jet connections to premium passengers. These services are featured-based rather than fee-based, such as baggage or reservation changes. New initiatives being considered include an airline adding multiple icons that travelers may click on to gain more information about various features such as the types of meals available, the degree of seat recline and the width of the seat, as well as details relating to in-flight entertainment. The idea now is to go far beyond simply providing flight times and fares.

Multiple Brands: Subsidiaries, Alliances, Mergers & Acquisitions

The branding element has become complicated due to the establishment of subsidiaries, codeshare flights, alliances, and mergers & acquisitions. In the case of subsidiaries, for example, Delta launched a very successful brand, Song—a single-class airline focused around the needs of style-conscious professional women travelers. The newly created brand was so successful that it raised the expectation of passengers traveling on the parent brand, expectations that the parent brand could not deliver. Three years after Song's launch, Delta decided to reconfigure its subsidiary's fleet into two classes and incorporate it into its own fleet, in part, to reduce its costs and emerge from bankruptcy. On the other hand, Qantas also launched a successful subsidiary, Jetstar, with a clear business strategy based on simplicity. Unlike Delta, Qantas carefully controlled the expectations of passengers traveling on Jetstar and allowed Jetstar to grow even if the growth of Jetstar was at the expense of Qantas. Learning from these failures and successes, other airlines are now trying to establish new brands—Singapore with its four brands, Air Canada with its Rouge brand, and Avianca Holdings (a combination of Avianca and TACA) that has seven subsidiaries.

In the case of codeshare flights, airlines place their codes on other airlines' flights to "virtually" extend their own networks. British Midland was a champion of this strategy, capitalizing on its 13 percent of the slots at London's Heathrow Airport. As of the beginning of 2014, JetBlue is capitalizing on its valuable network out of New York's John F Kennedy Airport and out of Boston's Logan Airport to codeshare with 32 airlines. While the codeshare agreements do expand the networks, they also raise branding issues related to inconsistencies in the services provided by different carriers. Should airlines with *real brand awareness and real brand appreciation* either not codeshare or codeshare with other airlines with similar brand attributes?

Are there any insights from the experience of Mercedes-Benz that put its "Star" on the Mercedes-Benz Citan Van built by Renault (a derivative of Renault's Kangoo Van) in its plant in Maubeuge, France? It is reported that the car performed poorly in a EuroNCAP crash test,[13] reflecting on the brand of Mercedes. Are there any insights for airlines from this "codeshare" car? What was the experience of buyers of Mercedes cars built by Chrysler? In terms of extensive codesharing agreements within the airline industry, can it be assumed that these airlines have accepted their products to be commodities? If this were to be a reasonable assumption, then could it be possible that an outside integrator of travel with a "non-airline code" set up a global network of flights under the integrator's brand without operating its own aircraft?

In the case of alliances, while alliances do provide the network that travelers need, there is little consistency in branding across the members. Part of the problem relates to the huge number of airlines in each of the three global alliances, the size variation among the members, the technology capability among the members, and the differences in culture. Leaving aside the lack of consistency among members within an alliance, the three major alliances have also not distinguished themselves to stand out from each other in the eyes of the traveler. This factor, in itself, is a huge missed opportunity—branded alliances.

Then there is the disconnect between branding and business strategy related to mergers & acquisitions. In the past, when airlines considered mergers, the focus seemed to be on economies of scale and scope to yield cost and revenue opportunities as well as efficiency of operations. What was missing in these considerations was the branding factor. What would be the new blended culture from the viewpoint of branding, especially when two very different cultures were being brought together? What would be the result? Mediocrity, at least for a very long time, exemplified by the experience of US Airways and Piedmont, and later US Airways and America West. In recent years there has been some focus on the branding issues resulting in decisions by some airlines to keep the brands separate after consolidation (for example, Air France and KLM, British Airways and Iberia, and Lufthansa with its multiple brands) and some to integrate the brands as quickly as possible (for example, Delta and Northwest and Continental and United). In the case of United, the airline is revisiting its old tagline from the 1960s "Fly the Friendly Skies" emphasizing being "flyer friendly" in an effort to "re-establish United's position as the world's leading" customer-focused airline according to Tom O'Toole, United's senior vice president for marketing and loyalty. Also according to United's O'Toole, the purpose is to "say to customers, co-workers and competitors that United is back in the game in a big way."[14] As highlighted on United's website, some of the components of this initiative include putting the passenger first from takeoff to landing, the ability to manage travel on the go, new and improved in-flight entertainment, creating one of the most modern and reliable fleets, getting passengers to more places, and working to meet travelers' needs.[15]

Branding Challenges and Opportunities

Design Thinking

There is a growing focus on *design thinking* in business to meet customer needs. What exactly is design thinking and what is its significance for businesses? Design thinking relates not only to the creation of significant economic value and meaningful differentiation but also improved customer experience. It can be used to "unlock hidden value in existing products, services, technologies, and assets—thereby reinvigorating a business without necessarily reinventing it."[16] Think about IBM that, under the leadership of Louis V. Gerstner, Jr. (CEO from 1993 to 2002), rebranded itself from a manufacturer of computers to a business that truly focused on the customer by developing and marketing user-based solutions and enabling other businesses to participate in e-commerce. In the case of airlines, Northwest, for example, tried to rebrand itself in the late 1990s as a digital airline with the promotion of e-ticketing and self-service kiosks at airports for check in.

"For the most part, branding firms over the years emphasized visual design as opposed to the other, more important, elements which influence whether a customer is loyal or not. Customer service empathy, personalization, clarity of communications and the intuitiveness of the experience is where the real impact happens, not just a handsome plane tail," said Siegel+Gale's Jason Cieslak. Airlines just now are beginning to broaden their branding design to design thinking for the business as it relates to choice and the overall customer experience that, in turn, can enable it to distinguish itself from other offerings and break out of the commodity trap that leads to the need to match prices. Think about Hawaiian Airlines that totally redesigned its business after it emerged from bankruptcy in 2004, capitalizing on its incredible leisure destination and a brand that could be enhanced to appeal to customers. The branding initiative was aligned with the business strategy that related not only to network, fleet, distribution channels, and workforce education, but, perhaps most important, to the product, especially to on-time performance (one measure of quality) and value for money.

With respect to value for money, for example, Hawaiian started to provide free meals in Economy Class (including a glass of wine) going against the direction of the airline industry. This product feature was important for vacationers paying their fares with their own money. Moreover, it put vacationers in a different frame of mind—guests, hospitality, and so forth.

Customer Experience

Although there are some areas where airlines have no control (the economy, the weather, the price of fuel, foreign exchange rates, for example), and some areas where they have some control (mechanical problems and airport congestion, for example), there are many other areas in which an airline has significant control over the experience created for customers. However, providing a superior customer experience in areas where airlines do have some control involves truly knowing and understanding customers in terms of their needs and wishes, and then, in turn, redesigning the systems and processes to provide the service in the way and manner that passengers want and is important to them. Customer experience is a "360-degree proposition," a truly "holistic" experience that involves the entire purchase cycle (as outlined in Chapter 4), and all the facets of the business.[17]

Co-Creation

A relatively new trend among progressive businesses is to co-create with their customers to design products and services instead of designing the products solely by internal teams. Although consumers have always been willing to provide input to sellers, now it is relatively easy given the advancements in communication and engagement technologies and the proliferation of social media. Sally O'Rourke, Managing Director Europe of Promise Communispace, provides some examples of companies undertaking co-creation.[18] McDonald's started to redesign its "restaurant of the future" through co-creation, working closely with targeted customers, resulting in "digital play areas, electronic kiosks for ordering food and varied seating options." Barclays co-created its "Barclaycard" by engaging with targeted customers that provided valuable input in such areas as loyalty rewards, and "pricing and supporting customers with payment problems."

Some recent examples of co-creation within the airline industry include the Finnair and Finavia (the operator of Helsinki Airport) initiative—"Quality Hunters 2013"—working with customers to improve the product, "the fastest and shortest connections between Asia and Europe." Previous engagements with customers led to the development of The Helsinki Airport Book Swop and vegetarian meals on long haul flights.[19] Another example of co-creation is the development of BalticMiles (launched in 2009), a multipartner loyalty program in Northern Europe and Russia, developed through engagement with customers who provided input on benefits as well as partners.

One critical success factor in the co-creation process is an open engagement among three groups—customers, various levels of internal staff (executives as well as customer-facing employees), and the branding team. Customers are looking for experience. A report cited that, according to a consumer trends survey conducted by JWT Intelligence, 73 percent of respondents indicated that they would rather spend money on an experience than on a material item.[20] Co-creation can ensure that companies gain the insight into the *type* of experience consumers want. With respect to the type of experience, recall the advice that Dixon, Freeman, and Toman provide that it is more important to solve a customer's problem than to delight the customer.[21]

Segmentation

If there is to be an alignment between business strategies and branding strategies, then the process needs to start with segmentation, a subject that has been addressed in Chapter 3. In the case of airlines, some have begun to seriously reexamine their targeted segments while most seem to be conducting business as usual. JetBlue is one example of an airline that is exploring segmentation options. The carrier is reported to state that it is not going after either the ultra price sensitive travelers or the Road Warriors (except for a limited group in Boston and in New York). Given its cost structure between the low cost carriers and the legacy carriers, and its significantly high score on the NPS Scale (see the discussion below), JetBlue sees itself targeting the "High Value Leisure" travelers and the "Mixed Wallets," a term describing travelers who fly for business and leisure.[22] See Figure 3.5 in Chapter 3. As for the limited subsegment of Road Warriors, JetBlue is offering a premium product in transcontinental markets at an impressive price point.

As some airlines are beginning to revisit their segmentation positioning and the implications for branding, there are two segments that need special focus, the Millennials and the "Connected" generation. Specifically, it is important to consider their expectations, interests, and needs. Consider the unique characteristics of Millennials with respect to travel. First, it has been reported that this segment is a much more ethnically diverse group relative to other generations and therefore international travel may be appealing to them. It has also been reported that they tend to be more interested in urban destinations rather than resorts, they are more likely to travel with respect to an activity or interest, and this segment is more likely to travel with friends in organized groups.[23] However, given that the members of this segment have grown up in the digital age, they are quite at ease conducting business through technology, unlike previous generations who may have been apprehensive or just less likely to be adaptors of such technology.

Let us also not forget about another important segment, one that is not defined by age or other traditional demographics. Rather, this segment, referred to as "Generation C" by author Brian Solis is comprised of people in a myriad of different generations as it refers to anyone who has "crossed over to the digital lifestyle."[24] This segment is "always on" and requires an entirely different approach to reach them. Engaging with this unique segment will, and already does, require new skill sets. Experience is key to this segment; they are influenced by the shared experiences of "like-minded strangers." What does this mean for businesses? Solis encourages that now is the time to determine how the customer landscape is changing and to recognize the level to which "traditional and connected consumers discover and make decisions differently."[25]

Branding in the Digital Era

It is well known that digital technology is greatly changing the way in which consumers are engaging with brands throughout the purchase cycle. Four new digital marketing models that have been identified by Booz & Company are described in an article in *strategy+business*: (1) Digital Branders, (2) Customer Experience Designers, (3) Demand Generators, and (4) Product Innovators. While it is indicated that these models are not industry-specific and that companies within the same industry may choose different ones, the following descriptions, including typical types of companies following the model, are given. Consider the "Digital Branders" that are often consumer products companies. Coca-Cola, having identified teens and young adults as its largest customer segments, is investing in implanting itself into popular culture. The company "identifies experiences that are consistent with its brand, creates content around those experiences, and then encourages its community of users to share additional content (aka experiences) that they create through social engagement." An example is a Coke Zero contest through social media for "my favorite dance moves" that involved the winning dance, having the Coke Zero brand integrated into the content, going viral around the world. Consider also the "Customer Experience Designers" that may include airlines, financial services, hotels, and retailers. Turning to the airline industry, Virgin is investing in an in-flight experience that is more interactive and personalized. For example, specialized content including such information as reviews for restaurants around the Piccadilly area might be provided to a passenger who travels to London often. Furthermore, travelers could also interact with a concierge service during the flight. Finally, leveraging information such as beverages purchased, meals purchased, videos watched, and so on, user profiles can be constructed to further personalize the experience.[26]

There is also the challenge of maintaining consistency across channels. Consider the challenge of maintaining consistency in the retail sector between the in-store experience and the online experience. Retailers are working to "digitize" the product so that consumers can "picture" it while shopping online. For example, when looking at a woman's coat on Nordstrom's website, a consumer can change the color of the coat displayed on the model, zoom in on the product, choose different "still" images (such as illustrating the front and or back of the coat), and even click on an image of the model "moving" making the product seem as if it were in "real" life. These type of digital experiences help replicate the customer being in a store setting. Brick-and-mortar stores are also leveraging digital experiences such as using mirrors that reflect images of a product in different colors (a dress) or different products (a blouse and a skirt) while the shopper stands in front of the mirrors. Adapting this concept to the airline industry, could airlines "digitize" the product online? Making such information as seat pitch "come alive" by enabling the shopper to click on the seat showing such a feature, as well as other features such as In-Flight Entertainment (IFE) systems, power outlets available, and so forth?

Managing Brand Reputation

One way to determine brand sentiment is through the concept of the NPS developed by Fred Reichheld, which represents the measurement of the number of promoters of a product or service minus the number of detractors. Many factors go into the decision of a passenger to become a net promoter of an airline. Achieving a positive score could be based on an airline doing the basics very well—such as on-time performance or an overall score of experience at all touchpoints shown in Figure 4.1 in Chapter 4 and Figure 5.1 in this chapter. JetBlue and Southwest have been achieving very high NPSs. A report by Dennis Schaal showed a survey in which JetBlue received the highest ranking within the US airline industry, receiving a NPS in the mid-60s range compared to the larger carriers receiving scores in the minus 5 to plus 10 range.[27] In another study conducted by Satmetrix and reported in PRWeb, Southwest received the highest NPS, ranking in the mid-60s range.[28] Other companies receiving high scores included USAA, Costco, Amazon.com, Trader Joe's, and Marriott. Another criterion could be an index developed by the Temkin Group that shows the forgiveness ratings. For example, according to the results published by the Temkin Group in the first quarter of 2013 Consumer Benchmark Survey, of the 10,000

US consumers surveyed, whereas 48 percent would be willing to forgive Alaska Airlines, only 14 percent would be willing to forgive US Airways.[29]

In both cases (the NPS and the Temkin Index), the percentage of passengers satisfied and the percentage dissatisfied, the sentiment depends on many factors, including the lack of performance relating to basic functions as well as frustration in other areas. In the case of the latter, if an individual only redeems miles for travel-related transactions (upgrades, free flights, and so forth) then an airline should know this *and* act upon this knowledge by not sending offers and catalogs for clothing and other items to that traveler but rather send relevant travel-related offers. Taking this point one step further, some travelers feel that they are bombarded with offers to purchase co-branded credit cards that not only do not interest them, but also create hassles in terms of having to shred the pre-printed personal information, thus actually causing damage in terms of the annoyance factor. Another pain point for some travelers is the abundance of surveys. This raises another important question. What is the right number of surveys—after a certain period of time or after each interaction with the airline? Some travelers do not wish to be bothered while others are more than willing to provide feedback. Airlines need to ensure that they are capturing (1) the frequency desired, (2) the manner in which consumers wish to interact (phone, email, mail, social media), and (3) the content of the communication with the airline, to promote loyalty rather than detract from it due to the annoyance factor. In today's environment it is so easy for customers to give feedback and for airlines to receive feedback. What is needed is timely action on the feedback received, along with a prioritization of the measurements of costs of actions and values of customers.

There is also the issue of trust. Trust can help retain customers in bad times, when things go wrong, but for this to happen the relationship must be well established beforehand. Think of Johnson & Johnson that overcame the Tylenol scare in the early 1980s and then nearly three decades later the recall of multiple over-the-counter medicines. Think also of Amazon that builds confidence with its policy to give a refund on pre-orders if the price of the item drops between the order time and the end of the day of the release date.[30] Trust can start, like most initiatives, with the internal culture, and then cascade out to customers and partners. These circumstances involve customers trusting the brand. However, it is also important to consider the reverse— companies trusting customers. For example, some companies offer extremely liberal return policies. Doing so means that companies have to have trust in their customers that the majority will not abuse the system.[31] Costco offers generous return policies and guarantees. In terms of membership, according to the company's website, if a member is dissatisfied, the company will refund the member's membership fee (in full, at any time). In terms of products, the company guarantees a member's satisfaction on every product that the company sells with a full refund (there are certain exceptions such as some electronics items which must be returned within 90 days of purchase for a refund).[32] Furthermore, at ALDI, if a consumer is not completely satisfied with a product, ALDI offers a "Double Guarantee"—they will not only replace the product, but also refund the customer's money (the "Double Guarantee" does not apply to non-food Special Buy items, alcohol, or national brands).[33] Do airlines offer any such programs that instill a sense of trust, confidence, and ease in travelers to develop a distinguishable brand? Alaska Airlines did. If passengers did not get their baggage at baggage claim within 20 minutes of their airplane parking at the gate, they were entitled to a $25 discount on a future Alaska Airlines flight or 2,500 bonus miles in their frequent flyer programs.

In a time when social media presence is extremely powerful, especially within certain segments such as the Millennials, as well as the availability of a myriad of other online information providers, what would be the effect of a star rating system (much like those already used for hotels) on airline brands? Would such a system actually help distinguish stronger brands from weaker ones, rather than the general negative attitude toward airline brands, especially in the US? Star ratings are done to some extent in the airline business, but they seem to be dependent on a list of "physical" service features. On the other hand, based on the popularity of TripAdvisor, consumers appear to be valuing user ratings, as with hotels.

Branding for the Future

A key differentiator in branding highlighted in this chapter is simplicity. Research conducted by Siegel+Gale shows that an investment in a stock portfolio of the top ten global brands worldwide has "beaten" the major indexes in the last five years. See Figure 5.2. These top ten brands were rated by consumers. As such, one would assume that a major criterion from consumers' perspective would be the ease of doing business, again a vote for simplicity. "As businesses become complex, those that can maintain simplicity will stand out in their financial performance, as well as in branding," said Brian Rafferty, Siegel+Gale's Global Director of Research Insights. Furthermore, according to Siegel+Gale, simplicity brings clarity instead of confusion, decision instead of doubt, and it inspires trust and loyalty.[34] In the case of the airline industry, simplicity can be examined with respect to each touchpoint in the travel cycle. See Figure 5.1. "Airlines can examine these touch points to identify the areas that fall within their scope and capitalize on these opportunities to strengthen their brands to provide choice and experience," said Rafferty. According to the information illustrated in Figure 5.1 the area that needs the most improvement would be the resolution of customers' problems, relating to, for example, itinerary changes and lost baggage. Focusing on the experience of passengers at each touchpoint will improve the NPS and, in turn, a customer's likeliness to make a recommendation.

Branding Insights from Other Businesses

Apple

Apple has led the way to the transformation of many *businesses* (including some *industries*, such as music), assembled a loyal customer base, and created a powerful and profitable global brand. The products, the packaging and also the unique design of Apple's retail stores all truly focus on the user experience factor. Huge tables filled with products are available for customers to browse, test, and ask questions of knowledgeable and friendly staff. Instead of traditional checkout counters and lines, one can

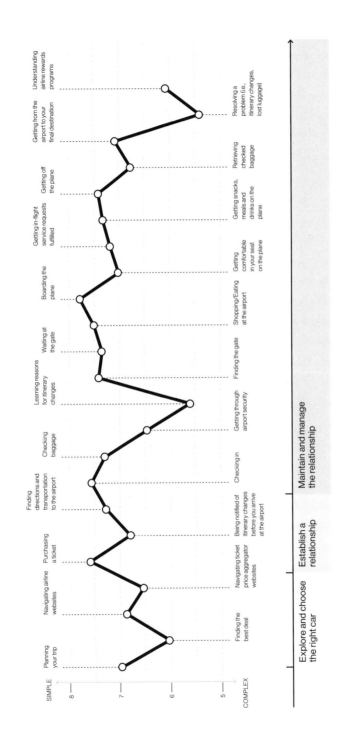

Global Brand Simplicity Index 2013

Figure 5.1   How people rated touchpoints of the airline experience

Source: Siegel+Gale

Percentage of growth of index/portfolio
since the beginning of 2009

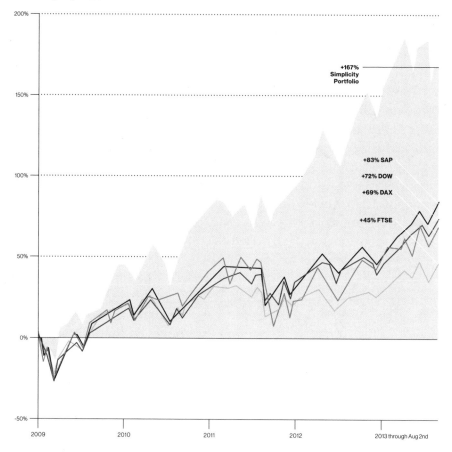

Figure 5.2   Simple brands top major market indexes
Source: Siegel+Gale

make the purchase right where one is standing, as employees bring the merchandise from the back to the customer and are equipped with mobile devices to accept payment and email a receipt. The stores are sleek and user friendly, very much in alignment with the products themselves, the packaging, and the company's overall strategy of providing a limited number of products. Remember the pyramid with three layers articulated by Manning and Bodine with Forrester Research, discussed earlier in this chapter—meeting customer needs, making it easy to do business, and making the shopping process enjoyable.

Burberry

Burberry is an example of a company that has worked to reinvent its brand. In an article in the *Harvard Business Review*, (now former) Burberry CEO Angela Ahrendts discussed the company's challenges and its turnaround. Ahrendts became CEO of Burberry in mid-2006, when the company faced a myriad of challenges, including losing its focus while expanding globally and not leveraging its historical core (the trench coat). Even the top employees were not wearing the brand and, as such, they were not living the brand. There was a lack of consistency across the globe, and it was trying to be something for everyone rather than focusing on the exclusivity factor of the brand. To address some of these challenges, Burberry changed its organizational structure to centralize all design under one global design director. With respect to customer segmentation, the company shifted from targeting everyone to targeting what they refer to as the luxury customers of the future, the Millennials, as they believed that this segment represented a possible "white space" for the company, given that they believed that this segment was being overlooked by competitors. The company recognized the need to rethink their marketing initiatives for this segment, capitalizing on the digital experience. In doing so, the company consolidated the few regional websites that they had from earlier on, and redesigned everything on one platform, exemplifying every aspect of the brand. The new marketing initiatives were designed to "speak" to the Millennials through "emotive brand content: music, movies, heritage, storytelling."[35]

The LEGO Group

Think about the Danish children's toy brand, LEGO, the name being an abbreviation of the Danish words, "leg godt" meaning "play well."[36] Note how this "play well" concept resonates with P&G's idea of improving people's lives. While the signature "brick" has been around for decades, in terms of segmentation, the company has been segmenting based upon affinity to the brand, distinguishing customer experience in the form of a pyramid. For example, the "top" of the pyramid represents consumers, both adults and children, who interact most with the brand, to the point of co-creating—an important element in design thinking, as highlighted earlier in the chapter. The next "layer" represents those consumers with whom the company has an ongoing dialogue. The following "layer" represents those who spend time on the company's online collaboration platform, and the "base" of the pyramid consists of those that have purchased the company's products. There are also subsegments, such as the LEGO Certified Professionals, that consists of those who are interested in turning their LEGO hobby into a part-time or full-time business, and LEGO Ambassadors that consists of individuals who arrange LEGO events worldwide. The LEGO group gains valuable insights with respect to which experiences and product features that its fans desire by interacting with them.[37]

Marriott

Some hotels are focusing on the element of design thinking in order to distinguish their brand. One example is Marriott, discussed in Chapter 3 with respect to its "Travel Brilliantly" campaign, which is pursuing co-creation in terms of designing with some of its customers at its Innovation Lab—a 10,000-square-foot facility located in the Marriott International headquarters. Michael Dail, vice president of Global Brand Marketing for Marriott Hotels explained, "Rather than someone at the company coming up with the idea and letting consumers validate it, with co-creation the idea starts with the consumer."[38] This is a new twist on the traditional focus group. This new collaborative initiative is a way to address the more empowered and demanding traveler, who has arisen as a result of the proliferation of social media. It is also a means of targeting the Millennial travelers, who have "unique habits that are influencing hotel design."[39]

Compare the strategies and, in some cases, brand transformation of these companies with most legacy carriers that try to be everything to everybody. The discussion on brand transformation continues in later parts of this book. Chapter 7 includes two more examples of brands that have been transforming themselves, Macy's and Netflix, in terms of leveraging analytics to gain customer insights. Furthermore, Chapter 9 also includes Thought Leadership Pieces, one by an executive of the Hertz Corporation on the company's transformation and one by an executive of Qantas on the use of analytics to get customer insights.

Takeaways

- Building a strong brand involves aligning branding and business strategies.
- Branding messages must be clear in the mind of the traveler — make it easy for the traveler to remember what the airline stands for and to distinctively stand out among all of the choices in air travel.
- Focus should be on the longer term overall experience as experience trumps material items in the new marketplace.
- Design thinking, incorporated in the business strategy, will be a brand differentiator.
- Leading brands are co-creating with their consumers to truly put them at the center of the process, exemplified by the strategies of LEGO and Marriott.
- Airlines should keep their eyes on the "white space," especially, as it relates to the Millennials and their needs which are very different from those of other generations.
- Focus should be on cross-channel consistency and digitization of the product.
- With all the information and choices available, ease of doing business leads to simplicity and can be a real brand differentiator.
- Trust can help forge lasting relationships between brands and consumers.

Notes

1 Eric V. Holtzclaw, *Laddering: Unlocking the Potential of Consumer Behavior* (Hoboken, NJ: John Wiley, 2013), pp. 148–50.

2 Gordon Bethune with Scott Huler, *From Worst to First: Behind the Scenes of Continental's Remarkable Comeback* (NY: John Wiley, 1998).

3 Nirmalya Kumar and Jan-Benedict E.M. Steenkamp, *Brand Breakout: How Emerging Market Brands Will Go Global* (NY: Palgrave Macmillan, 2013), p. 209.

4 Rafat Ali, "The Most Valuable Airline Brands of 2013," *Skift*, October 4, 2013.

5 http://www.theemiratesgroup.com/english/our-brands/air-transportation/emirates-airline.aspx (accessed March 2014 online).

6   http://www.emirates.com/us/english/about/emirates-sponsorships/sponsorships. aspx (accessed March 2014 online).

7   Jim Stengel, *Grow: How Ideals Power Growth and Profit at the World's Greatest Companies* (NY: Crown Publishing Group, 2011).

8   "Global Brand Simplicity Index 2013: Demonstrating the Impact of Simplicity on Revenue, Loyalty, and Innovation," Siegel+Gale, New York, 2013, pp. 20–1.

9   http://www.southwest.com/html/travel-experience/index.html?int=GFOOTER-SWA-TRAVEL-EXPERIENCE (accessed April 3, 2014 online).

10   Laurence Vincent, *Brand Real: How Smart Companies Live Their Brand Promise and Inspire Fierce Customer Loyalty* (NY: AMACOM, 2012), p. 14.

11   Harley Manning and Kerry Bodine, *Outside In: The Power of Putting Customers at the Center of Your Business* (NY: Houghton Mifflin Harcourt, 2012).

12   Matthew Dixon, Karen Freeman, and Nicholas Toman, "STOP Trying to Delight Your Customers," *Harvard Business Review*, July–August 2010, pp. 116–22.

13   Matthias Krust, "Mercedes Citan Performs Poorly in EuroNCAP Crash Test," *Automotive News Europe*, April 26, 2013.

14   Jane L. Levere, "Old Slogan Returns as United Asserts it is Customer-Focused," *The New York Times*, September 20, 2013.

15   https://hub.united.com/en-us/flyerfriendly/Pages/default.aspx.

16   Idris Mootee, *Design Thinking for Strategic Innovation: What They Can't Teach You at Business or Design School* (Hoboken, NJ: John Wiley, 2013), p. 16.

17   Based on the material in Kelly McDonald, *Crafting the Customer Experience for People Not Like You: How to Delight and Engage the Customers Your Competitors Don't Understand* (Hoboken, NJ: John Wiley, 2013), pp. 8–9, 12.

18   Sally O'Rourke, "Why Smart Companies are Turning to Co-Creation," CMO. COM, Digital Marketing Insight for CMOs, October 8, 2013.

19   http://www.finnair.com/FI/GB/qualityhunters2013 (accessed February 2014 online).

20   Maria Lenhart, "Travel Trends 2014: Unplugged, Imperfect, Fast," www. travelmarketreport.com, January 3, 2014.

21   Matthew Dixon, Karen Freeman, and Nicholas Toman, "STOP Trying to Delight Your Customers," *Harvard Business Review*, July–August 2010, pp. 116–22.

22   Dennis Schaal, "Why JetBlue Doesn't Target Road Warriors and Doesn't Plan to Anytime Soon," *Skift*, March 20, 2013.

23   Robin Amster, "Six Travel Trends to Watch in 2014 & Beyond," www. travelmarketreport.com, November 14, 2013.

24   Brian Solis, *What's the Future of Business?: Changing the Way Businesses Create Experiences* (Hoboken, NJ: John Wiley, 2013), p. 32.

25   Ibid., pp. 32–5.

26   Matt Egol, Michael Peterson, and Stefan Stroh, "How to Choose the Right Digital Marketing Model," *strategy+business*, January 27, 2014.

27   Dennis Schaal, "Why JetBlue Doesn't Target Road Warriors and Doesn't Plan to Anytime Soon," *Skift*, March 20, 2013.

28 "USAA, Costco, Apple, Amazon.com, Southwest Airlines, Trader Joe's and Marriott Among the Highest in Customer Loyalty in the 2013 Satmetrix Net Promoter Benchmark Study," Press Release by PRWeb, San Mateo, CA, April 24, 2013.

29 "2013 Temkin Forgiveness Ratings (TFR), Top and Bottom Firms" Source: Temkin Group Q1 2013 Consumer Benchmark Survey.

30 Dr Linden R. Brown and Chris L. Brown, *The Customer Culture Imperative: A Leader's Guide to Driving Superior Performance* (NY: McGraw-Hill, 2014), p. 205.

31 Barry Berman, *Competing in Tough Times* (Upper Saddle River, NJ: Pearson, 2011), pp. 130–1.

32 http://www.costco.com/returns-replacements-refunds.html (accessed March 2014 online).

33 https://www.aldi.us/en/new-to-aldi/double-guarantee/ (accessed March 2014 online).

34 "Global Brand Simplicity Index 2013: Demonstrating the Impact of Simplicity on Revenue, Loyalty, and Innovation," Siegel+Gale, New York, 2013, p. 3.

35 Angela Ahrendts, "Burberry's CEO on Turning An Aging British Icon into a Global Luxury Brand," *Harvard Business Review*, January–February 2013, pp. 39–42.

36 http://aboutus.lego.com/en-us/lego-group/the_lego_history (accessed March 2014 online).

37 Reza Soudagar, Vinay Iyer, and Dr Volker G. Hildebrand, *The Customer Experience Edge: Technology and Techniques for Delivering an Enduring, Profitable, and Positive Experience to Your Customers* (NY: McGraw-Hill, 2012), pp. 83–7.

38 Nancy Trejos, "Guests Help Design the Hotel of the Future," *USA Today*, November 15, 2013.

39 Ibid.

Chapter 6
Addressing the Role of Loyalty

How is it that companies like Apple have created such a strong sense of loyalty that people anxiously anticipate the announcement of new products and new versions of products and then stand in line for them without expectations of discounts or loyalty points? Consider Trader Joe's, a store that does not use many of the marketing elements that traditional grocery chains do—such as coupons or loyalty cards—yet still retains a strong customer base. And how about Costco which actually charges its customers an annual fee to shop in its stores and still enjoys a membership renewal rate of nearly 90 percent (89.7 percent for North America and 86.4 percent worldwide according to one report in March 2013)?[1] How do airlines compare with these businesses? According to a recent survey by Deloitte on consumer loyalty in the airline industry (all passengers, those travelling for business and for leisure) the current loyalty programs ranked 19 out of 26 attributes in terms of importance.[2] This chapter on loyalty explores what airlines have done, and what they can do, in order to build a loyal customer base and premium-price-commanding brands which will allow them to achieve the success that companies in others industries have enjoyed. This chapter has a strong linkage to the previous chapter on branding, in terms of loyalty to the brand.

Some Background

Loyalty programs in the global airline industry, as we know them today, began in 1981 when American Airlines introduced its AAdvantage program. This program was developed for four primary reasons. First, deregulation of the airline industry in the

US led to the proliferation of price competition and the potential value for airlines to develop marketing initiatives to reward their repeat customers. Second, after deregulation, low cost, low fare airlines (for example, New York Air, founded in 1980) became competitive threats to traditional airlines. It is interesting to note that People Express came into business in April 1981 and American introduced its frequent flyer program in May 1981. Third, major network airlines were just beginning to build their information technology capability—with the exception of American Airlines that was willing to invest much more in this area in order to manage the huge size of its loyalty program, track miles flown by passengers from PNR data, and, eventually, to include partners such as car rental companies and hotels. Fourth, with its high fixed costs and load factors in the 70–80 percent range, airlines could use the spare capacity to support its frequent flyer program at marginal cost.

Initially, the basic reward was a free ticket on the airline. Over time, the reward system was expanded to include free products and the services of partners (car rentals, hotel rooms, and so on), upgrades to premium cabins, and, subsequently, to include access to airport lounges, free tickets on alliance partners, priority check in and boarding, baggage allowance, elite bonus miles, access to elite customer service agents, and so forth. The other major development in the airline frequent flyer loyalty programs was the monetization of loyalty programs through the sale of the miles to third parties—banks, for example. As such, these loyalty programs represented both a cost and a revenue dimension. On the cost side were the costs for administration, the (carefully monitored and dynamically managed) cost associated with displacement of fare-paying passengers, the fees paid to partners to provide free travel to loyal passengers, the incremental costs to transport the free ticketed passengers— extra fuel, meals, insurance, passenger facility charges (PFCs), and any (allocated) reservation, check-in and gate/lounge facility costs. On the revenue side were the sale of miles to third parties (primarily banks, where miles formed a resilient and valuable foundation of full-fledged product suites of personal and business cards), revenues from partner redemptions, as well as the attributed revenue generated through an increase in share of wallet, lifetime value, and recommendations, initially through word-of-mouth and, more recently, through various types of social media. Accounting for revenues and costs associated with these programs has changed over time, most notably with the progressive introduction of reporting requirements in most accounting conventions.

The other desire driving the enhancement of the loyalty program was the ability to gather more information on customers. Increasing technological sophistication and more recent focus on big data has allowed airlines to capitalize on the value of customer data captured by the program. Apart from complete recorded detail of travel history and travel plans, coalition programs (where multiple partners from various industries cooperate) hold powerful data that is increasingly being sought after by marketing partners and the airlines themselves.

Over the past decade a further dimension of FFP monetization has started to take place—internally (via point sales to partners), partnerships/JVs, spinoffs, and outright IPOs. The concept of spinning off frequent flyer programs makes sense in that the programs are more profitable than other components of the airline and their value can be recognized more clearly through separation. The concept of selling off the more profitable division of the business is not new within the airline industry, exemplified by AMR's decision to spin off AMR Services (now Sabre), Lufthansa's decision to divest its stake in Amadeus, the GDS, and the former Swissair to sell off Gate Gourmet. FFPs are an important source of profits to modern carriers (sometimes amounting to 50, 80, and even 120 percent of the underlying carrier profitability), and an increasingly important source of revenue (ranging from 6 to 10 percent of topline revenues). The value of FFPs also increased after being spunoff. For example, the value of three FFPs of three airlines (Air Canada, Latam, and GOL) increased by factors of two, eight, and 13, respectively.[3]

Fundamentally, programs are monetized by the presale of points to partners, in addition to share of wallet improvements and customer retention. Banks are interested in buying these points because of the significant uptick in credit card use for products in the point programs of well-known airlines. According to the Affinity Capital Exchange, in some markets, notably Australia, the uptick is even higher, prompting Qantas multiple non-exclusive relationships with banks in the country. For banks, however, who see the immediate impact of loyalty programs, the question remains whether to continue spending on miles or establish their own currency to reduce costs and improve customer choice. Affinity Capital Exchange estimates that loyalty program revenues from point sales top $40 billion annually, with banks accounting for over $25 billion dollars (63 percent) of these revenues.[4]

These loyalty programs became extremely successful within the traditional network carriers. Based on the success of the loyalty programs of traditional full service carriers, one would assume that if schedule, product, and price are similar, membership in a loyalty program could be the deciding factor. One would also assume that this effect would become stronger as a member holds a progressively higher status. This would be true in the case of frequent travelers (on business or leisure). The survey conducted by Deloitte cited above found, for example, that 44 percent of airline travelers fly more than 75 percent of air miles on their preferred airline.[5] Low cost carriers did not initially embrace the frequent flyer programs, partly to keep costs low by avoiding complexity, and partly because they neither had the data nor the know how to capitalize on this resource. The basic assumption was that low fares themselves developed loyalty, a valid assumption for certain segments of the traveling population. On the other hand, Evert de Boer and Ralph Browning of Aimia, a loyalty management company, point out that low cost carriers that choose not to offer loyalty programs are overlooking two key points: (1) the programs do not have to add to net costs (especially when the benefits of incremental travelers and incremental mileage are factored in), and (2) the programs bring new business partners, affiliate revenue, and a potential for added profit to the low cost carrier.[6]

With increased competition not only between low cost carriers and full service carriers, but also among the low cost carriers themselves, loyalty programs began to emerge even within the low cost sector, exemplified by Southwest's RapidRewards, Virgin Australia's Velocity, and AirAsia's BIG. The need for viable loyalty programs continues to solidify as the business models of the two sectors converge (a result of the low cost carriers' desire to penetrate the business market in the domestic, regional, and intercontinental sectors). Within this segment there is the willingness and the ability to pay higher fares. Moreover, if an airline offers a co-branded credit card, those who acquire the card are likely to spend more on it, resulting in increased revenue streams for the airline/loyalty program. It has been reported that eight of the ten largest low cost carriers have some form of loyalty program.[7] An Affinity Capital Exchange forecast suggests that profits from loyalty-related businesses at low cost carriers may soon outgrow profits generated by ancillary products sold at these airlines.

There are no hard numbers relating to the penetration of loyalty programs within the airline industry. It is estimated that between 30 and 50 percent of passengers traveling with full service airlines in mature markets such as North America, Europe, Japan, and Australia are members of loyalty programs. The percentage in developing markets is estimated to be less than 30 percent and growing fast as programs and offerings gain momentum. And the percentage of passengers traveling with low cost carriers would be less than with full service carriers, with the exception of Southwest. Therefore, to remain competitive, airlines feel the need to offer loyalty programs. However, they need to differentiate their programs, especially with respect to making them customer value oriented.[8]

Current Landscape

The focus of loyalty programs more recently has been on the "earning and burning" aspects of miles, in some cases to the point of playing a "game." It appears that, while successful in the past, the loyalty programs in their current state have been losing their sense of excitement and, as such, they now need to be reviewed due to a myriad of issues, including:

From the airlines' perspective:

- Frequent flier programs have become businesses in themselves and have their own objectives that may be different from the objectives of the airline.

- An airline may lose control over its loyalty program in that travelers may earn points through many different channels, and thus may be less loyal to a particular airline, unless the airline decides to be selective on the partners to be included.
- Many travelers are members of a number of loyalty programs. One study, for example, indicates that 28 percent have membership in three or more different programs, and nearly 22 percent are in two airline loyalty programs.[9] Consequently, there can be a low engagement with any single frequent flier program, except for preference of passengers for an airline influenced by their home airport representation of airlines.
- While there are many partners included in these programs, most members appear to only be aware of a few of them, thus leading to low utilization and suboptimal revenue generation for the airline.
- Airlines need to identify the values that travelers are seeking and distinguish whether travelers are loyal to their airline or to the frequent flyer program. Airlines need to make investments to measure these values, specifically: (1) what travelers value, and (2) did the travelers receive it and did the airline benefit from it.
- Even though a disproportionate share of revenues and profits come from passengers in the loyalty programs, airlines may also want to focus on passengers that are *not* in the frequent flyer program, including by actively encouraging sign-ups in the program. What are their needs, preferences, and interests? Relating to the discussion in Chapter 3, perhaps a customer-centric airline should take steps to determine the needs of this segment and create an attractive offering to meet these needs rather than the more traditional loyalty program offerings.
- Liability management is becoming an increasingly greater issue as the estimated amount of unredeemed miles continues to rise. This aspect became even more important with new accounting rules that forced airlines to only recognize revenue from the frequent flyer programs when the miles are redeemed.

- There are many interpretations of loyalty, even within a single segment such as those traveling on business, and airlines may be missing out on these differences in the preferences among travelers.

From the passengers' perspective:

- Many passengers feel that it is becoming increasingly difficult and costly to redeem miles for travel on traditional airlines — reward travel is not available for the destinations or the dates/times needed, not to mention the fees that are now incurred for accessing and, when necessary, changing reward travel. Some airlines are even thinking about setting a minimum amount of money spent each year on travel to obtain even a low level of status. On the other hand, according to surveys, value airlines (such as Air Berlin, GOL, and Southwest) rank high with respect to reward seat availability.[10]
- Expanding upon the point above, for some leisure travelers, the expectations of attaining award travel (free trips or upgrades) is unrealistic in today's environment due to sophisticated yield management and high load factors, unless passengers are willing to be flexible in planning their award travel. In the US, airlines typically now allocate about 10 percent of the available seat miles for award travel. However, airline revenue management and space control systems vary this proportion dynamically on flight/date level, rendering busy routes inaccessible on reward seats.
- Passengers find that programs differ widely in terms of all-in cost of award travel, driven primarily by the levy of the so-called "fuel surcharge" introduced by carriers over the last few years.
- Less frequent travelers could be interested in joining these programs as even a low number of accumulated miles (for example 10–15,000) may allow a passenger on some airlines to obtain a one-way flight, or redeem rewards in low season where most airlines reduce reward levels.
- While loyalty programs have been augmented to include various offerings (everything from credit cards and

merchandise to iTunes downloads), many airlines are still pushing out offers through mass marketing without paying attention to who is interested and in what offer, and at what time. Consider one study that indicates that 35 percent either rarely or never redeem promotional offers received from airlines.[11] The progressive airlines are beginning to change these tactics as they invest in extensive analytics on large data sets collected from partners, social media, and campaign management solutions.

- There is also the issue of taxation of frequent flyer program benefits, as being explored by various tax authorities.
- For some segments of passengers, an airline should provide more opportunities than simply "earning and burning" miles. It should become a travel solution provider for these segments to earn their loyalty.

Let us start with what motivates loyalty and raise two fundamental questions: First, does an airline distinguish between *true* and *perceived* loyalty? Suppose the situation represents a virtual *monopoly*—the only carrier with the majority of attractive flight options out of a given airport. In this case, patronage cannot be confused with loyalty. Many frequent travelers would purchase a ticket on the almost monopoly airline because they have no other *viable* choice. The second question: Is the airline *buying* loyalty or truly *earning* it? Many frequent flyers say that the airline is buying their loyalty through *bribery*, for example, through upgrades and early boarding, to reduce pain.

It is also important to distinguish between behavioral and emotional loyalty. Bryan Pearson points out that behavioral loyalty reflects purchasing behavior and is usually motivated by rewards. The consumer is generally satisfied with prices, products, and service, but if something better is offered, the consumer will likely go elsewhere. While this type of loyalty is a strong indicator with respect to factors such as price advantage and convenience, and perhaps a lack of feasible competition, it does not serve as a strong indicator of customer engagement. Emotional loyalty, on the other hand, exists within a continuous customer relationship and involves the company's ability to acknowledge the customer's contributions directly. In this case the customer is committed to the company, even if he or she is presented a better option by another company.[12] Consider the emotional loyalty that Johnson & Johnson built with young mothers with respect to the care of their young babies in their famous taglines.

One business executive points out that people often talk about, particularly with regard to loyalty programs in the travel industry, *rational rewards* — "If you do this, I will give you that." While acknowledging that there is a very clear linkage in this type of message, he also notes that there is a lot of value in loyalty programs when they also are capable of delivering *experiential rewards*. This type of reward is different in that one does not always receive it, but when the person does, he/she is surprised and delighted.[13]

Along the lines of the earlier discussion regarding what motivates loyalty, data, specifically relating to behavior, can be leveraged to determine where travelers are in terms of their level of commitment. Is a traveler: (1) indifferent — that is, will leave for a better offering, (2) middle of the road — that is, will take an airline even if a competitor offers a nonstop or a slightly lower fare, or (3) totally committed — that is, will go out of his way to take the airline by changing travel plans to accommodate the airline's service schedule to a particular destination? Regardless of a traveler's point in the loyalty spectrum, one thing is for certain — no one prefers poor service. Thus, airlines must get the basic service components right (such as reliability and minimum customer service levels) before hoping to earn a true preference. As discussed in Chapter 2, an airline might consider 80 percent on-time performance to be reasonable. What is acceptable from the viewpoint of customers, not just those by categories (such as those on business, leisure, or VFR), but by each individual on an airplane immediately after completing the trip? Tools and systems are now available to derive this information almost effortlessly. Would courier service providers, such as Federal Express and UPS, be able to get away with 80 or even 90 percent on-time delivery performance?

Leveraging Data

The key to rethinking loyalty is to *leverage* data to engage
with travelers at the segment level and or the individual level,
depending on where the carrier has determined it should be on
the customization spectrum outlined in Chapter 3, and to tailor
the services offered and provided accordingly. As seasoned
travelers state, intelligent and loyalty-capturing opportunities
can be created even by leveraging the data that airlines already
possess to offer meaningful and relevant information to travelers
on a segment or even individual basis. What is truly meaningful
varies by traveler and therefore a "one-size-fits-all" approach
is no longer applicable, even within higher tiers. For example,
a person who travels several times a week may value priority
boarding each time for the opportunity to obtain a place for his
bags over the opportunity to earn a free trip in the future. To
another frequent traveler, it could be some assurance that if she
misses her connection, the airline will reaccommodate her on the
next flight, regardless of whether the very next flight is on the
airline itself, or an alliance partner, or a competitor. Some low
frequency travelers may prefer to have an airline simply reduce
the fare on the next flight based on the number of points that the
traveler has accumulated.

For example, it is reported that Etihad allows passengers
to spend every mile they earn, right from the start, toward the
purchase of the next flight.[14] One way to overcome the issue of
people who would rather have an alternative option to a free
flight is a mobile wallet, as launched by Loylogic, a Zurich-based
company, that enables a person to convert points or miles to cash
that may in turn be used at any point of sale.[15] Some airlines
are beginning to offer merchandise and or gift cards, effectively
enabling members to buy the products and services they desire.

Another way of leveraging data and analytics, either in the
area of promotions or service recovery, is to focus on three
aspects of the consumer engagement: "multichannel, multistep,
and closed loop." The multichannel component is already being
used by airlines to communicate with the customer. The multistep
component relates to finding out why the receiver did not respond
or, if they did respond, the information provided, and finally, the

actions taken. For example, suppose an airline sends an email letting a customer know of a change in a connecting flight. If the customer does not respond, should the airline follow up to ask if the customer, in fact, even received the email and if the change was acceptable? This leads to the closed loop component that, in turn, relates to the two-way conversation. For example, in a service recovery scenario, if an airline were to rebook a passenger on the next flight available, should the question be asked if such a move on the part of the airline was acceptable? If not, should other options be presented?

Consider the following example of a company outside the airline industry that leveraged data to provide meaningful and relevant information to its customers. Bryan Pearson gives the example of Shell's Canadian operations that had too many and outdated stations in the mid-1990s. Shell, in partnership with AIR MILES, leveraged data relating to buying behavior and temporarily redirected its customers through the renovation and or closures to new locations by incentivizing them with additional miles. Shell and AIR MILES mined and used data to determine and change customer behavior through relevant rewards and communications in a business that is extremely sensitive to price and convenience, such as the airline industry.[16]

Another aspect of leveraging data to grow new segments to the loyalty program lies in the selection of partners that would bring in new segments. An airline could work at both ends of the retailing business, for instance. The low cost retailers could help to attract a new segment at the low end that would consist of non-frequent travelers. Working with the high end retailers could provide access to segments that, even if they did not fit into top tier flyer status, would fit into the premium-fare flyers category.

Since the crux of the Shell example above relates to the availability and use of information, this raises a new question: Are airlines losing or gaining information from their relationship with buyers of miles, for example, banks/credit card providers? Admitted, airlines gain enormous revenue from credit card providers for miles purchased, but have they been removing themselves from the data on actual travelers in terms of valuable information to fuel loyalty? However, the relationship with banks could provide more than just financial return if airlines could make different arrangements and, in fact, were to gain additional insights about the behavior of new buyers via the bank. One example is the recent ten-year financial credit card agreements between Aimia and the Canadian Imperial Bank of Commerce (CIBC) and the TD Bank Group (TD), effective January 1, 2014.[17] This begs the question: Leaving aside, for a moment, the matter of privacy, can such programs, as they are administered today by most airlines, truly provide additional information about the buying behavior patterns and attitude of passengers, and if so, are most airlines acting upon this information?

Rupert Duchesne of Aimia states that the new currency is consumer data. He cautions, as has been stated on other occasions throughout this book, if a company does not leverage its customer data, other companies will. Understandably, if airlines do not deliver the right offer, other businesses will. And as Duchesne states, standing by on the sidelines is no longer an option, giving the following call to action: "Every consumer-facing company in every industry must develop, execute and evolve a data-based customer loyalty strategy in order to maintain control of and build value into their customer relationships."[18]

Rethinking Segmentation

By leveraging data, large network airlines can now begin to focus, for example, on specific subsegments of the broader leisure segment from the perspective of loyalty. The importance of this new focus is based partly on the enormous size of the leisure market, and partly on the downward trend in the percentage of travelers buying premium fares to increase profitability. It is the expected growth in the lower fare traffic in emerging markets that represents the real opportunity. And, in the case of the leisure segment in developed markets, it is the perception of the gap between the value received and the fare charged. A solid and positive difference between these two aspects will enhance loyalty and, in turn, strengthen the brand.

Another value-adding piece of information in the segmentation process would be the life cycle of travelers. While it is reasonable to focus on the loyalty of top travelers that provide a disproportionate amount of revenue, and possibly profitability, airlines also need to consider the loyalty of those new in their careers but who are very likely to increase travel as they progress in their careers. Consequently, while the top tier cannot be ignored, airlines must start placing a greater emphasis on the next or "up and coming" levels—especially their needs and their willingness to pay for certain products and services versus what they report they would like (as discussed in Chapter 2), as well as whether the airline has the resources to provide the required service features to make them loyal. One airline is, for example, selling lower fare prepaid vouchers for travel to students while they are still in graduate business schools for travel between their schools and their homes to increase their awareness of the airline and its products and, in turn, loyalty.

Having analyzed the conventional segments, an airline can also explore some "specialty" segments, such as:

- Less frequent travelers who are not currently enrolled in the carrier's loyalty program. How would an airline motivate the individual already flying on the airline to join its loyalty program, given that only 30–50 percent of the passengers traveling on global airlines are in their frequent flyer programs? Consequently, there is an opportunity to conduct a comprehensive analysis (using internal and external sources of information) of the remaining 50–70 percent to identify and engage with the next attractive segment. To obtain their loyalty, airlines may entice them with free baggage and or no fees for changing reservations. Interestingly, hotels are facing a similar challenge and an opportunity. They have also been catering to the needs of business travelers whereas 75 percent of the expenditures are now being made by the leisure segment.
- Individuals in a competitor loyalty program which could be targeted to make the switch. Some airlines already offer matching status levels for switching—this may be feasible in a market where two carriers have a dominant presence and a high frequency business traveler could be persuaded to make the switch. If a high frequency traveler with KLM moved from Amsterdam to Munich, how would Lufthansa

be able to extract this information to pursue this traveler? Such tactics could invite the type of "gaming" behavior from members as highlighted earlier in the chapter.

- Frequent travelers living in cities where there is no hub for a particular airline. Until recently, Boston, Massachusetts, for example, had no one dominant airline. And, even though JetBlue has begun to develop a major hub in Boston, it will be some time until it builds up its scale and scope comparable to the other three major US airlines.

- Passengers who are not yet enrolled in an airline's frequent flier program, but have purchased infrequent but full fare, one way, and or made last minute reservations in business markets. Such activities indicate potential viable high value travelers and could be pursued with relative ease. A few airlines do have high value predictor models that rate passengers based on such criteria, enabling airlines to fast track new members to a higher starting level.

- Past high frequency and or value travelers who have stopped traveling on a carrier. Some progressive airlines have tried to engage with these customers relating to the reduction in their travel (recurrent dissatisfaction with the service provided, retirement, relocation, and so forth). Based on such an engagement, these airlines have developed appropriate strategies.

- Millennial travelers (approximately ages 18–30). This group represents a different challenge as (1) more of them tend to combine business and leisure travel, (2) they heavily leverage their mobile devices in terms of search and booking, and (3) they do not hesitate to share their negative reviews. However, on the positive side, it is reported that this segment travels a lot more than young adults (approximately ages 31–45) for both business and leisure.[19]

How could an airline target some of these segments? Again, this is where data and analytics come into play—to identify appropriate targets and to develop appropriate value propositions. Figure 6.1 breaks down customers in two segments into two basic groups, members and non-members in an airline's loyalty program. Consider, for a moment, the customers who are not members in the loyalty program. Further, consider a subsegment in which the customers are new to the airline. This subsegment provides an opportunity to reach for new sources of business, through social media, a channel that has only become available in the past few years. There is also an opportunity to sell new products to this subsegment. The key insight enabled by new digital technology is information relating to marketing attribution. For example, which part of the shopping process led to the purchase decision—the social media channel (such as Facebook) and a specific click (such as an advertising banner or a product review). Similar insights and campaigns could be developed for the other segment in that group as well as the other group and its segments.

Many airlines have already tapped into various aspects of the social media world, including Facebook, Twitter, and YouTube, to connect with and gain insights from customers. One example of a new way that airlines are connecting with people is Etihad, which has created a new mapping tool in connection with LinkedIn enabling travelers to display their LinkedIn connections on a map and easily interact with them as they travel, a concept that may have been developed by Satisfly. A second example would be KLM which has developed an engagement technique that enables different passengers to sit together on the same flight. Qatar, a relatively young airline, launched its service on Facebook in April 2011 and had more than two million fans by the end of September 2013. The airline has capitalized on this component of social media to promote itself through exclusive airfares and sponsorship of popular football clubs.

Consider some of the programs that hotels are offering, as outlined in Chapter 3. Could airlines determine the "pain points" of passengers and implement programs to help alleviate some of them in an effort to shift the value proposition—value *for* travelers as opposed to value *from* travelers, thus increasing revenues from loyalty more than the refunds given or forgone revenue from additional fees charged? It comes down to a question of the balance of increased costs versus increased revenues from loyalty. Would a significant increase in loyalty bring more revenue than costs? The bigger question may be: is loyalty a cost center or a profit center?

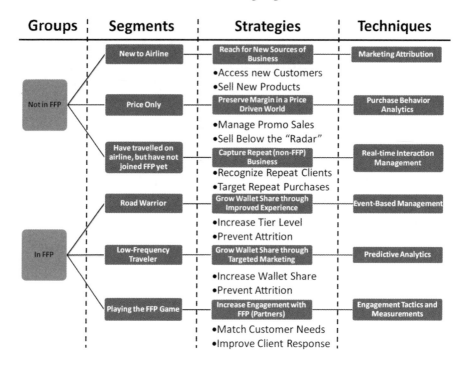

Figure 6.1   Leveraging business intelligence and analytics to re-design segment strategies

In the spirit of becoming more like a retailer, as discussed in Chapter 4, why not offer a one time price adjustment within 14 days of purchase if a traveler finds a lower fare for the same flight on the same carrier in the same fare category after making a purchase? An example of an airline that has already adopted this concept is Jetstar, as illustrated by its "Price Beat Guarantee." If a passenger finds a lower fare online for comparable travel, it will not only match the fare but also offer a 10 percent additional reduction.

Beyond Traditional Incentives

Rajat Paharia describes the evolution of loyalty as follows. Loyalty 1.0 included the standard loyalty programs such as frequent flyer programs that provided well defined benefits—a free ticket after a certain number of miles flown. There was very little information on customer behavior other than the number of trips, the time of ticket purchases prior to travel, price of the tickets, and class of travel. Passengers presumably got excited when they joined the programs and when they redeemed the miles for free tickets. There was virtually no information on behavior and very little emotional activity in between the two events relating to brand loyalty other than simply the accumulation of miles. Loyalty 2.0 involved some segmentation and personalization, for example, through direct marketing with the use of direct mail and email. Businesses started to leverage data to better connect with their customers, but, as a result, customers started to become bombarded with, mostly, irrelevant communications. Now, Loyalty 3.0 combines the powerful forces of big data, gamification, and motivation, according to Paharia, to make both customers and employees more active, more engaged, and truly loyal.[20]

Motivation provides information on what influences consumers to do or not do things. This information, generated through the use of big data to move toward Loyalty 3.0, provides an opportunity for the business to understand and engage with its customers, a process that enhances loyalty. Gamification involves leveraging the motivational techniques from video games and applying them to non-game situations. Gamification is a way to engage users rather than merely pushing out content to them, such as through an email. For example, an airline could leverage gamification to "teach" travelers about a new product or service rather than just push out an email that could easily be overlooked or ignored. In October 2012, Gartner reported that 70 percent of business transformation initiatives are unsuccessful due to a lack of engagement, and went on to predict that by 2015, 40 percent of companies (of Global 1,000 organizations) will leverage gamification as the main tool in business operations transformation.[21]

As Paharia points out, gamification is not a new technique. Rather, what is new is the role of big data in gamification that allows it to be automated and scaled, with real time feedback, to motivate players and their experience at levels that were not previously possible. The goal of gamification is not to provide entertainment, but to meet the goals of the business, such as to inform players about some product features or brand values. The "game" part is to get the user interested and to keep the user engaged on the basis of experience. The mechanics of the gamification process can vary from one business to another and from one situation to another. Correctly, he cautions about those who follow the hype and jump on the bandwagon without a true understanding of the concept, mentioning that the top reason for failure is poor gamification design, the result of a lack of understanding as well as a lack of experience and a proven process.[22]

Consider two examples of gamification, both in the travel industry, one for engaging customers and one for engaging (potential) employees. First, KLM created "Aviation Empire" that allows customers to experience managing an airline—including selecting flight destinations, investing in aircraft and landing rights, and developing airports.[23] Second, Marriott launched "My Marriott Hotel" that allows potential employees to manage a virtual hotel restaurant kitchen, focusing on various operational elements. Such an initiative helps the company as it expands into new markets and also aids the targeting of the Millennials.[24] According to an online article in *tnooz*, a recent study by Gigya showed the following: "gamification improves engagement by one-third, with online commenting improving by 13%, social media sharing improving by 22%, and content discovery improving by a whopping 68%."[25]

Another way to rethink loyalty, as presented in a paper written by Peeter Kivestu of Teradata, is to reposition loyalty with respect to engaging customer experiences. Specifically, he highlights four components to consider in reframing loyalty: (1) 360-degree view of the customer experience, (2) measures of customer value, (3) correlations of customer value and experience, and (4) experiences designed to drive value growth. The first component involves augmenting traditional transactional data gathered by an airline with behavioral data. This also means covering all online channels to gain information before the transaction— behaviors can add context to transactions. The second component, measures of customer value (both value provided and value received, as highlighted earlier in this chapter), includes such elements as contribution by the customer and their social network presence and value. The third component involves the correlation of specific experiences with changing customer value. Different methods of determining such correlations include direct measurement (measuring growth in customer value over time), marketing attribution (measuring impact of various marketing messages in directing a consumer to a purchase), behavioral analytics (measuring the likelihood that customers will chose specific offers), and following analytics (evaluating customers' behavior on one or more devices toward a specific action). The fourth component involves offering different customer segments specific experiences created to improve customer value.

Kivestu highlights that one critical success factor in developing loyalty is to pursue knowledge at the individual level. He stresses starting out simply, such as in terms of developing metrics and targeting just a few customer value components. Finally, he summarizes that continuous testing, measurement, and the implementation of continuous improvement facilitated by the appropriate processes, technologies, and corporate culture is critical to reframing loyalty.[26]

This chapter addressed two of the three components of "Loyalty 3.0" as outlined by Paharia, namely gamification and motivation. The third component of loyalty, big data, will be discussed at greater length in Chapter 7. Airline loyalty programs would have performed much better if airlines had engaged in more meaningful ways with their customers (for example, how they plan and book their travel and what attributes they value) and then promoted the desired behavior with relevant awards. This engagement comes with the use of big data and analytics, the subject of the next chapter.

Takeaways

- In an industry of high-fixed costs, overcapacity and capital constraints, loyalty programs play an increasingly important role, straddling financial and marketing benefits to operators and sponsors.
- It is necessary to clearly define and determine travelers' behavior and attitudes with respect to loyalty (behavioral and emotional) as well as their level of commitment. Are

airlines truly earning their customers' loyalty? Are airlines rewarding and, possibly, penalizing the desired behavior, at least by segment, if not by individual?

- Airlines must consider the many "next" and or "up-and-coming" segments and how they can engage with them to attract them and to inspire other potential loyalty.
- Tools such as gamification can be used to better engage with all segments.
- Airlines should think about moving beyond the "earning and burning" mentality and think about the delivery of relevant products and services throughout the customer travel cycle and at different touchpoints. For some segments, an airline should become a travel solution provider to earn their loyalty.
- Customer insights, gained through data and analytics, as well as improvements in customer experience, will lead to more relevant and energized loyalty programs to, in turn, generate more value for both the customer and the airline.

Notes

1 Trefis Team, "Costco's Earnings: Steady Sales Growth And Expanding Membership Base In Focus," *Forbes*, March 11, 2013.

2 "Rising above the Clouds: Charting a Course for Renewed Airline Consumer Loyalty," Deloitte & Touche LLP, 2013, p. 8.

3 Based upon an interview with Atanas Christov, President of the Affinity Capital Exchange, April 4, 2014.

4 Based upon an email communication from Atanas Christov, President of the Affinity Capital Exchange, April 7, 2014.

5 "Rising above the Clouds: Charting a Course for Renewed Airline Consumer Loyalty," Deloitte & Touche LLP, 2013, p. 5.

6 Evert de Boer and Ralph Browning, "The Legacy Effect: Rethinking Loyalty for Low-Cost Carriers" Aimia Inc., 2013, p. 2.

7 Ibid., p. 1.

8 Ibid.

9 "Consumer Loyalty in the Airline Industry," Deloitte Development LLC, 2013, p. 23.

10 Fourth Annual Switchfly Reward Seat Availability Survey, quoted in an *IdeaWorks* publication.

11 "Consumer Loyalty in the Airline Industry," Deloitte Development LLC, 2013, p. 18.

12 Bryan Pearson, *The Loyalty Leap: Turning Customer Information into Customer Intimacy* (NY: The Penguin Group, 2012), pp. 65–8.

13 Based upon a presentation given by David Trimm of the Hertz Corporation at the International Airline Symposium in October 2013.

14 Michele McDonald, "A Question of Loyalty," *Air Transport World*, November 2013, p. 43.

15 Ibid.

16 Bryan Pearson, *The Loyalty Leap: Turning Customer Information into Customer Intimacy* (NY: The Penguin Group, 2012), pp. 53–6.

17 Aimia News Release, September 16, 2013.

18 Rupert Duchesne, "Joining the Datarati: How Customer Data Will Redefine Loyalty Management," Aimia Inc., 2012, p. 2.

19 Nancy Trejos, "Young Travelers Spend—and Are Hard to Please," *USA Today*, October 14, 2013, p. 3B.

20 Rajat Paharia, *Loyalty 3.0: How to Revolutionize Customer and Employee Engagement with Big Data and Gamification* (NY: McGraw-Hill, 2013), pp. 10–13.

21 Gartner Press Release, "Gartner Reveals Top Predictions for IT Organizations and Users for 2013 and Beyond," October 24, 2012.

22 Rajat Paharia, *Loyalty 3.0: How to Revolutionize Customer and Employee Engagement with Big Data and Gamification* (NY: McGraw-Hill, 2013), pp. 65–93.

23 Press Release by KLM, "New: KLM game 'Aviation Empire'," June 28, 2013.

24 Jeanne Meister, "Gamification: Three Ways To Use Gaming For Recruiting, Training, and Health & Wellness," *Forbes* (online), May 21, 2012.

25 "The Rise of Gamification in Hospitality and Travel," tnooz.com, September 4, 2013.

26 Peeter Kivestu, "Leveling Up on Loyalty: Capturing ROI from Customer Experience Management," Teradata Corporation, 2013.

Chapter 7
Driving the Business Through Technology

Progressive airlines have always managed to face challenges and capitalize on opportunities through the use of technology — relating to aircraft, communications, or information — in all of their functions, operations, commercial, administration, and so forth. And, with the use of technology in different areas, airlines have been able to "do more with less." Consider the following as some examples, from a historical perspective.

- In the 1950s, with growing passenger traffic, American Airlines, facing a challenge to speedily handle passenger reservations, developed Sabre (Semi-automated Business Research Environment) — a computer reservation system — to automate the process of booking reservations.
- In the 1960s, Eastern Airlines and Delta Airlines pioneered the hub-and-spoke system that enabled the transportation of more passengers and a reduction in the number of empty seats.
- In the early 1980s, American, faced with growing competition from low cost airlines, figured out how to compete with them by offering low fares through the development of an advanced analytic technique, known, at the time, as "yield management." The airline also used information contained in the PNR, based on the amount of travel, to develop a loyalty program that set a trend worldwide in the airline industry and many other businesses.
- In the early 1990s, Northwest Airlines and KLM, faced with increasing competition across the Atlantic, developed the first innovative strategic alliance to carry more traffic with less capacity through their smaller hubs. Using information

on traffic, capacity, and fares, the two carriers used advanced analytic techniques (along with a change in corporate culture) to truly integrate their three hubs in Amsterdam, Detroit, and Tokyo to generate incredible profits.

- In 1994, United Airlines figured out how to issue e-tickets. With 100 percent e-ticketing achieved by 2008, the industry was able to achieve more revenue power, more control over distribution with lower expense, and lower distribution lead time.

- In 1995, Continental Airlines installed a self-service kiosk at Newark Airport, enabling passengers to check in faster and airlines to reduce the cost of checking in passengers compared to using ticket counter agents.

- With the use of e-ticketing, airlines were able to offer value-adding services from last minute, low fare email specials, and self-service check in.

- In the latter part of the first decade, airlines started to merchandise their products and services, realizing that they could not easily grow the line-haul revenue. They began to generate incremental revenue through the sale of ancillary products and services.

- In 2012, Qantas Airways, faced with increasing competition from the relatively new three full service Persian Gulf-based carriers, developed a game changing relationship with Emirates Airline to "do more with less," specifically, serve multiple destinations in Europe, the Middle East, and Africa with less ultra long haul aircraft. Data on traffic and capacity as well as advanced network, fleet, and schedule planning techniques were used to totally overhaul the network of Qantas, virtually creating a new airline to achieve more market share with less long haul flying.

- In the mid part of the second decade (around 2014), the really ambitious airlines, realizing that they were having increasingly less control of customers, began initiatives to get increasingly greater control of information to enable better engagement with customers, leading to better customer experiences.

Going forward, airlines need to continue to do more with less for at least five reasons. First, with average load factors running at the 85–90 percent level, it is not realistic to try to accommodate more passengers within existing capacity. Consequently, airlines need to figure out how to get more revenue per seat. Second, given the increase in competition, for example, for legacy carriers (from the Persian Gulf-based airlines, from low cost carriers expanding in longer haul markets, in the new regional markets from lower cost subsidiaries such as Jetstar), the legacy airlines need to figure out how to capture more premium fare paying passengers with less relative market presence on the one hand, and the newly created middle classes in emerging markets, on the other hand. Third, with the focus of customers changing from operations and products to customer experience, airlines need to figure out how to deploy emerging technology (mobile and social, for example) to provide more emphasis on customer service. Fourth, with the actual and potential entry of Internet-focused businesses, airlines with customer-centric ambitions need to redesign their marketing, sales, and distribution functions to maintain engagement capabilities with customers. With the adoption by the full service carriers of many processes of low cost carriers, there is a need to trade up or be even more firm on managing costs. And, fifth, some airlines, individually, or in groups, will develop sought-after brands, necessitating the rest to find new ways to acquire, connect with, and retain loyal customers.

Facing these challenges, how can airlines capitalize on emerging opportunities? One answer is to continue to be able to do more with less. All airlines can use technology as an enabler of business strategies. A few can use technology as a driver of business strategies.

Airlines viewing technology as an enabler can focus on operations and products, and use technology in such areas as maintenance, flight operations, and ground operations with respect to operations, as well as in the area of network and fleet planning with respect to products. As an example of enabling technology with respect to operations centricity, an article in *Harvard Business Review* highlights PASSUR Aerospace's RightETA that leverages multidimensional data to provide airlines more accurate predictions of estimated flight arrival times versus actual arrival times. Such a data-driven tool is integral to the airline industry where every minute matters.[1] Consider two other examples in related businesses, GE and UPS.

First, GE is making jet engines not just more fuel efficient, but also more intelligent by embedding sophisticated sensors (to collect and analyze very large quantities of data) to extract, structure, and "predict" the right information about engine performance and get it delivered to the right people, at the right station, and at the right time. This initiative will reduce the "downtime" of the aircraft and enable the airline to provide better on-time performance to its passengers. Moreover, this data-analytic-driven capability can help aircraft engine manufacturers to expand their "power-by-the-hour" component of their engine business to capitalize on lower maintenance costs. The new-generation aircraft (such as the Boeing 787 and the Airbus 350) are totally connected aircraft, not just from the viewpoint of increasing operational efficiency, by providing real time information to crews and the maintenance departments, but also from the viewpoint of passengers.

Next, UPS is using big data and analytics to constantly improve its drivers' delivery routes. The process takes into consideration not only information coming from sensors embedded in the trucks and online maps, but also data on the packages themselves—time of shipment, delivery commitments, and so forth. The next step in improving the route recommendation process would be to factor in forecasts of weather and road conditions. This capability clearly saves fuel used by the trucks but also provides better delivery service for customers.

Those airlines viewing technology as a driver of business strategies need to use technology (big data, analytics, mobile, and search) to develop deep customer insights that, in turn, can be used to develop and market mutually beneficial value propositions, strong brands, and relevant loyalty programs. The starting point is to go beyond the use of transactional data that airlines have leveraged to this point. Now they need to use behavioral and attitudinal data to develop new revenue streams. By engaging with customers in their early stages of planning cycles, airlines can become more proactive in (1) increasing the value of currently attractive customers (by delivering a better experience and generating higher levels of ancillary revenue), (2) acquiring new valuable customers (by identifying customer behaviors indicative of high worth), and (3) warding off the defection of valuable customers (again, by identifying behaviors indicative of defection and by taking appropriate actions prior to defection). The key to being able to provide better experiences (by leveraging big data and analytics) is to connect a very broad spectrum of pieces of information to get insights on customers that are *actionable* and to make search and the use of mobile devices easier. However, airlines will need to (1) take into account the issue of privacy discussed in Chapter 1, and (2) change the organizational culture (just as they did with the use of yield management and e-ticketing), (a) to build organizations around the new imperatives of information and analytics (including the deployment of information technology staff with knowledge of businesses, briefly discussed in Chapter 8), and (b) to design processes to maximize the value derived from information (faster than competitors and in a more repeatable fashion than competitors).

Technologies Driving the Business

Given the increasing power held by customers, focus should now be on the *Customer Managed Relationship* (CMR) and not Customer Relationship Management (CRM) as consumers now decide what they buy, when they buy, from whom they buy, under what terms they buy, and with emphasis on experience. Successful CMR requires even more customer insights than CRM using big data and analytics. Providing better experience requires a focus on technologies that relate to mobile and search. There are two primary ways for obtaining information from customers. First, analytics can use past behavior to predict all sorts of interactions both with the airline and in other areas such as social media and credit card usage. The second approach is with customer managed data, where a loyal customer describes her travel intentions with respect to a destination, time of the year, and other product feature preferences and allows a user-driven search to find exactly what she wants for the specific trip. The search can be made by a smart machine, or a smart physical agent, or a combination. And, it is the data smart and data-driven airlines, competing with the use of big data and analytics, regardless of the segment of the industry (legacy, low cost, or hybrid airlines) that can achieve substantial competitive advantages.

Deploying big data matched with analytics, a few global innovation led legacy airlines could redesign their businesses and transition from being providers of air transportation services from airport-to-airport to selling travel experiences, or becoming total travel facilitators by connecting the dots and by working with new third party players. And, it is through the integration of data (connecting the dots) that new value will be generated (including, if necessary, working with third party partners).

Big Data

Big data, coupled with analytics, enables businesses to go far beyond traditional business intelligence. It provides access to far more data than the traditional realm of business intelligence. Every time a consumer uses a mobile device or participates in one of the many social media channels, or purchases a product or service online (or even just browses for products and services online), data is generated that can be analyzed and correlated with the use of sophisticated analytical techniques to identify, develop, and implement short and long term strategies, and not just for all customers, but for segmented and targeted customers to provide, almost customized products and services. Data has become such an important element in businesses that some are calling it the "new oil" or the "new currency of the digital world." One author compares the value of oil and data as follows. Data is much easier to transport and one cannot run out of it. Keeping the comparison going, he also points out that, in 2012, Apple sailed past Exxon Mobile, the world's largest oil company.[2]

In the case of airlines, data, in general, has referred to large quantities of structured data, controlled by airlines and derived from traditional sources (such as PNRs, FFPs, and, in some cases, CRM). This transactional data was derived mostly from bookings—names, addresses, telephone numbers, origins and destinations, dates of travel, class of travel, fares purchased, and so forth. The initial data sources in the 1970s were the airline reservation systems and the check-in systems. Then, in the 1980s, two new sources came in, surveys and loyalty programs.

The unstructured data, that the airlines did not focus on until very recently, comes from a myriad of interactions—conversations with call centers, activity on websites, and communications through social media (blogs, reviews, posts, Tweets, photos, and videos). Consider sources such as emails, sensors, and even voicemail. Information from web browsing, for example, is made up of an analysis of words used during a search and the ultimate destination, schedule, and fare selected. Since the beginning of this century, particularly since the beginning of this decade, a few data-driven airlines have begun to collect additional information via the segmentation process through customer profiles developed with the use of information from shopping, mobile communications, and social media. It is the synthesis of both structured (transactional) data and unstructured data that can lead to the development of definitive and actionable segments. And, it is the use of analytics on the synthesized data that can predict the likelihood of purchase of various offers by various targeted segments.

The concept of data is not new even though the phrase, "big data," was coined more recently. Businesses have always had and used large volumes of data even within the airline industry. Recall the competitive advantage American developed by using the PNR data back in the early 1980s to develop its loyalty programs and it's, at that time known as, yield management program. In fact, it was not just the collection of data, but rather it was the creative use of data that American introduced through the integration of three essential pieces of data—passenger bookings, flight availability, and demand (disaggregated by willingness and ability to pay). What is now new are the following eight features and challenges related to the use of big data and its integration through analytics.

1. The quantity of data (both structured and unstructured). Figure 7.1 shows that the quantity of data is now beginning to be measured not in peta, or even zetta, but yottabytes.[3]

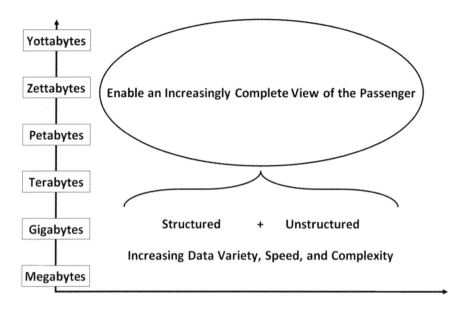

Figure 7.1   Potential of data-driven marketing

2. Data is now becoming increasingly connected.
3. The digitization capability makes the collection, integration, and analysis of the data much easier.
4. Data is now being generated and transmitted at incredible speeds.
5. The size is now so big that it is not necessary to deal with samples.[4]
6. The availability of data in two forms, structured and unstructured, has led to an enormous increase in complexity.
7. The analysis of big data shows *what* is happening not *why* it is happening and not what is *causing* it to happen. Causality is not implied—just correlation.[5]
8. The availability of technology (a wide array of data collection devices and ubiquitous computing) to derive unique insights from the data about consumer preferences, behavior, and attitudes.

Consider the first point with respect to quantity. Think about the enormous and rich data available from monitoring shopping behavior compared to just the data on the transactional aspects of the booking itself—"click" streams and travel reviews, for example. With respect to complexity, it is not only that customers are now more connected through their mobile devices and social media, but also that their individual purchases are connected to their overall buying patterns—online and offline, cross-product purchases, payment methods, recommendations by others (colleagues or strangers).

Some of the aforementioned challenges relate to the gathering, warehousing, and mining of data to convert, in real time, the raw data into meaningful and actionable information to understand and anticipate future behavior of segments of customers, as well as individual customers within a segment. However, big data also presents opportunities. As mentioned, because vast quantities of data are available, it is not only unnecessary to work with samples, but an airline can now work with customers on a one-to-one basis (if appropriate for the airline's situation as outlined in Chapter 3). And, collecting and analyzing very large volumes of data can reveal information to produce valuable insights benefitting both airlines and customers in terms of the value provided and value the received—again, the ability to do more with less. In alignment with Chapter 2, customers can be segmented based on needs. The VFR segment is not likely to need rental cars, whereas the leisure segment might. It is possible to subsegment the business segment into those who may need a taxi versus those who may need a limousine. Customers can be analyzed based on needs and predictive analytics can be used to make relevant marketing offers that are of interest to customers and that make money for airlines.

Currently, airlines are at an early stage of leveraging big data and analytics. One only needs to analyze the content of emails containing almost irrelevant offers—flights to destinations or sale of products in which the receiver has virtually no interest. Such emails do not lead to economically viable sales and they generate instead irritation on the part of the receiver—along the lines of the discussion in Chapter 5. The important point is to build detailed and action-oriented customer profiles based on information collected at various touchpoints and integrated from different departments within an airline (marketing, sales, loyalty, reservations, for example) and the field (airport check in, and lost and found baggage, for example). Virgin Atlantic uses a taxi service system in which it identifies passengers on a given flight who are planning to stay at the same hotel to share cabs and costs.[6]

Assuming that an airline has started monitoring and collecting the relevant data, the next step—analytics—includes identifying influencers and trends and responding to them, all in real time and on a continual basis—actionable insights. This step relates to not only relatively new sources of data such as social media, but also analytics that produce, for example, customer sentiment analysis to extract feelings, trends, and so forth—"social intelligence"—at the point they are occurring. If a key requirement of airlines is to find and acquire customers, then the use of big data and analytics is the answer. As one expert points out in simple terms, "Big data analysis can be compared to finding the needle in the haystack."[7]

Analytics

Most airlines have not fully leveraged big data and analytics to (1) customize their value propositions with respect to the value provided to a customer and the value received from a customer, and (2) equip their customer-facing employees with the quantity, quality, and timelessness of information to provide a personalized customer experience. Moreover, the use of "social analytics"[8] can even help an airline connect its relevant staff to engage and interact at the relevant times with the relevant customers. If an airline takes months to analyze the data, then it will most likely be too late, for example, to implement service recovery.

What are analytics? The area of analytics is about sensing patterns through the integration of data, particularly behavioral data. Analytics are processes for analyses for improving the business, not an assortment of software techniques or algorithms. In other words, they are sophisticated ways for making sense of data to gain an understanding or insight that they may not have before. One example of an analytic is Google Analytics that tracks visitors to a website, coming from different sources— direct visits and referring sites as well as referrals from search optimization engines and social networks. It can create a wide array of statistics about the traffic on the website—sources of visitors, their geographical locations, length of time spent on the site, and so forth. It also provides information on conversions and sales.

As for the use of analytics by an airline, it must, first, be clear on its business objectives. The necessary data and the techniques for analyses come next. Suppose an airline found some customer segments that it had overlooked. Data and analytics can be used to identify the segments by value and the appropriate marketing campaigns. The concept of analytics, like data as mentioned earlier, is not new. Businesses have been deploying analytics to make better decisions for decades. So, what is new? In the case of analytics, airlines have access to advanced techniques. The traditional predictors of buying behavior have been the most recent time when a purchase was made, the frequency with which purchases were made, and cross-product purchases. Now, analytics build upon these basic predictors, and analyze what is being recommended in the social media channels with which a particular individual engages, interactions during the travel value chain in past travels, and the degree with which businesses fulfilled their promises in the area of customer care.

Just as there is a linkage between big data and analytics, there is also a linkage of these two and the Cloud, given that many social platforms are hosted in the Cloud, where connections are made not only among people, but also among businesses. The key to getting actionable customer insights from big data with the use of analytics and the Cloud is not just the ability to develop agile pricing strategies and predict purchase behavior, but also to design various elements of the business (for example, websites) to enhance the customer experience and analyze customer sentiments. Think about the value of using the Cloud to provide results to an online shopper's inquiry based on the shopper's preferences (not just the price, but also the quality of the product) and using it to predict purchase behavior (from browsing to purchase phases). The quality of the product can relate not just to the schedule and the seat (nonstop flight with a lie-flat bed), but also to the brand of the airline, evaluated on hard data (such as on-time performance and Net Promoter Scores), and opinions expressed in user-generated content and social media.

Consider the following example given by one business writer that highlights the power of the Cloud. If one needed an auto part, most likely the consumer would choose a search engine that would produce a list of suppliers, ranked based upon (1) sponsored ads, and (2) relevance to search criteria (type of auto part, type of automobile, and so on). If the consumer were to use a supplier's site, ratings by other consumers might be available. In the Cloud, the search could include other related aspects, such as past buying preferences based upon shopping history, knowledge of vehicles the consumer owns, knowledge of the mileage on vehicles via sensors, maintenance records, as well as a prediction of how long a consumer may keep the vehicle based on its condition and the user's behaviors. These aspects can be taken even a step further such as the type of credit card that the user has and that the seller accepts.[9]

Consider a somewhat different example. Search Engine Optimization (SEO) is normally related to content, namely, optimizing the relevancy of the information and making it meaningful for shoppers. However, it can also be about optimizing the search for customers by segmentation based on their characteristics and patterns—preferences, attitudes, behaviors, and consumption patterns. The idea would be to work backwards. Instead of a specific segment of customer using search keywords to find content, a business could use search keywords to find a specific segment of customers, sometimes called personas. For example, which segments participate in social media, in general, and what type of social media in particular. This would be a new way to use technology to find and acquire new customers. Consider Google that can provide personalized advertisements based on browsing history and typed key words or Google's ability to predict influenza occurrences by following searches on the Web for influenza symptoms and related topics.[10] Consider also Amazon that can provide personalized recommendations for products based on past browsing and purchases.

Previously, the analyses of data would only show how businesses performed—descriptive analytics. In the next phase, the sophistication in data and the prevailing analytic techniques enabled some businesses to be able to predict (anticipate) the behavior of customers to certain marketing campaigns and tactics. Now, the combination of complex data (structured and unstructured) and analytics can help businesses identify and implement optimal strategies based on the segments selected, the profiles of customers within the segments, and the value propositions offered. This approach can allow an airline to do controlled experiments—provide a unique offer to a target audience. Then, based on the outcome, an airline can "predict" what the response would be if the offer was made available to a larger segment of the marketplace, and, eventually anticipate the response from the whole market. Plus, an airline can go much more deeply into a particular area, say segmentation. For example, an airline can segment based not just on similar customer profiles (say, the Millennials, or wealthy seniors, or the "active-and-interactive" tourists), but also "basket segmentation" within "customer segmentation" and "affinity purchases" within "basket segmentation." Basket segmentation relates to different product features and services purchased with each trip. "Affinity purchases" refers to the purchase of cross-products. Let us say there are a number of similar passengers with respect to their purchase of trips, say the Millennials. However, not only may the passengers within this segment differ with respect to the ancillary products purchased, but there may also be some relationships between the ancillary cross-products.

Although most Millennials are likely to be heavily equipped with mobile devices, some may decide, for example, not to turn them on, at least for brief periods of time, and simply enjoy the travel experience "unplugged." At the other extreme, there may a subsegment that wants all kinds of "on-demand options" to deliver services around the clock, not to mention fast and seamlessly. Thus, a specific subsegment of Millennials (looking for "active-and-interactive" tourist facilities and services) may choose accommodations through Airbnb, staying with a local family rather than at a chain hotel, visiting urban rather than resort destinations, and using local residents as tour guides rather than professional guides, as highlighted in Chapter 8. Analytics used in these types of analyses can be descriptive in that they can describe and show information—how many passengers bought tickets in given fare buckets based on advance purchase. Analytics can also be predictive in that they can help to predict the likelihood of an event—how likely is it that a particular passenger will defect given that this is the third negative incidence with the airline.

Take, for example, analytics that can help identify, understand, and obtain insights into (1) what happened in the past, (2) what is currently happening so that an airline may react in real time to provide value to the customer, and (3) to anticipate what could happen to become more proactive in providing options and solutions. For example:

- Three different departments could be working with a particular passenger (lost baggage, refund, and loyalty) and yet not know that it is the same passenger. Consequently, connecting data from different areas to create a unified and complete view of this passenger may indicate future behavior, such as defection. The use of advanced analytics would enable management to anticipate such a scenario and take appropriate action.

- Data and its analysis in the traditional environment could indicate that 85 percent of flights for a given airline were on time during the previous day. But, what about the 15 percent of the flights that were not on time? An analysis must, therefore, be performed with respect to the 15 percent that were not, at the individual flight level, *at the individual passenger level on each of the late flights*, and how each passenger's buying behavior is likely to change given the previous day's occurrences *combined with* any other past service issues that each affected passenger may have previously incurred.

- Big data and analytics can be used to integrate previously unintegrated brands. For example, many airlines developed low cost subsidiaries that they closed later due to cannibalization of traffic. Big data and analytics can now be used to simulate the proposed value propositions of each subsidiary of an airline and not only anticipate and predict the response, but also optimize the different value propositions. Imagine the value of *customer-related information* for an airline like Singapore with its four subsidiaries (Singapore, SilkAir, Tiger and Scoot) or to Delta with equities in a growing number of airlines (such as GOL, AeroMexico, and Virgin Atlantic).

- Airlines can not only leverage big data and analytics to derive deeper insights for passengers, but also for competitors. For example, instead of just monitoring fares offered by competitors (and often simply matching them), they can gain insights with respect to the rationale behind the fares offered by each competitor in real time and simulate different scenarios for an optimal response. The last step would require measurements, reviews, and constant iterations.
- It is also possible to use "discovery analytics" — an area that comes into play when an airline may not have, or want, a data warehouse. In this case the idea is to "throw all the data into a hopper" (structured and unstructured data, coming from streams, web clicks, call centers, airport kiosks, and so forth) and then to use tools (such as Hadoop) to find nuggets of information and take appropriate actions.
- Finally, there is also the area of "experiential" analytics. An example of this type of analytics is considering the experience in trying to actually research a flight and book via the mobile channel.

Consequently, the use of analytics on big data offers many opportunities for airlines to create value, including finer customer segmentation, thus yielding more customized products and services to accommodate the needs of not only a single personality and behavior of a customer, but multiple personalities and behaviors of the same customer in different situations. This management initiative (coupled with the use of mobile) would lead an airline to sell services and not just seats. See Figure 8.1 in Chapter 8. As reported in a *Harvard Business Review Blog Network* regarding the retail industry, "Research shows that personalization can deliver five to eight times the ROI on marketing spend and lift sales 10% or more."[11] Such personalization can differentiate an airline and therefore create an opportunity to increase margins, as well as enhance satisfaction, thus augmenting loyalty to the brand. For example, if a customer places a phone call into an airline's call center but does not make a reservation or if a customer browses a website but does not book a ticket, would making a personalized offer right on the spot have helped? Such tactics can be easily analyzed on a controlled experimental basis for those airlines seeking higher levels of customization. The key is to monitor the behavior of a web browser *prior* to the decision to make a purchase.

Airlines can become smart-data-driven organizations. As reported in an article in the *Harvard Business Review*, "companies in the top third of their industry in the use of data-driven decision making were, on average, 5% more productive and 6% more profitable than their competitors."[12] Take, for example, the area of revenue leakage—the gap between revenue shown from bookings and revenue generated by bookings flown. The gap results from no-shows and late cancellations. Airlines, of course, use overbooking tactics to counter the impact of no-shows and late cancellations. However, both aspects, no-shows and overbooking, can lead to lost revenues and dissatisfied customers. Airlines have used a variety of data analyses to reduce the severity of the no-show and the late cancellation problem. Airlines look at the booking data to identify multiple bookings (on the same flight or different flights and violation of booking rules). However, a much greater success can be achieved if airlines were to use advanced mining techniques and analytics on customer behavior. Traditional revenue management techniques try to optimize based on revenue booked (through the sale of seats in various buckets at various prices). However, the revenue realized after the aircraft has flown could easily be very different, not only because of no-shows and cancellations, but also because some passengers change their bookings several times and in different buckets. Analytics can improve not only the quantity of demand based on bookings, but also the quality of demand based on information on the passengers making the bookings.

The smart-data-driven airlines are just beginning to comprehend the opportunities to use analytics on big data to identify, acquire, develop, and market to specific segments on their specific personalized needs. The segments selected go beyond the traditional segments based on usage. They are behavioral segments, based on behavior and attitude relating to the amount purchased, the brand selected (which one of the four within the Singapore Airlines group or a strategic partner, for example), the communication and distribution channels used, and the features selected. Moreover, segments selected are based on both *functional* needs as well as *emotional* needs.

Since travelers are armed with the means to make informed purchasing decisions, it is necessary for airlines to deploy predictive analytics to rethink their strategies on their offers. Are current revenue management processes and systems sufficient to maximize revenue? Are current loyalty programs sufficient to retain customers? Should status in the loyalty programs be the differentiator of services provided? Given that passengers are now not only constantly connected and tech-savvy, but also global, meaning that they now have information from worldwide sources to make detailed comparisons (on products, prices, operations, brand values, and customer service performance), how can airlines adapt proactively to the rapidly changing consumer shopping and purchasing behavior? The answer could be to use prescriptive analytics[13] and offer customized products/services. Consumers get their information from all kinds of sources, online and offline, from a broad spectrum of social media channels, and from suppliers and third parties. The use of analytics can help make airlines more proactive rather than reactive on their part.

If airlines are to provide customized products and services at any level of the spectrum, they will need analytics deployed on big data—the finer the level of customization, the greater the need for information and data analytical capability. Much more analyses are needed, for example, relating to price–seat comfort sensitivity and how much different customers pay for various levels of comfort *with adjustments* made for stage lengths, crossing of time zones, the timing of the trip during the 24-hour period, demographic characteristics of the customer, including the ethnic background and physical stature. With respect to the latter, for example, there could be a wide variation among the responses of Japanese, versus British, versus Americans, versus Chinese travelers. Analytics can help identify relationships using past data to predict future behavior by ethnicity. Then predictive analytics can be used to provide customized offers, just as grocery stores have been doing for years.

Analytics can also be used to mine data to target passengers who are not in the loyalty program of an airline. For example, non-member passengers can be identified by behavior and attitude (see Chapter 6) and the targeted passengers can be presented with customized offers. An airline could combine its CRM loyalty data with the newly captured web browsing data, and possibly data coming from third parties, to offer the most relevant content and tailored user experience in real time. Analytics can enable an airline to plan and execute differently with respect to value propositions for the non-members. For example, since passengers engage through social media (through user-generated content and sharing experiences), since they are at ease with both multichannel and omnichannel experiences, and since they tend to have multiple personalities when they travel at different times, airlines can use analytics to gain meaningful customer insights and their business value on an individual basis so as to subsegment, develop, market, measure, test, and revise unique value propositions across different channels.

The challenge shown in Figure 7.1 is not, in some ways, related to the quantities of data or the speed with which it is being accumulated, or even its complexity, but the capability to analyze this data, virtually in real time and to link the data at the individual customer level. If airlines do not analyze this data, some other laser-focused businesses will get close to consumers on a personalized basis—not just to upsell and cross-sell, but to understand and meet their needs. Kayak has already proven that they can and benefit from it even with the deployment of relatively simple analytics. Now the emerging data miners can go a lot further by analyzing web browsing history and shopping behavior that goes far beyond the traditional CRM analysis. Think about the Amazon recommendation engine that results in making recommendations as soon as a customer signs on, based on past buying, past web browsing, and based on similar patterns of others in similar segments. On its website, an airline has significant control not only regarding the content presented dynamically, but also with respect to the user experience. The idea is now to use analytics to develop a meaningful product differentiation and a competitive advantage.

Analytics Insights from Other Businesses

Netflix Netflix is in the entertainment business—a content-distribution powerhouse. It enables people initially to (1) get DVDs by mail at a flat rate that includes, shipping, and, later (2) see on-demand, through streaming, selected movies and TV shows, commercial free, on their Internet-connected screens (televisions, computers, or mobile devices). Initially, Netflix faced competition from the Blockbuster chain—a giant in the video rental industry, Wal-Mart stores, and small mom-and-pop rental stores. Netflix's competitive advantage was to have a large inventory to attract customers and to enable customers to get their first choice on DVD rentals. The challenge was to keep track of requests and availability. So, data was needed to be an effective competitor. Then technology enabled Netflix's customers to stream content with only a click, at a low cost and on the customers' preferred devices—smart TVs, smartphones, computers, iPads, and so forth.

Blockbuster, the giant competitor, which did not anticipate competitive threats ahead of time, had an opportunity to use its resources, either to buy out Netflix or embrace the new technology. Instead, it allowed Netflix, a data-centric and data-analytic business, to keep pace with the changing consumer desires. People did not want to make trips to the store for renting and returning, not to mention possible fees for late returns. Netflix not only eliminated the need to go to a store but also allowed renters to keep the DVDs as long as they liked based on subscriptions. Technology and lack of vision brought down the giant Blockbuster and technology, coupled with the right vision, led Netflix to have over 40 million members in more than 40 countries.[14] Management has developed partnerships with the US Postal Service for the delivery of DVDs and Amazon for streaming content.[15]

Netflix built a loyal base of fans through personalization—giving people what they want and when they want it plus rank ordered recommendations. For example, recommendations on movies and TV shows appear on the first screen—similar to Amazon's recommendations and Google's optimization of search. Netflix provides relevant content on the first screen based on individual tastes. The company constantly engages with people to improve the recommendation process—the rating and the ranking systems—and uses techniques such as the A/B testing system to learn about people's preferences and to identify high margin customers. Management is very focused on users and users' experience. They track behavior data—who is watching, which program, when, on which device, length of time, including early closure on selected titles, and return to selected titles. Netflix also gets data from third parties such as Nielsen[16] and is reported to integrate data also from social media (Facebook, Twitter, and so forth).[17]

Netflix continues to monitor changes in the entertainment business. For example, TV, while still very popular, has limitations from the viewpoint of users. While the number of channels has grown, different channels air shows at selected times and not all shows are readily available on transportable screens. Some viewers find the use of remote control devices to be non-user friendly. The use of Digital Video Recorders (DVRs) can help viewers watch the shows at times they want, but the service can be costly. In light of these limitations, the demand for Internet on-demand TV is increasing, facilitated by an increase in (1) the speed and reliability of the Internet data transmission, and (2) sale of smart TVs, tablets, and smartphones as their prices decrease. While Netflix recognizes that it cannot compete with the likes of "Comcast, Sky, Amazon, Apple, Microsoft, Sony, or Google," with respect to the breadth of entertainment, it plans to compete on the basis of user experience, wide ranging content, personalized recommendations, the flat fee unlimited viewing commercial-free value proposition, easy to do business philosophy (exemplified by the no hassle online cancellation feature, any screen, any time viewing capability), and the "fun of indulgent viewing" philosophy.[18] From the perspective of user experience, consider just one area. A viewer can watch a TV show when it is convenient for the viewer rather than when the channel decides to air it on the day of the week and at a time decided by the channel. The Netflix customer can watch not only a given episode at any time, but also the whole series rather than one episode per week. Consequently, Netflix is providing not only relevant content but also enabling different viewers to optimize their individual times.

Macy's Since retailers work with razor thin margins, having the right product (in sizes, styles, and colors) and the right quantity at the right time in the right store can mean the difference between profit and loss. This aspect of retailing has become more challenging with the changing dynamics of buying and selling. The Internet and mobile devices have empowered buyers to be in the driver's seat. Now some retailers can capitalize on relevant information made available through the use of analytics not only to get in the driver's seat, but to provide a better customer experience, build customer's trust, and strengthen loyalty, as well as to outperform competitors.

Macy's is a 150-year old established department store in the US, known for its Thanksgiving Parade in New York City and Fourth of July fireworks. It owns Bloomingdale's Department Stores. During the financial crisis in 2008, noticing that sales at brick-and-mortar stores had been declining while sales through the online channel had been increasing, the question was if each channel could complement the other based on the strengths of each and provide customers with convenience, choice, and experience. For example, online shopping can enable a customer to compare prices more easily. On the other hand, shopping in a store can enable a customer to try on different outfits and see how they fit and feel.

As a result, Macy's decided to focus on customer centricity and to implement an omnichannel retailing strategy. The customer-centricity initiative was substantiated by the appointment of Julie Bernard, Group Vice President of Customer Centricity to transform its business from being product focused to being customer focused, based on customer insights derived from customer data (coming from multiple sources such as loyalty programs and credit card usage), and not, for example, from Point of Sale (POS) data.[19] The plan was to look at not just products and prices, but also experiences. The objective of the omnichannel strategy was to make the shopping experience "more engaging," the same whether the buyer shops online or in a store. The key attributes relating to the online shopping experience are functionality and content. Macy's introduced the "True Fit" concept that helps shoppers select the clothes that appeal to their individual bodies and their personal tastes. This feature enhances the customer experience by reducing the concern about how the apparel would fit after it has been purchased online and delivered to the shopper. While it is true that a buyer shopping online can compare prices of competitors, online features such as "True Fit" can keep the buyer interested in Macy's product.[20] It is interesting to note that according to Macy's analyses, an improvement in online shopping improved experience in the store, and vice versa.[21]

The idea was to capitalize on the strengths of each channel to improve customer experience. One example of such an experience would be for a customer to buy online and, if necessary, return the item in a store. Along this line of thinking, it is reported that Macy's analytics department enabled it to (1) analyze buying behavior and preferences (including, not only *tracking clicks through conversion*, but also seeing how people discuss their shopping experience through social media), and (2) facilitate the company's merchandisers and planners to not only get access to real time information, but also information in formats to meet individual user's needs to develop effective marketing initiatives.[22] One example of behavioral analysis would be to identify the relationship, if any, between online browsing and in-store purchases. As for information available to different merchandisers and planners, each department head can not only "slice and dice" the information to suit his or her needs, but also access information from other sources to conduct ad-hoc analysis. Macy's is reported to be using predictive analytics to analyze and manage its inventory.[23] It has been reported that Macy's use of data and business intelligence led to the company achieving sales above industry average since 2010.[24]

Mobile

The mobile space is changing rapidly, partly because of the proliferation of mobile devices (smartphones, tablets, e-Readers, and so forth), and partly because of the incorporation of technology

(Near Field Communication (NFC), RFID, Wi-Fi onboard aircraft, and so forth). As a result, the changing mobile space can (1) enhance the customer experience by reducing stress, (2) generate revenue opportunities for airlines, (3) reduce operating costs, (4) enable airlines to get more data, and (5) provide a storage place for lots of data.

Not too long from now, passengers could go to the airport and board an airplane with nothing more than a passport and a mobile device, and, possibly, not even a passport in the future. The mobile device already serves as a boarding pass. Some carriers, such as Lufthansa, have had the systems for mobile boarding passes for about five years. Currently the barcoded boarding passes have to be visible on the device and the device needs to be pointing to the reader. The devices with advanced technology incorporated may not need to point to a screen to be read, in fact, they may not even need to be turned on to transmit the information on the boarding pass. Boarding passes on mobile devices can help airlines to board passengers at much greater speeds. Theoretically, even a large aircraft with 500 seats could be boarded in well under 10 minutes. However, mobile devices without reliable biometric user data embedded cannot be the sole source of information as in many countries photo IDs are also required to confirm the identity of a traveler. Some airlines are leveraging mobile devices, specifically tablets, to get issues resolved quickly while onboard the aircraft in an attempt to provide better service. Given the availability of onboard connectivity, crews are being equipped with tablets to perform a myriad of functions.

As for enhancement in revenue, there are many opportunities for upsell and cross-sell with the capability to make payments through the mobile device (with multicurrency functionality). Besides the opportunity to upsell and cross-sell, the use of such mobile devices can provide sellers with powerful data on buying behavior—what they buy at each touchpoint, for example, and how they respond to timely and customized offers.

As for the storage capability aspect, the mobile device can store all kinds of information relating to travel documents (such as boarding passes as previously discussed, as well as visas), loyalty cards, and commercial papers (such as coupons). Consequently, mobile is a facilitator (for companies such as TripIt) for enabling better travel experiences for passengers (more seamless) and more revenue streams and lower costs possibilities for airlines (and airports). The capability for a mobile device to have connections between online and offline systems is important, for example, in providing information related to check in and loyalty status and privileges as well as in-flight connectivity (with access to Wi-Fi, tablet armed cabin crews). Through on-ground and in-flight connectivity, it is possible for an airline to upsell and cross-sell products and services. While at an airport, for example, a passenger could use his mobile device to browse the duty free store and purchase an item, then simply collect it on the way to the plane.

Let us go back for a moment to the use of mobile tablets onboard by flight attendants, as highlighted earlier. The deployment of such two-way communication devices in the hands of properly trained and incentivized cabin crews can provide solutions to passengers' problems through contextual support. Specifically, the availability and strategic deployment of relevant and timely information to relieve passengers' concerns, on a one-to-one situational basis, can serve as an opportunity to improve passenger satisfaction and build loyalty through service-driven decisions, not to mention the capability to raise additional revenues through the sale of a much broader assortment of products and services. Leaving aside the revenue aspect for a moment, the main function of the tablets is for crews to work with paperless systems, with information on passenger names, their status on FFPs, and the status of their luggage, as well as information on passengers making connections, information on immigration/customs forms, and useful information on destinations. And if crews do not have the needed information to engage with passengers, they can obtain it easily through the apps included in the tablets. Crews can help provide customized service, for example, to passengers with tight connections. Crews can first identify such passengers. Next, they can use their tablets to find information on connecting flights, gates, transfer times, and so forth. Finally, they can request assistance from ground staff at the arrival airport to meet and assist passengers.

However, such endeavors require changes in the business model, beyond the acquisition of new devices and technologies.

It requires a redesign of the business—redesign of vital processes and organizational structures to mine meaningful and integrated data and to design appropriate services. Cabin crews might say, for example, that the new proposed responsibilities relating to in-flight tablets are not covered within the negotiated union contracts. They may also say that they neither have the time nor the knowledge to help passengers, for instance, make new reservations during times of irregular operations. These are the areas where management must make HR-related changes to realign business models—restructuring of departments, organizational structures, individual roles and responsibilities, training, and compensation schemes to go beyond being merely customer focused, and move toward customer centricity, and even perhaps, personalization, as outlined in Chapter 3.

If an important reason for the use of technology is to reduce stress (resulting from lack of control, lack of information, and, to some extent, even lack of time), then self-service devices (enabled by mobile technology) is one answer. However, until recently some of these self-services have not been able to meet the needs of customers. For example, passengers have not been able to check their own bags. There are now two solutions. The first is for passengers to be able to print the bag labels and then drop off the bags at selected locations. The second option is to use the mobile device to encode the flight information on the equipment embedded into the luggage. See Figure 7.2 that illustrates electronic bag tags created by Airbus.

Electronic bag tags could become operationalized by as early as the end of 2014, a development that will improve the experience for customers and reduce costs for airlines. Passengers would be able to upload the information on the bag tags (relating to destination) using their smartphones. The tag can look like a regular paper tag but be made of material that is much more durable. It can be attached to different bags with different information uploaded for different journeys—an electronic tag. Or, the tag can be embedded permanently (with an RFID chip) into a specific bag. Either way, there are different options for placing itinerary information on the tag. It can be sent via a smartphone with the use of GSM, Bluetooth, or NFC. Although the technology is already available, the challenge is that the

Figure 7.2a   BAG2GO: New-generation bag tags
Source: Airbus

**Figure 7.2b   BAG2GO: A self-weighing and mobile-enabled bag
                    tag**
Source: Airbus

standards are not uniform around the world. This requirement is necessary for worldwide operations and for interline connections. The electronic baggage tags can be sold by airlines or given free to their high value customers. This technology will improve the customer experience and enable airlines to provide better service in tracking, handling, and delivering baggage. Just to recap: the information on this type of tag can be loaded from a remote location, it can "weigh" itself, it can not only "track" itself, but also upload information relating to other modes of travel as well as to specific non-airport destinations such as specific hotels.

Search

Passengers want an enjoyable experience when shopping and making the purchase. One way to achieve a higher level of buying—shopping and booking—experience is to have access to relevant information. Thus airlines can start with providing sufficient and trustworthy information on products and services. However, the collection, packaging, and delivery of such information requires knowledge of the customer profile. Next there is the need to reduce the complexity of the information provided, and the ability to make booking faster. Finally, there is the presentation style, for example, "opt-in" versus "opt-out" options, "forced choice" methods, and "hidden surcharges." An example of a "forced choice" method is a prepaid change fee. A "forced choice" method or "opt-out" option may have the possibility of generating an additional $15 in revenue but also the possibility of losing a passenger who could have purchased a $300 ticket.

Let us step back and examine shopping channels. It is estimated that about half of the travelers in the US book via airline websites whereas about one third book via online travel agents. The number varies slightly for leisure and business travelers. Leisure travelers tend to use search engines to plan their travel online whereas business travelers tend to use supplier sites. Airlines need to dive deeply into each source—how long did it take for the passenger to conduct his search, the number of "clicks" leading up to the reservation, and so forth. The other key consideration is related to the experience when using mobile devices to perform search.

Existing mobile websites are difficult to read and navigate. The ease of booking is poor in terms of speed. There are also security concerns.

Again, if airlines do not significantly improve the area of search, the use of big data and analytics will lead some innovative technology companies, such as Google and Apple, to grow within their travel verticals to implement new business initiatives that manage the passenger travel experience. First, they could offer truly comprehensive content, not just the offers from an airline, or a hotel, or a car rental company, but all of them simultaneously. Second, they can integrate information from different travel-related businesses (airlines, hotels, and car rental companies) for particular individuals for particular itineraries. Third, data can be gathered on the real time location of an individual to provide a real time and context-sensitive concierge service based on local conditions and services such as traffic jams, on-the-spot promotions being offered by local vendors (stores and restaurants), and expected weather conditions (based on information gathered from local meteorological services). Fourth, they can add a new dimension to their value that airlines cannot provide. For example, these tech-savvy companies could offer even more sophisticated advice using their own algorithms or those provided by third parties (such as Kayak and Momondo) on when a customer should purchase the ticket based on the "buy now" or "wait" recommendations to take advantage of fare changes. This dimension can be applied not just to airline fares, but also to the price of hotel rooms and car rentals, and, in turn, provide enormous value to travelers with some flexibility.

Organizational Structure

If big data, analytics, the Cloud, and mobile are to play a key role in an airline to redesign its business to do more with less and become a data-driven marketing powerhouse (product, price, and the brand), then the airline must transform the information technology function from a data collection and report production center to one that facilitates collaboration, communication, and integration within all areas of the airline. Such a transformation requires a different mindset, a different set of skills, and appropriate data-related architectures. One challenge for becoming a smart-data-driven airline, even more than the investment in technology, is the change in organizational structure and culture. As for organizational structure, there is now a critical need for a new function — Big Data and Analytics. Take, for example, the use of the Cloud. Some individual departments or functions within the organization are beginning to go to the Cloud to make available the use of some servers or software, and so forth. The potential problem with this approach is that it eliminates the need for individual departments or functions to meet within the organization to integrate data and "connect the dots" to identify value-adding initiatives. And, it should be the responsibility of the CEO to establish a department — Big Data and Analytics — where "dots can be connected" to identify actionable insights. This department must report directly to the CEO. The change in culture is needed to acquire and retain people with the appropriate skills as well as the identification and implementation of the appropriate processes. The use of analytics, for example, involves the right people asking the right questions to, in turn, implement the right decisions.[25] The right questions relate to necessary improvements in databases and the required analytics technologies for the changing marketplace and the role of big data and the management of big data to manage all elements of the marketing mix. See the discussion in Chapter 9 in the Thought Leadership Piece by the Qantas executive.

In the past, data analysts have analyzed traditional data to help airlines make operational and commercial decisions. There is, however, a difference between being data *driven* and data *analytic*. Davenport, Barth, and Bean suggest, for example, that data-driven organizations have data *scientists* rather than data *analysts*, that they follow real time data to increase the probability of the success of an event in a timely manner, and that analytics are shifted from information technology functions and integrated into the business functions and processes.[26] Data-driven airlines will need to employ data scientists and analytics leaders, people who can analyze clickstream data and web browsing behavior to predict consumer shopping behavior (purchases and loyalty). These people can not only help an airline to use the data to analyze what happened in the past, and what could happen in the future, but to determine what the optimal strategy and tactics should be—now known as descriptive, predictive, and prescriptive analytics, respectively.[27]

Takeaways

- Technology can be an enabler for all airlines to "do more with less" in the areas of operations and products. But for a select few airlines it can be a driver of businesses by generating more revenue from passengers who are no longer within the control of airlines and by redesigning parts of their businesses to maximize mutual value—value provided to targeted customers and value received from the targeted customers.
- All airlines can use technology to make it easier to shop and enhance the travel experience.
- If technology is to play a key role in the redesign of an airline's business, then the airline must transform its information technology function from a data collection and report production center to one that facilitates collaboration, communication, and integration of information within all areas of the airline to obtain and act upon detailed customer insights.
- The key aspect of big data and analytics is not just to collect and analyze data to improve internal decision making, but to enable an airline to redesign its business, for example, to provide customized service, predict buying behavior based on data-driven customer preferences, and enhance an airline's capability for upselling and cross-selling.
- Intelligence gained from the use of big data and analytics, as well as leveraging mobile technology, can be monetized and will be deployed by innovation-led third parties to produce value with respect to customer acquisition through the "connection of dots" and implementation of actionable insights.
- While information can be leveraged to provide more customized service and experiences to travelers, it can also be a concern to travelers in terms of privacy.

Notes

1 Andrew McAfee and Erik Brynjolfsson, "Big Data: The Management Revolution," *Harvard Business Review*, October 2012.

2 Eric Siegel, *Predictive Analytics* (Hoboken, NJ: John Wiley, 2013), pp. 79–80.

3 Data will soon be measured in petabytes, zettabytes, and yottabytes, numbers with 15, 21, and 24 zeros, respectively, after them.

4 Viktor Mayer-Schönberger and Kenneth Cukier, *BIG DATA: A Revolution That Will Transform How We Live, Work, and Think* (NY: Houghton Mifflin Harcourt, 2013).

5 Ibid.

6 "Getting Personal," *Airlines International*, IATA Issue 46, October–November 2013, p. 40.

7 Christopher Morace with Sara Gaviser Leslie, *Transform: How Leading Companies Are Winning with Disruptive Social Technology* (NY: McGraw-Hill, 2014), p. 42.

8 Ibid., p. 43, and pp. 152–3.

9 Thomas M. Koulopoulos, *Cloud Surfing: A New Way to Think About Risk, Innovation, Scale, and Success* (Brookline, MA: Bibliomotion, 2012), p. 95.

10 Howard Rheingold, "Three Harbingers of Change," *strategy+business*, Winter 2013, p. 73.

11 Josh Leibowitz, Kelly Ungerman, and Maher Masri, "Know Your Customers Wherever They Are," *Harvard Business Review Blog Network*, October 26, 2012.

12 Andrew McAfee and Erik Brynjolfsson, "Big Data: The Management Revolution," *Harvard Business Review*, October 2012.

13 Thomas H. Davenport, "Analytics 3.0: In the New Era, Big Data Will Power Consumer Products and Services," *Harvard Business Review*, December 2013, p. 70 and Thomas H. Davenport and Jinho Kim, *Keeping Up with the Quants: Your Guide to Understanding and Using Analytics* (Boston, MA: Harvard Business Review Press, 2013), pp. 3–5.

14 www.netflix.com.

15 Cindi Howson, *Successful Business Intelligence*, 2nd Ed. (NY: McGraw-Hill, 2014), p. 150.

16 Phil Simon, *Too BIG to IGNORE: The Business Case for Big Data* (Hoboken, NJ: John Wiley, 2013), p. 58.

17 Derrick Harris, "Netflix Analyzes a Lot of Data about Your Viewing Habits," June 14, 2012.

18 www.netflix.com.

19 Bob Thompson, "From Big Data to Big Decisions: Three Ways Analytics Can Improve the Retail Experience," *Customer Think Corporation*, an article on the web, October 5, 2012.

20 Joseph Dennis Kelly, "Reclaim Your Edge: How Advanced Analytics is Helping Macy's Transform the Customer Experience," an article on the web, January 29, 2013.

21 Len Lewis, "Something for Everyone," an article on the web, May 2011.

22 Ibid.

23   Robert L. Mitchell, "How Macys.com Visualizes the Future," an article on the web, August 10, 2011.

24   Cindi Howson, *Successful Business Intelligence*, 2nd Ed. (NY: McGraw-Hill, 2014), p. 108.

25   David Meer, "The ABCs of Analytics," *strategy+business*, Issue 70, p. 6.

26   Thomas H. Davenport, Paul Barth, and Randy Bean, "How 'Big Data' is Different," *MIT Sloan Management Review*, Fall 2012, Vol. 54, No. 1, pp. 43–6.

27   Thomas H. Davenport, "Analytics 3.0: In the New Era, Big Data will Power Consumer Products and Services," *Harvard Business Review*, December 2013, p. 70 and Thomas H. Davenport and Jinho Kim, *Keeping Up with the Quants: Your Guide to Understanding and Using Analytics* (Boston, MA: Harvard Business Review Press, 2013), pp. 3–5.

Chapter 8
Preparing for Tomorrow

Although there are many forces affecting the aviation environment, from airlines' perspective the top three, in terms of challenges and opportunities, would be, (1) changing consumers, (2) changing competitors, and (3) changing collaborators. Customers will use the ever increasing market research tools available to them in order to obtain the best value for money. A decision to purchase a product or service will be made based on (1) a strong brand, acquired through the cheapest channel, (2) being available to purchase through a trusted retail site (such as Amazon) or a comparison rating site, or (3) connected products and services (a complex vacation or a business trip) available via a trusted "Total Travel Facilitator." The business-to-consumer distribution could easily be replaced by consumer-to-business shopping.

As for competitors, the "competitive space" is being stretched, with competition not only increasing within air carrier sectors and between air carrier sectors, but also from new information loaded businesses that are circling the distribution landscape. As for full service airlines, one can see not only the past expansion of the three Persian Gulf-based carriers and their future expansion plans, but also the quality of their product, the level of price, and the attraction of their brands. Some airlines are trying to become "powerhouses" by focusing on product centricity, for example, Emirates Airline. Some are planning to do so by focusing on customer centricity, for example, British Airways. As for the low cost carrier sector, competition is becoming hypercompetitive. Not only do the three large low cost airlines have more than 200 aircraft each (easyJet about 200, Ryanair about 300, and Southwest about 600), but there are now numerous other airlines growing rapidly. Lion Air from Indonesia has almost 100 aircraft and AirAsia from Malaysia, Jetstar from Australia, and IndiGo from India, each have about 75 aircraft. These new airlines have low costs, they are growing fast, and they are much more agile than most full service airlines.

As for the potential power of new distributors (who could also be collaborators), one only needs to see how consumers are embracing the likes of Hipmunk, Kayak, and TripAdvisor. There is also the incredible potential power of a Total Travel Facilitator—this could be developed by powerhouses such as Google, Apple, Facebook, or Amazon, driven by as yet unknown upstarts, or indeed led by some of today's airlines growing the scale and scope of their products and services. Consumers want access to integrated information that can enhance the totality of their travel experience.

What are the options for various categories of airlines in an increasingly competitive marketplace? To different degrees, and in different ways, those that want to succeed can use the available transformative technology at least as an enabler, if not as a driver. Some can choose to remain product centric and continue to focus on the physical attributes of the product (networks, fleet), costs, and support from digital assets that can help in the acquisition of customers. And, they can provide brand value through reach and price. Others can focus on customer centricity through digital product innovation (with digital integration) to enhance user experience for the customer who is in control (through information). They provide brand value through reach and value added, as opposed to price. And, they use data, analytics, mobile, and search to formulate customer strategy, to engage with customers, and to measure the results of their strategic and tactical initiatives. Both groups (with product centricity and customer centricity) can make profits. There is, however, uncertainty of profits for airlines that decide to straddle the centricity spectrum and try to be between the two, product and customer centricity.

For both groups, technology can help to stretch the way in which an airline can add value. See Figure 8.1, which represents the initial basic product, the seat, depicted in the figure as the center of the "onion." The growing layers of the "onion" represent all of the value that has been generated over time, radiating from that initial core product. Finally, the outermost layer illustrates the new and future opportunities in terms of technologies that are benefiting, and will benefit, customers. However, the effective

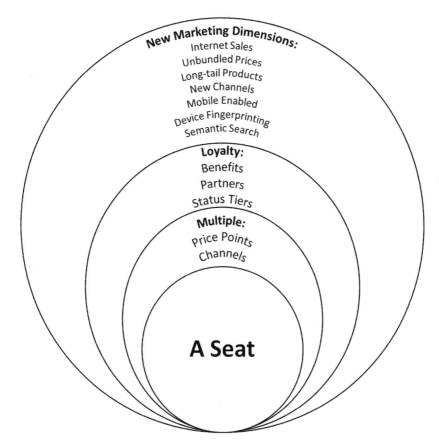

Figure 8.1   Expanding value generation

deployment of technology requires not only a different mindset, but also dramatic changes in many systems and processes as well as organizational changes, involving functions, people, and skills. Such a mindset is particularly important for those airlines interested in becoming customer centric. And, it all starts with the leadership that does not accept averages and mediocrity and is determined to achieve extraordinary performance, through true customer centricity and team performance.

Consumers

To begin with, consumers are changing even in the area of fundamental demographics. Consider the ramifications. The rising middle class in China alone (see Figure 1.2 in Chapter 1) is changing the geopolitics within the aviation industry. Table 8.1 shows a forecast of the compounded average growth in domestic passenger traffic in China compared to a selected number of other countries. If this rate continues during the next ten years, the total airline domestic passenger traffic in China would surpass the level of the domestic traffic in the US. What are the expectations of travelers not just in China, but also in India, or, for that matter, in Asia relating to comfort, for example? According to the survey cited throughout the book, the Asians consider the important criteria of comfort to be "relaxation, sleep, and wellbeing."[1] Consider another forecast relating to the Millennials in the US (with very different life, work, and travel styles). What if this segment of the population forms 75 percent of the workforce by 2025?[2] What are the expectations with respect to value—product, price, brand, experience, the degree of personalization, and willingness to pay? How do the Millennials in North America differ from those in Europe, Asia, Latin America, or Africa? What are their views not only with respect to the commercial side of products and services, but also with respect to the use of social media, engagement with sellers, and the provision of personal information?

Table 8.1   **Domestic passenger growth (2012–2017): selected countries**

		CAGR (%)	
Country	**2012**	**2017**	**2013 over 2017**
United States	607.4	677.8	2.2
China	291.9	487.9	10.8
Brazil	90.4	122.4	6.3
Russian Federation	35.7	50.5	7.2
Turkey	26.3	43.4	10.6
Mexico	25.9	33.3	5.2

Source: International Air Transport Association, Airline Industry Forecast, 2013–2017, October 2013, pp. 33–5.

Competitors

Competition is becoming much fiercer within airline sectors and among airline sectors. Take the full service sector. The three Persian Gulf-based carriers as a group, and Emirates in particular, are not only growing at an incredible rate, but they are providing enticing products, prices, and brands. At the end of 2013, Emirates had a fleet of over 200 aircraft (all wide body) with about 40 Airbus 380s, almost one third of the total number in service worldwide. Moreover, the airline has an additional order of almost 400 aircraft, about 150 to be Airbus 380s. It is noteworthy that Emirates would be replacing some of its older Airbus 380s with newer Airbus 380s before most other airlines in the world would have even acquired any Airbus 380s. The growth of Emirates's hub activity can also be gauged from the growth of Dubai Airport, with the story line, "Connecting the world." In terms of seats offered, it is approaching the rank of number four in the world, after Beijing, Atlanta, and London Heathrow.

The Persian Gulf-based airlines are also in a favorable position in terms of their cost structure. Again, take Emirates as one example. Figure 8.2 shows the Cost per Available Seat Kilometer (CASK) (in US cents) against Average Trip Length in 2012 for selected European legacy carriers. Emirates has lower unit costs than Virgin Atlantic despite the higher average stage length of Virgin. Emirates also has lower unit costs than British Airways, but British Airways has lower average stage length. According to a recent comprehensive analysis by the CAPA-Centre for Aviation, based in Sydney, Australia, relative to Virgin and the International Consolidated Airlines Group (IAG), Emirates has significant cost advantage in the areas of labor, maintenance, fuel, and catering, despite cost disadvantage in the areas of depreciation, selling, and corporate overhead.[3] Emirates has a strong management team demonstrated by its cutting edge initiatives in areas ranging from bilateral partnerships (for example, with Qantas) and branding (for example, through the sponsorship of sports teams and stadiums worldwide).

Next, consider the emerging competition for traditional full service airlines from newer generation low cost airlines in long haul international markets. Take three airlines alone with very different business models, Jetstar (a division of Qantas), AirAsia X (a division of AirAsia), and Norwegian Air Shuttle. Jetstar and AirAsia X have already proven the power of their business models and their brands, both operating in Asia and Oceania. Norwegian is planning to launch new international routes out of London Gatwick during the summer of 2014 and has ordered more Boeing 787s. See Figure 2.4 in Chapter 2. Norwegian also takes Jetstar's concept of establishing local crew bases around the world one step further, with planned bases in Ireland, the US, and Thailand. Others could easily follow the likes of the Indonesia-based Lion Air with some experience in operating Boeing 747s, the Philippines-based Cebu Pacific with some experience in operating the Airbus 330s, and the Japan-based Skymark Airlines with six Airbus 380s on order and applications to serve New York's John F Kennedy and London's Heathrow airports. If not these, other even newer generations of low cost airlines could succeed in long haul intercontinental markets, the last high margin product line of full service airlines.

Leaving aside the breathtaking competition among airlines, it is the information-based businesses that will change the competitive landscape by penetrating the distribution arena. As mentioned throughout the book, consumers now have incredible power to conduct market research, on their own, or through facilitators, armed with big data, analytics, search engines, access to services of the Cloud, and indepth and working knowledge of social media. The situation for many passenger airlines could easily be the same as in the operations of air cargo capacity offered by passenger airlines. The introduction of, initially, powerful and well integrated traditional freight forwarders, followed by marketing-savvy, third party logistics, and finally, information technology-embracing, fourth party logistic businesses, made many passenger airlines offering cargo capacity to be "truckers" in the sky. Now, the new information-armed and customer-centric distributors could easily make many passenger airlines "buses" in the sky. A few large global airlines are aware of this development and are preparing competitive responses.

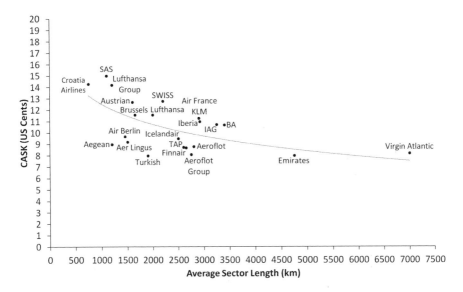

Figure 8.2   Cost per Available Seat Kilometer (US cents) and Average Trip Length for selected European legacy carriers: 2012

Source: "Unit Cost Analysis of Emirates, IAG, and Virgin; About Learning from a New Model, not Unpicking it," CAPA–Centre for Aviation, January 10, 2014.

Even a few low cost carriers are monitoring the situation. Ryanair, for example, has partnered with Google to enable passengers to shop on Google Flight Search. Instead of browsing dozens of different sites to search for flight and fare information, a passenger can go to Google Flight Search and view Ryanair's flights and fares and how the fares compare with other airlines. If a passenger decides to purchase, the booking can be made directly on Ryanair.com through Google Flight Search. According to the airline, passengers will also be able to have mobile boarding passes starting from the first half of 2014.

Collaborators

One way to achieve a greater share of wallet is through customer centricity; the keys to personalization are (1) the acquisition and creative deployment of wide ranging information to obtain a comprehensive view of targeted customers, and (2) innovation competency to redesign the airline business to offer the right product to the right customer at the right time, and at the right price. The right product is not just the sale of a seat in a given market. It could be the provision of solutions related to travel needs, for example, door-to-door service or the service of a 24/7 travel concierge, or the resolution of a travel challenge caused by an irregular operation—a solution that meets the needs of a traveler, not just the capability of an airline to reaccommodate the passenger on the next available flight of the airline or its alliance partner. The question is: Should airlines develop the needed technologies, the innovation competencies, and gather and analyze the needed timely information internally, or go outside their own organizations to collaborate with third parties?

Airlines are already collaborating on the operations side and on the commercial side, but mostly among themselves. For example, rather than flying their own aircraft, they are beginning to set up virtual airlines, as in the case of Qantas, as previously discussed. On the commercial side, some have just begun to sell seats differently, as in the bidding process to buy upgrades, using platforms developed by outsiders. However, should they now collaborate more aggressively with not just third parties, but also customers, to redesign their businesses to generate ancillary revenues beyond the fee-based processes, through personalized value-based options? This step requires the acquisition and integration of information (some of which already exists internally, complemented with additional information from internal and external sources), coupled with analytics to understand and anticipate customer behavior so as to be proactive in meeting customers' stated and perceived needs. As stated earlier in this book, the threat is that if airlines do not become proactive, other customer-centric and information-savvy companies (say, Google) could step in, perhaps even in an alliance with other collaborators (say, Facebook), to generate and capture traveler value through leveraging situation-based behavior to offer personalized services. This threat also exists as currently airlines tend to "push" less relevant information and customers prefer to "pull" more relevant information.

Collaboration is hardly a new concept in today's environment. There are collaborators leading to such developments as crowd-sourcing, crowd-funding, and consumer co-creation (co-production). As mentioned earlier, there is also the new trend—"socialstructing"[4]—people coming together to engage in collective action to change their lives. Relating this concept of "socialstructing" to the travel industry, consider the launch of Airbnb, discussed below.

The main potential area for collaboration is in the digital space to improve the customer experience in every facet of the travel cycle—from using information to inspire consumers about travel and destinations to tracking their baggage. Such collaboration, among the employees of an airline, among alliance partners, as well as third parties, can be facilitated with the use of technologies, surfacing from the confluence of mobile, big data, and the Cloud. Penetrating the digital and mobile spaces through internal and external collaboration would certainly be one way to improve the travel experience and provide, and charge for, various levels of personalized services.

Leadership

To face the multiple and converging challenges and to capitalize on a wide array of opportunities, airline leaders must now really develop a customer-centric, or at least a product-centric, vision and articulate it in terms of a "story line" to focus on the aforementioned three forces. If Google's "story line" was to organize the world's information and make it accessible and useful, and Dubai Airport's story line is "Connecting the world," what would be an equivalent story line of a global airline? Could it be "Travel Solution Provider" or "Total Travel Facilitator?" Within the airline industry, the need is now critical to shift the focus from optimizing around constraints and constantly putting out today's fire(s) to finding ways to mobilize organizations to acquire, engage with, and retain customers. There are now new listening posts (many forms of social media, for example) and new ways to receive and mine timely information (big data, analytics, and mobile, for example), and new potential partners (innovation-driven information companies, for example) to redesign airline businesses. The key is to use analytics as an integrative function and collaborate with third parties.

If Google can offer real time advertisements and track their performance also in real time, then airlines should be able to make dynamic offers and track their performance. In 1997, IBM's computer, Deep Blue, beat the world chess champion after a six game match. In 2011, IBM's supercomputer, Watson, defeated two human champions at Jeopardy. IBM, in partnership with Lionbridge, is offering "GeoFluent," an online application that instantly translates conversations between customers and troubleshooters who speak different languages.[5] In light of such advances being made by technology companies, it makes sense to develop partnerships that would enable airlines to provide value to targeted customers and receive value from them.

After the development of a customer-centric vision, the next critical success factor is determination to bring about change, particularly in corporate culture to embrace customer centricity, cross-functional integration, and new skills. The determination also relates to the execution phase. The starting point in this cultural change might be a shift in practice from philosophy to pragmatism. There is no such thing anymore as "a" model, let alone a "good" or a "bad" model. It is a circumstantial or a contextual question. At any time, and for a given airline, there can be several options instead of "the" model, in terms of failure or success in the long term. Success, instead, is likely to come from using an iterative process to redesign the airline business and be agile in the development of products and services, for example. The mindset of "introduce it now and perfect it later" would work if an airline is ready to listen to and understand its customers, and more importantly, act upon the feedback from customers to refine, in an iterative manner, products and services that enhance customer experience—the emerging expectation.

One factor that is very difficult to change, particularly within airlines, relates to people, because changes in systems and operations, no matter how complex they are, cannot be made unless the people are willing to change. Consequently, changes in business models require changes in how executives and frontline staff think about the business. They have to think differently about their customers and their products and services. For example, from one segment of customers' point of view, the important part is the total transportation from one point on a globe to another. Another segment of customers now has a dilemma, to drive or fly in shorter haul markets in the US because it now takes too long to get through the entire process. For another segment, a published 45-minute connection is simply not enough given that a 15-minute delay is still considered to reflect on-time performance. Connections are a significant concern given that for about 50 percent of travelers in the US and about 30 percent of the travelers on a worldwide basis it is necessary to make connections to complete the air part of the trip. Yet, another segment continues to look at an airline product as a commodity. And these are just a few customer-centricity issues relating to the subsegment level. Think about the size of the issues at the individual traveler level!

Currently, while it is one thing for almost every airline to want to be a retailer, it is another thing for most airlines to actually be able to get into a retailing mindset. Does *everyone* within the airline have the mindset of a retailer? Does management know how to execute retailing initiatives? Is management implementing the retailing initiatives *throughout* the airline? Retailing in the airline industry in the past was limited to a discussion on products, pricing, and distribution, and more recently, it is related to the merchandising of ancillary products. Consider the element of the product for a minute. While the focus has been mostly on the physical attributes (such as the seat and even that mostly in Premium Classes), airlines now need to explore the digital aspects of products and experience. As to pricing, whereas the challenge in the past may have been with respect to transparency, the opportunity in retailing relates to personalization. Similarly with distribution, the focus in the past may have related to the proliferation of channels (including the matter of direct versus indirect), from the retailing viewpoint the challenge and the opportunity relates to the potential new group of third party distributors that airlines must deal with, given their information and analytics capabilities. The use of data and analytics must, however, respect the privacy concerns of consumers. The use of personal data to research past shopping behavior and to predict future shopping behavior can be seen as a "double-edged sword" as discussed in Chapter 1.

While becoming a retailer is a valid vision for redesigning the airline business, it requires a laser-like focus on all of the phases of the retailing cycle shown in Figure 4.1 in Chapter 4. Specifically, the objective now is to improve the digital experience in the shopping, planning, and buying phases so that passengers can experience the physical products. Within this context, challenges and opportunities relate to the mobile and social domains. And the control regarding airline choice is in the hands of digital passengers, their social networks, and user-generated content. The competitive landscape is clearly being stretched. From a distribution perspective, hotels were not only competing with Priceline, but now Priceline is competing with the likes of HotelTonight and Airbnb.

Driving Transformative Technology

For all airlines, technology is an enabler of business strategies. For the innovation ambitious it can even be a driver of business strategies. Think about the initial success of two new travel-related businesses, Uber and Airbnb. These two companies built their entire businesses facilitated by technology. In the case of Uber, the business strategy was driven by the deployment of mobile technology to connect drivers with customers and the payment system. In the case of Airbnb, the strategy was to connect hosts with guests (in an online community marketplace), matching the profiles and needs of both hosts and guests.

Uber's business, "Moving People," connects people with drivers at the click of a button on a mobile device. The company collects a fee for connecting drivers with passengers. With the customer's location identified through the GPS information on the mobile device, the driver knows the exact location and the customer does not even need to provide an exact address. The customer can use the mobile device to track the driver on a map and the name of the driver as well as the description of the vehicle can become available on the customer's mobile device. The customer can get a quote for the fare by providing the pickup and dropoff locations. Some drivers have implemented "surge pricing" in which they can change the fare based on demand — high fares during periods of high demand. The fare can be charged to the credit card that is already on file with the company. A receipt can be emailed to the customer. This is clearly a business that has been designed to provide seamless connectivity using mobile technology. Launched in 2009, as of the end of 2013, Uber provided services in 69 cities in 26 countries. Vehicles range from standard cars to luxury cars and from sedans to SUVs.[6]

Airbnb, launched in 2008, is an online service that connects hosts with space to rent with guests looking for space to rent for short periods. The accommodations offered, in almost 35,000 cities in almost 200 countries, represent an extremely broad array of properties—rooms, apartments, boats, castles, and, even treehouses. Hosts need to provide comprehensive information on their properties (descriptions, photos, prices, rules, and so forth) as well as their profiles. Similarly, guests also provide a comprehensive list of their needs—type, price, location, amenities, reviews, neighborhoods (local transportation, shopping, eateries, nightlife, and so forth), as well as their profiles. The objective is to match the profiles and needs of hosts on the one hand and guests on the other hand. Moreover, Airbnb introduced "Two-Way-Ratings," where not only properties are rated by guests, but also the hosts rate their guests. Thus, travelers can build up a reputation as "qualified guests," making it easier for them to be accepted. Security and privacy considerations on both sides (hosts and guests) are given high priority. For example, IDs from both sides are verified and personal information is protected. The service provided is easy to use and seamless. For example, search allows the user to provide numerous filters as well as local guides.[7]

One final thought: Could an airline deploy disruptive technology, coupled with a willingness to "think in a *new* box," to develop and implement a "quantum strategy"—high quality product or service achieved with a lean cost structure? One writer provides two examples of companies able to implement such a strategy—Apple and Singapore Airlines.[8] The idea is not new. Toyota succeeded in implementing such a strategy decades ago by improving quality, for example, through the zero-defect mandate and by reducing costs through the Just-In-Time inventory concept. ALDI did it through embracing simplicity not just to provide higher quality, but also through low costs.

Amazon did it with higher quality service (ease of shopping, reliable and fast delivery service, personalized services) and lower costs through optimized logistics. In the case of airlines, while Qantas and Singapore Airlines may not have been able to develop such strategies relating to their mainline operations, they seem to be experimenting with the concept through their multibrand approach, Qantas through Jetstar and Singapore Airlines through SilkAir. SilkAir is now reported to be a full service carrier catering to the needs, from check in to touch down, of well-traveled global customers.[9] In light of the commitment shown by a few innovation ambitious carriers it is just a matter of time until some major mainline carriers succeed in implementing quantum strategy along the lines of ALDI, Amazon, and Apple.

Takeaways

- Contemporary businesses, such as Uber and Airbnb, have leveraged technology as a driver of their strategies, coupled with leadership determination and creativity to resolve challenges facing users.
- Balance can be achieved between the value provided by a business and the value received from its customers, as discussed in Chapter 2. In the case of Airbnb, the exchange in value is between each individual host and each individual guest. Think also about the length to which Disney has gone to engage and interact (as discussed in Chapter 4) with customers to improve their experience through the entire cycle, from shopping to post-resort visit.
- The way forward is customer centricity and personalization, as discussed in Chapter 3. Airbnb not only offers an enormous variety of rental spaces but is able to offer a customized search result to meet the needs of a particular guest.
- Branding and business strategies should be integrated to build strong brands, as discussed in Chapter 5. Think about the businesses ranked by consumers as the top ten in the world with simplicity as the common denominator. ALDI was number one. Now, Uber appears to be branding itself as a company that is moving people, with ease, at reasonable prices, and with style.

- The role of loyalty is changing. It must be earned, not bought, as discussed in Chapter 6. Neither Apple, nor Uber, appear to be discounting their prices, but instead are providing products and services to meet the physical and emotional needs of their customers.

- Technology, particularly mobile, can be an enabler for all airlines and, possibly even, a driver of business strategy, for some airlines, through the digitization of not only products and services, but also of experience, as discussed in Chapters 4 and 7. Now, airlines with mobility as the center piece of their redesign can achieve significant benefits by deploying a "Completely Mobile" service chain.

Notes

1 Martin Raymond, "The Future of Comfort: Asia," *The Future Laboratory*, London, UK, February 2014, p. 23.

2 Brian Solis, *What's the Future of Business?: Changing the Way Businesses Create Experiences* (Hoboken, NJ: John Wiley, 2013), p. 30.

3 "Unit Cost Analysis of Emirates, IAG, and Virgin; About Learning from a New Model, not Unpicking it," CAPA–Centre for Aviation, January 10, 2014.

4 Howard Rheingold, "Three Harbingers of Change," *strategy+business*, Winter 2013, p. 74.

5 Erik Brynjolfsson and Andrew McAfee, *The Second Machine Age: Work, Progress, and Prosperity in a Time of Brilliant Technologies* (NY: W.W. Norton, 2014), p. 23.

6 Information synthesized from the official Uber website.

7 Information synthesized from the official Airbnb website.

8 Loizos Heracleous, "What Do Apple and Singapore Airlines Have in Common? Quantum Strategy," Companies & Industries, *Bloomberg Businessweek*, July 31, 2013.

9 "SilkAir's New Brand Campaign Embraces the Joy of Flying," by SilkAir, as reported in *Air Transport News*, February 17, 2014.

Chapter 9
Attaining Market Leadership: Thought Leadership Pieces

ALDI: CRM by Simplicity

Dieter Brandes
Former General Manager and Board Director, ALDI

and

Nils Brandes
International Consultant, Hard Discount Retail

ALDI can be considered not only the most successful Hard Discounter in food retailing but also the most customer-oriented one.

ALDI is certainly the most successful Hard Discounter. It has 9,500 stores in 20 countries, sales of more than US$80 billion, 1,300 stores in the US, and a constant profit before tax of more than 4 percent, not to mention large real estate assets and no bank credits at all.[1]

How is it possible that a company which has never carried out customer research, has no Marketing department and carries the smallest range of all retailers can be so successful and considered extremely customer oriented? Research in Germany—where the brothers founded the company after the Second World War, adopting the discount concept in 1960—showed that 80 percent of all customers were, more or less, regularly shopping at ALDI. This research was not carried out by ALDI but by competitors, suppliers, and others.

Let us look at the ALDI business principles—just six points which can be easily understood by every cashier and warehouse worker:

1. a limited product range;
2. goods which reflect basic consumer needs;
3. all goods are easy to handle in terms of operational requirements like logistics;
4. best possible qualities—measured against leading brands;
5. the lowest possible sales prices;
6. high number of private labels.

A clear business concept like this helps to give everyone in the organization and even suppliers direction. These principles provide in themselves a very customer-oriented basis for the company. Successful projects and businesses start with a clear strategy and explanation, "why should the customer come into my store?" If this question is not answered, there will be no success, never mind any customer orientation.

Taking into account the limited range it carries, ALDI is even larger than the largest retailer in the world, Wal-Mart. How does ALDI compare with Wal-Mart? ALDI sells about 1,800 items and generates worldwide sales of $80 billion. Wal-Mart sells about 120,000 items and the worldwide turnover is more than $450 billion. This means the average sales per item in ALDI is 12 times the Wal-Mart average.

How does ALDI achieve such an incredible customer acceptance? We will give a little insight by using some vivid examples of how ALDI runs its business.

If You Don't Like the Product, Bring it Back

No explanation is required—the customer always receives his money back if he returns an item. The wine bottle may even be almost empty. According to his job description, the store manager has to accept the customer's wish. This is not only very customer friendly, it is actually a matter of simplicity and good organization. The store manager is fully in charge of taking back the product and must not question the reasons or justification of the customer's request. There are no exceptions allowed. Others may fear that the number of returns may ruin the company but in reality very few returns actually occur. The products are of good quality and trust between employees and customers means that not many customers misuse the policy.

Easy to Shop

ALDI stores are designed to accomodate easy and fast shopping without any psychological concepts or product placements which tempt the customer to buy high margin products placed at eye-height. Instead the store layout relates to logistical ideas. Products are sold out of boxes ("box store") and—as an example—heavy boxes are just put on the lower shelf level.

Furthermore, one finds only one product per type of product. More than one type is only found when there are different qualities. The customer does not need to choose between ten or more different brands. Some hypermarkets carry 40 or even more different brands and types of toilet paper. Studies have shown that customers find it difficult to decide when choosing between lots of brands—this can result in them not making a choice at all because they feel uncomfortable and want to avoid making the wrong decision. A larger assortment actually leads to fewer sales because it is so customer unfriendly.

The Range Stocked is Not Dictated by the Purchasing Department or Suppliers

It is standard practice in most retailers that the range of products stocked is influenced by good offers from suppliers along with additional listing fees. Listing a new item has nothing to do with the customer. The decisions are supplier-driven.

ALDI never select their product range in this way. New items make it into the assortment because all the responsible managers make their own decisions on what would be of interest to the customer. Their ideas are then followed up using the "Three-Store Test." Margin does not play any part in this process, the only proof of customers' demand for a product is sales.

The "Three-Store Test"

This test not only avoids the high cost of market research, it also gives a good idea of potential sales and volumes with real numbers very quickly. Not requiring much preparation, this test is extremely reliable and provides fact-based numbers on which to make final decisions. The test gives important information on the acceptance of a product by customers. It also provides an opportunity to test a supplier, as well as other important factors such as handling of a product or possible shrinkage.

Everyday Low Prices and Information Instead of Promotion

ALDI customers can expect the lowest possible price every day. This is a great simplification and builds trust. The ALDI principles and the ALDI pricing strategy was only once explained by ALDI co-founder Karl Albrecht as follows:

> Our only consideration when we are working out a product's price is how cheaply can we sell it.

There is no Marketing department to invent, calculate, and negotiate the next promotion designed to allure customers. Customers are treated like adults and can simply approve the quality and price with no time pressure or temptation placed upon them. The trust ALDI has built up over decades is one of their greatest assets. Most retailers work out the highest price they can sell a product at—the highest possible margin that will not affect the volume. They then use promotions to attract customers and create a low price impression of the product. This is not a clear strategy and again is not supplier-focused and not customer-oriented. A large and expensive Marketing department is responsible for thinking up the next "kick" and how they can increase the "drug dose" in order to keep customers addicted— which is not the same thing as loyal.

In addition, ALDI only "informs" customers about its quality and prices. Like a serious newspaper, ALDI's communication is designed to make customers compare the quality and price of its products with those of brands and competitors—thus building trust in ALDI's quality and assortment. ALDI's advertisements are legendary for their headline "ALDI inform." This is a completely different approach and a totally different understanding of marketing and customer orientation.

Consistency and Price Leadership

ALDI pursues its strategy with consistency. Where other companies are often tempted by activities which are nice to have and are considered to somewhat "help," ALDI sticks to its principles like a religious dogma. Every decision is related to its very basic business principles.

This can mean that ALDI lowers the sales prices of an item even when the new cost is not yet valid, having been negotiated with the supplier for the very near future. The new price is immediately passed on to the customer who benefits from the negotiations. ALDI's business principles result in customer-oriented decisions.

Creativity and Responsibility: Regional Items

Another intelligent method used by ALDI to reduce complexity and encourage responsibility by managers is the so-called "regional items. " Each ALDI region, comprising 50–80 stores, is organized as a fully functioning company. The Accounting department is responsible for a monthly balance sheet. The Warehouse, with its truck fleet, distributes the merchandise to the stores, the Sales organization manages the stores, the expansion manager searches for new locations and is in charge of construction of new stores. The regional purchaser orders all goods which are needed in the stores from the supplier, to be delivered to the warehouse.

Each of these regions can fully independently select up to 30 regional items. The selections can be very creative and sometimes are so successful they are transferred to the standard ALDI product range. Here, ALDI makes use of the power of decentralization which goes along with high autonomy and responsibility. These are the essentials to create simplicity and to manage complexity. Each regional manager wants to improve the results of his region and by this contributes to the whole company.

Everybody is a Potential Customer

It has never been ALDI's aim to segment its customers or find out who their specific target customer is. ALDI just makes an offer: a very limited assortment with excellent quality and the lowest possible prices. This was not based on a study or a selection of potential customer groups. Instead of doing what everybody else did, ALDI followed a strategy of being different in everything. They have done this to the best of their ability. Decades ago, ALDI ignored the fact that customers may want fresh milk and made UHT milk famous by offering the lowest price in the market. This allowed the company to avoid all the difficulties related to investments in refrigerators, logistical challenges and the shrinkage which normally goes with fresh dairy products.

The traditional way would have been to follow the marketing experts and offer what everyone recommends and what seems to be customer expectation. By going a different way, ALDI created a market for their products and avoided lots of complex problems.

Summary

ALDI's success is the result of sticking to the very essentials of the business—winning the customer's trust by pursuing a very special business concept. ALDI omitted all the "nice to haves" and concentrated on what really makes a difference to the customer and what is in line with its company principles. ALDI was never familiar with sophisticated vocabulary such as "customer-centricity" or "customer-focused." ALDI invented CRM by using the concepts of simplicity. It all came down to what improves quality and cost and what does not—what is important and what is reasonable. Real numbers and testing gave an indication of successful decisions. Without really being aware of the "scientific" implications of complexity, ALDI developed a successful business using the simplest business procedures possible.

Hertz Reinvents Car Rental for a Customer-Centric World

David Trimm
Executive Vice President and Chief Information Officer, Hertz Corporation

Hertz operates its car rental business through the Hertz, Dollar, Thrifty and Firefly brands from approximately 11,200 corporate, licensee, and franchisee locations in 150 countries throughout the world. It is the number one airport car rental brand in the US and at 120 major airports in Europe, as well as being the largest worldwide airport general use car rental brand.

For the past few years, Hertz has been on a transformative mission to operate as a customer-centric organization. Whether a company is customer-centric can be determined by how time is allocated in the organization: if it is primarily allocated to selling a limited range of products to an ever-expanding customer base, the company is probably product centric. If, on the other hand, time is mostly spent on understanding and meeting the needs of a specific customer or group of customers, the organization is probably customer-centric. This distinction matters because, in a future driven by more personalized choices made by consumers and increased visibility of their purchasing options, the companies which most accurately know and anticipate their customers' needs will win.

Companies must have a very clear idea of the customer(s) they intend to serve and their most critical needs, and this insight must be grounded in facts and data, and not based on purchases by previous customers or management's beliefs. This research should include sizing and segmenting markets based on consumer needs, and making rational resource allocation decisions to create experiences that are relevant to and reach chosen target segments.

Hertz has a longstanding reputation for quality and service. Starting in 2011, the company committed to also becoming well known for speed of service and the range and quality of vehicles that they offer. In fact, Hertz is seeking to reinvent the car rental experience by becoming the first choice brand worldwide based on providing the fastest, easiest, and most valued rentals.

To uphold this brand promise, Hertz embarked on a major investment program which has, so far, spanned over 1,000 on- and off-airport locations worldwide. The investments involve innovations across the whole company including fleet, operations, human resources, sales, marketing, customer service, uniforms, facilities, and information technology. The overarching objective is to make the rental process faster and easier, and this manifests itself in very visible customer-facing innovations such as a pager system which replaces wait-lines (and is similar to restaurant line management), or video-kiosks to supplement serving (counter) positions when locations are busy. There are also subtler changes such as a more casual, approachable, and sporty look for employee uniforms or the way special cars are highlighted on prominent display ramps—each adding to the "wow" experience Hertz is attempting to generate.

The company has worked hard to eliminate roadblocks which hold customers up as they move through the rental experience, and, one-by-one, delays are being engineered out of the reservation, pickup and return processes. A good example is Hertz's award winning Gold service whereby customers by-pass the counter altogether, go straight to their car and from there to the exit gate and the open road. Some customers told the company that they wanted to choose their car, so Hertz provided them the ability to do just that on the rental lot. The concept of car choice was extended online by allowing customers to pre-select a vehicle from their smartphone or mobile device—a service Hertz calls Gold Choice and which triggers an SMS or email confirmation (called a "Carfirmation"). Customers also told Hertz they sometimes get delayed at the exit gate, which resulted in additional exit gates being constructed at busy locations. Additionally, only frequent travelers who had signed up and paid for Gold service received expedited vehicle pickup, so the company removed barriers to expansion of the program. The most notable changes were eliminating the Gold membership fee and integrating the sign-up process with the web booking process.

Hertz also removed automated voice response booking due to customer feedback that voice response slows the booking process for those who prefer to book by phone. Technology should enable or enhance the experience, not get in the way. Hertz intends to be not only "high tech," but also "high touch" where this is the more customer-friendly approach. Along this line were decisions to expand the range of "click to call" services direct from their website, and the large investment in training to help customer service agents resolve issues with just one call.

At its rental locations, Hertz is designing the experience to be more similar to retail than to traditional car rental. Locations have been redesigned with interiors which are bright, airy, and different. These important differences include individualized serving "pods," technology to add interest and provide information, and even an onsite "RoadTrip" retail store (see Figure 9.1). The Road Trip stores serve items that customers may need or may have forgotten like phone chargers, food and drink, or last-minute gifts. This enables customers to avoid stopping again after they leave the Hertz location, expediting their arrival at their ultimate destination. Additional features include a "Recharge" bar where customer's personal electronic devices can be plugged in and a children's zone to keep the little ones happy. The Road Trip stores also include copying, printing, or Fedex/UPS mailings, assisting customers with business services needs before they leave the rental lot.

Figure 9.1   Redesign of Hertz's car rental area
Source: Hertz

The entire organization has been engaged to activate this vision which has progressed hand-in-hand with the introduction of new products. These include a "dream-car" fleet (vehicles from prestigious or exotic brands that people aspire to drive and love to get close to—Figure 9.2), and "24/7" with vehicles placed for pickup away from traditional rental car locations or made

Figure 9.2   Hertz prestigious and exotic brands
Source: Hertz

available to them outside normal business hours to provide a true mobility service, not just traditional car rental. Hertz 24/7 (see Figure 9.3) is a revolutionary, universal car rental service because it combines the technology and on-demand service associated with car sharing with the operational and logistical capabilities of a global car rental company. In fact, the stated goal is to bring this user-friendly, round-the-clock service to all. 24/7 service also demonstrates Hertz's commitment to sustainable mobility solutions by making situational vehicle rental a viable option for all consumers. This vision hasn't been easy to implement and has required two acquisitions—a further proof-point to the organization that the company is serious about making the transformation happen.

Increasingly, the customer is familiar, and expects to interact, with technology. That insight is foundational for Hertz, despite the company's longstanding reputation for innovation which includes the first bookable website in the industry, and the introduction of GPS under the brand name Neverlost. Rather, the

Figure 9.3   24/7 on-demand functionality
Source: Hertz

intention is to use technology to strip away time and trouble from the customer's journey, optimizing speed of service, knowing that this is a critical requirement for the Hertz customer.

Along the way, not every innovation will succeed, and there must be a candid, facts-based review of each element of this program. Successful activation of a brand message requires cross-functional and whole-organization focus, requiring strong sponsorship from senior leaders and a unified, global leadership of this brand-altering initiative. Nevertheless, because this Hertz program is based on a customer-centric perspective and analytics, the prospects for its overall, long term success have been enhanced significantly.

The Influence of Megatrends on the Airline Industry and its Customers

Jonathan Kletzel

US Transportation Leader, PricewaterhouseCoopers LLP

The world is changing at an accelerated pace, and the airline sector is particularly susceptible to disruptive forces. Airlines operate globally, with thin profit margins and high operating costs, and rely heavily on fossil fuels. Global competition to capture market share is now greater than ever. Governments influence industry profitability through taxation, regulation, and infrastructure investments (or lack of investments), creating an uneven global playing field.

To better understand the implications of disruptive forces on industries, we have looked beyond short term, tactical threats and opportunities to focus on the underlying forces, or "megatrends," driving societal change and transforming the business landscape. These megatrends will likely shape the future of the airline industry. Those companies that best anticipate and adapt to the coming changes will be best positioned for the future

---

5 Megatrends

1. Shifts in global economic power
2. Demographic shifts
3. Accelerating urbanization
4. Climate change and resource scarcity
5. Technological breakthroughs

Working with airlines around the world, we are already seeing how megatrends are influencing the direction of the industry and how leaders are acting to their benefit.

Shifts in Global Economic Power

The global economic balance is changing rapidly. A number of developing countries are becoming consumption economies and influencing where companies are pursuing growth opportunities As indicated in Figure 9.4, by 2050, GDP in the E7 countries (China, India, Brazil, Russia, Indonesia, Mexico, and Turkey) is expected to be just $69 trillion.[2]

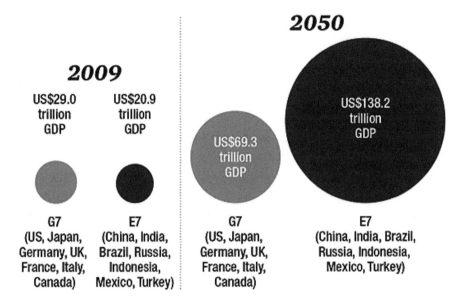

Figure 9.4   GDP of G7 and E7 countries at US$ PPP
Source: PwC Analysis

As large numbers of people in developing countries grow more prosperous, new air travel markets are emerging. Domestic carriers in these markets enjoy a natural competitive advantage, but history has shown that geographic advantage alone is not sufficient for success. Scale and speed are critical to adapt and deploy resources to new markets. Many smaller carriers are unprepared to take advantage of this rapid growth, while established, larger carriers may lack the brand awareness or cultural understanding to grow their operations in those markets. One potential solution to this challenge is cooperative competition or "co-petition."

Carriers with global ambitions are evolving to enter new markets and protect existing areas of strength. "Co-petition" is manifest in several business models including traditional codeshares, global alliances, targeted joint ventures, and direct equity investments. Regardless of the model chosen, successful airlines of the future will operate as integrated global partners with optimized route networks and a seamless passenger experience rather than loosely affiliated carriers simply trading passenger traffic.

Demographic Shifts

There is a dichotomy in population growth across regions. Some countries, such as Germany and Japan, are aging, while others, including India and countries in the African continent, are young and growing (see Figure 9.5).[3] We are also seeing the rise of the middle class, especially in Asia. Explosive population growth in some areas and declining growth in others has widespread implications, including shifts in economic power, resource scarcity, and changes in societal norms.

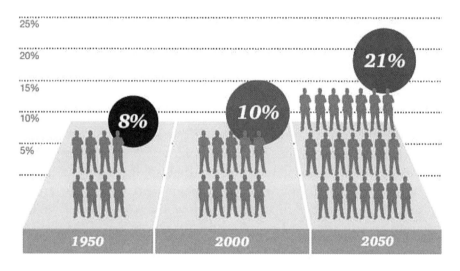

Figure 9.5   Proportion of the world population aged 60 years or more

Source: UN report, World Population Ageing 1950–2050

Demographic shifts present opportunities and challenges for airlines. Greater longevity and increased prosperity will contribute to 31 percent growth in airline traffic by 2017 compared to 2012, representing 930 million additional passengers.[4] These passengers will be more diverse than ever, with differing interests, desires, and expectations. They will come from newly emerging countries and across the demographic spectrum. For example, younger generations are more technologically-savvy (and dependent) than their elders and will demand real time connectivity on a host of portable devices.

Carriers that continue to focus on price, network, schedule, frequency, and or loyalty alone will not be the leading airlines of tomorrow. In addition to the traditional attributes, airlines must offer an increasing variety of products and services to attract and retain passengers in the future and focus on delivering a more personalized and tailored experience.

Accelerating Urbanization

Since 2007, the number of people living in urban centers has exceeded those living in rural areas. By 2030, it's expected that 60 percent of the world's population will be living in cities (see Figure 9.6).[5] The rate of urbanization is likely to increase most rapidly in countries with the highest population growth and where the urban proportion of the population is still relatively low, such as in sub-Saharan Africa and Asia.

Urbanization and prosperity go hand-in-hand; and strong middle class growth creates new customers and new markets for airlines. Network carriers are opening up new routes to

The world urban population is expected to increase by 72% by 2050

Figure 9.6   World urban population

Source: World Urbanization Prospects: 2011 revision, produced by the UN Department of Economic and Social Affairs

fast growing cities in China and other emerging markets. As opportunities expand, they will likely have a significant impact on fleet strategies, network planning, infrastructure investment, product development, and revenue management functions.

With more middle class flyers from emerging nations, airlines will have to consider and understand how the cultural and economic characteristics of new urban centers impact consumer purchase decisions. Balancing the needs of originating, destination, and connecting segments will become increasingly challenging. At the same time, consumers may be willing to pay a premium for personalized services, creating additional opportunities that airlines could potentially capitalize on.

Climate Change and Resource Scarcity

With a global population of 8.3 billion, by 2030, demand for energy is forecast to increase by as much as 50 percent, food by 35 percent, and water withdrawals by 40 percent (see Figure 9.7). As emerging economies modernize and become wealthier, more of their citizens will likely choose to fly, further intensifying the potential environmental impact of the aviation industry. With this as a backdrop, it is not surprising that airlines are under constant pressure to reduce their carbon footprint.

To avoid additional potential regulation and or taxation the aviation industry must address climate change as a whole. But doing so will require significant investment by individual carriers, including replacement of aging aircraft with more fuel efficient models, deployment of winglets and other new technologies that increase fuel efficiency, greater densification through less dependency on regional aircraft, and increased use of alternative fuels, among other measures.

In addition to the regulatory and environmental implications, airlines need to consider environmentally concerned consumers who are becoming more discerning about the companies with which they do business. Since taking care of the environment is becoming more important to passengers, making them aware of corporate sustainability can help win their loyalty and give "greener" airlines a competitive edge.[6] Airlines that are not

Figure 9.7   **With a population of 8.3 billion people by 2030, we'll need: 50 percent more energy, 40 percent more water, and 35 percent more food**

Source: National Intelligence Council: Global Trends 2030: Alternative Worlds

focused on sustainability, should be; and those that are, need to do a better job of communicating their initiatives and philosophy to consumers.

Technological Breakthroughs

From the inception of the airline industry, technological breakthroughs have driven its growth. Technology will continue to play this critical role as manufacturers develop more comfortable and fuel efficient aircraft, energy producers develop alternative fuel sources, and enterprise and personal technology shifts to expanding social, mobile, and Cloud capabilities (see Figure 9.8). With more data generated, collected, and analyzed, airlines will be enabled to connect aircraft, crew, passengers, and operations to deliver innovative products, a better customer experience, and stronger operational performance.

The issue of customer connectivity is presenting airlines with a very immediate challenge in meeting In-Flight Entertainment and Connectivity (IFEC) needs. With urbanization and shifting demographics, more flyers are expecting to use their sophisticated personal electronic devices on board aircraft. Carriers are finding themselves in a race to respond with offerings such as

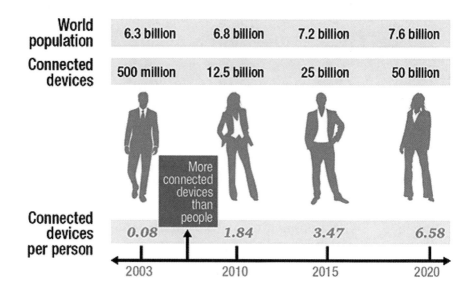

Figure 9.8   The rise of the "Internet of Things"

Source: Cisco Internet Business Solutions Group, April 2011

reliable Wi-Fi and streaming video. And the race may accelerate: a growing numbers of customers are looking for performance that already outstrips today's capabilities, such as access to subscription video services across multiple devices.

The proliferation of personal devices provides airlines with the ability to stay in touch with customers on a regular basis and provide helpful information as well as buying opportunities. Given the ubiquity of these devices, airlines cannot afford to ignore their potential as a critical information and distribution channel. Interactions with customers in real time also provide airlines with valuable customer information that, in turn, can provide input for designing a more personalized customer experience.

*****

These megatrends are not the only factors influencing the airline industry. Executives still need to focus on fuel consumption, operational efficiency, labor agreements, and the immediate competitive environment. Given all these issues, it can be easy to overlook the importance of long trends on the industry. But megatrends are real and will affect our future. Airline leaders need to think about how megatrends will impact their business and, more importantly, how they will impact the passenger experience.

Maintaining Competitive Advantage in the Face of Changing Competitive Dynamics

Vaughan Chandler

Executive Manager Strategy, Insights and Innovation, Qantas Loyalty

"Competition is increasing." Few would disagree with that statement. It is, however, unlikely to be true.

Commonly, competition in business is either defined as the effort between two or more parties to win a third parties' business, or the allocation of resources to their most highly valued uses. Under both of these definitions it is unlikely that your historical competitors were putting in less effort to win the business than today or that they were not allocating their resources effectively given the circumstances at that time. Simply ascribing the challenges faced by many incumbents to increased competition is both simplistic and convenient.

It would also be wrong, however, to assert that incumbent businesses do not face increasing challenges—therefore it becomes critical to define these challenges more specifically than simply "increased competition."

Changing Sources of Competitive Advantage

So whilst the intensity of competition may actually be unchanged, the sources of competitive advantage are changing. Historically, industry incumbents were afforded significant advantage by achieving scale. Scale brought cost efficiencies to operations and barriers to entry for competitors. Both of these advantages of scale are now being eroded by the increasing flexibility of operating infrastructure and the decreasing costs of (and capability to control) media.

Now for a new entrant to grow from niche to mass market the funding requirements for infrastructure present a significantly lower barrier. Cost outlay can now be matched closer to the realization of growth. For example, it is no longer necessary to implement an expensive enterprise information technology infrastructure upfront to create a business capable of massive scalability.

Similarly, if the product/service is a step-change product, the need to spend significant money on advertising and marketing (which has historically been almost mandatory to achieve mainstream market positions) has significantly diminished due to the emergence of social media.

Therefore, the investment and speed required to grow from niche to mainstream is one of the key factors that has changed significantly in recent years. This dynamic exists strongly in the airline industry and new entrants are able to build up mainstream positions with significantly less investment and risk than predecessors required only 20 years ago.

Another less recognized historical advantage of scale was the importance of the ability to fund large R&D budgets. While scale brought a widely recognized lack of agility related to organizational dynamics, it did bring a significant capability to innovate. Importantly, often the large R&D budgets were most needed not to invent, but to be able to bring inventions into the mainstream (with some notable exceptions such as the pharmaceutical industry). Put another way, large organizations were able to create strategic agility advantage through their scale.

Given that the cost of achieving mainstream market positions is reducing, it follows that the strategic agility advantage of incumbent businesses is also being eroded.

In summary, many of the key historical advantages of incumbency and scale—being cost efficiencies, barriers to entry, and capability to drive innovations to mainstream—are rapidly being eroded.

Maintaining Competitive Advantage

This then asks the question: how do incumbents maintain their competitive advantage in their respective markets in the face of these changing dynamics?

Once cost efficiency, innovation, and barriers to entry are extracted as competitive advantages, what are the key advantages that remain for most corporations against more agile and cost efficient new entrants that can now achieve scale? For many companies the key remaining advantages revolve around:

- brand;
- the volume of customer interactions being conducted; and
- the volume of data created by these customer interactions.

Leveraging brand is going to be very specific to each company and market and therefore hard to generalize. However, data and the management of customer interactions have a great deal of commonality across businesses and industries.

Large incumbent businesses often have millions of opportunities more than their competitors to interact with customers. Furthermore, these interactions create an historical footprint of data that is far more detailed, robust, and precise than a new entrant enjoys. Incumbent airlines often enjoy benefits in this area, as the data is usually identifiable back to an individual measurable over time and there is a strong richness of data created not just from the airline operations but from loyalty and ancillary businesses as well.

Data is, needless to say, one of the biggest current management topics. In practice, however, most organizations limit the value of data to generating a better understanding of their customers, which is a retrospective or backward looking approach. Therefore the focus of most companies is in creating a data strategy and or a customer reporting framework.

Rather than a retrospective approach, however, the combination of data and volume of interactions provides an opportunity to create significant change. Incumbents have an opportunity to create advantage by creating more change as well as more precise change than new entrants who lack these assets. To put this another way, there is a potential to create operational agility advantage.

Bringing all of these dynamics together, the historical advantage of the incumbent (being strategic agility) is now becoming the competitive advantage of the new entrant. Conversely, the historical advantage of the new entrant (being operational agility) is becoming a potential competitive advantage—and key defence—of an incumbent's business. Almost perversely, the biggest weakness of many companies is now becoming one of the key elements that will provide them with the potential to create competitive edge in the future.

Benefitting from the New Competitive Advantage

Whilst this theoretical or potential advantage may exist, the practical capability to leverage the advantage becomes a significant, often monumental, challenge. The last question then is how does a corporate shift from a lack of operational agility to realizing its hidden competitive advantage in this area?

Unfortunately, most organizations appear to be failing in this—presuming that data is the goal or objective. Creating change, however, should be the primary goal—particularly focused around the creation of operational as well as strategic agility.

A focus on data as the goal is common and often manifests itself with the initiation of large information technology implementations that have been structured using historical project paradigms geared significantly toward ensuring total accuracy—usually at the expense of agility, dynamism, and ongoing improvement. These projects often fail, or at a minimum take dramatically more time and effort to operationalize and provide significantly less benefits than expected.

Correctly developing both organization design and organizational dynamics will have far more impact than any particular system or technology; however these aspects are typically forgotten or ignored by most large organizations when they consider "data."

From an organizational design perspective, it is surprising to see how many organizations position their customer analytics teams either underneath marketing or within IT. These structures typically confine the scope of customer analytics teams to either direct marketing operations (if in marketing) or Business Intelligence (BI) reporting (if in information technology).

Advanced customer analytics has a pivotal role to play in every aspect of the business from the fundamental strategy creation of the business through to the most tactical customer service event. The organization design needs to reflect this role.

From an organization dynamics perspective, it is also important to recognize an important behavioral paradox. Training of data analytics experts coupled with a generalization of the personalities of analysts has been skewed toward using the technical skill set to create explanations and remove uncertainty.

However, to improve competitive position, it is important to establish the analytics team as one of the key change agents of the business. Creating change creates ambiguity—hence the paradox of training to remove uncertainty compared to the task of creating ambiguity.

Recognizing this and equipping these teams to tackle the paradox is an exercise not just in training and organization design, but also in building a culture that fosters the traditional analytical skill set and couples it with a non-traditional entrepreneurial mindset.

The ability to create this skill set/mindset combination at scale, with broad reach across a corporate entity, has now become both the key challenge and the necessity for how many existing mainstream companies are going to compete into the future.

Airline Retailing Research Summary

Stan Boyer
Vice President Solution Marketing
SabreSonic Customer Sales & Service
Sabre Airline Solutions

In 2012, *Sabre Airline Solutions*® conducted market research to better understand where airlines are in the retail life cycle compared to other travel-industry competitors as well as in comparison to companies more traditionally thought of as retailers.

A retailing strategy is increasingly important as more airline revenue is being generated from ancillary products and services. With the advent of these new ancillary opportunities come new challenges to airlines, namely in the realm of operations and pricing. As a preamble to the study, it's important to first focus on these challenges.

Operational Fulfillment Challenges

The fact that an airline sells ancillaries does not always mean there is post-sale automation in planning and day-of-departure operations to help ensure consumers actually receive the products they have purchased. In fact, many times ancillaries are supported by manual processes and workarounds whereby an airline may rely on gate agents or flight attendants to remember which ancillary products and services are included in a branded fare. This requires airlines to rely on human memory to ensure products and services are delivered to the consumer in flight, increasing the potential for errors and customer dissatisfaction.

Airlines have shown a willingness to allow these manual processes and workarounds as the margins associated with the ancillary sales often dwarfs the margins they receive from traditional ticket revenue. However, there is ample opportunity for improvement.

Assuming it is not always clear which products and services a consumer is entitled to on a good day, it is even more difficult to ensure consumers receive the products they have purchased in the event of a schedule change or other irregular operations — something that is not the least bit uncommon in the world of air travel.

Imagine a customer purchased a premium seat and was later reaccommodated to another flight because his or her original flight was cancelled due to inclement weather.

How does the airline ensure that the customer who already paid for a premium seat gets a premium seat on the new flight since premium seat inventory is not always available? If the inventory is not available, how does the airline ensure the consumer gets a refund or credit? Is this process automated, or does the airline rely on the customer to call the airline to ensure that he or she receives the appropriate credit — not the experience an airline wants for travelers, particularly their highly valued travelers?

Pricing Challenges

Most airlines possess sophisticated pricing and revenue management practices. They are extremely skilled at forecasting flight availability and price to maximize airline revenue. However, as more of their revenue is being derived from ancillaries, airlines are sub-optimally pricing an increasing percentage of revenue because they are not currently analyzing and optimizing ancillary revenue using the same methods they do for flight inventory. As a result, they are overlooking considerable opportunities to generate incremental revenue by applying analytics, forecasting, and pricing optimization to ancillary products and services.

Sabre Airline Solutions learned via its research into retail strategy that applying traditional retail practices and strategies can help airlines overcome these challenges.

Research Methodology

During the extensive research conducted by *Sabre Airline Solutions*, it was imperative to gather information from airlines as well as aviation industry experts and educators. And most importantly, it was vital to study successful retailers, entities focused on consumer products, as an example, to gain insight into the art and science of the practice. As a result of the research, four key themes were identified that paved the way to successful retailing:

1. Ease of use
2. End-to-end customer experience
3. Revenue optimization
4. Right systems

The following are examples of how these strategies are deployed in traditional retailing and suggestions for how airlines can deploy the principles to complete their transformation to successful retailers.

Ease of Use

Consumers have myriad methods for shopping and just as many options in terms of products and services, so ease of use is essential. In addition, they must provide relevant products and services at the very moment a consumer wants to buy. They also must give consumers the ability to easily shop online and offline with exceptional search and filter tools. They need to allow shoppers to focus by minimizing clutter.

Many retailers organize online and offline stores similarly to make stores easy to shop. For example, The Container Store organizes its brick-and-mortar stores by department such as travel, office, and kitchen in the same way it organizes its online stores to make it easier for consumers to find what they are looking for, which drives consistency across all channels.

Online retailers must provide superior search and filter tools to improve ease of use. For example, when searching for a men's coat at Nordstrom, the online site contained 582 different coats. However, if a consumer knows what he or she is looking for and selects a size, color, and price, the options can be narrowed down to 12. The approach of creating custom, personal shopping experiences based on personal preferences is called faceted navigation, and it is very common in the online retail space. It is quite different from the—low-fare search approach that dominates the travel industry and provides hundreds of price-driven flight options.

Implications for Airlines   To apply ease-of-use retail themes, airlines should cross-sell and upsell relevant offers and use advanced search and filter techniques. For example, an airline could use shopping-cart contents to cross-sell other products. If a traveler booked an overnight stay but didn't book a hotel at the same time, the airline could offer to sell the traveler a hotel.

If the airline does not offer non-air products, it can also create upsell opportunities for air ancillaries—using a rules-based methodology. For example, the airline could offer reduced bag fees if there is more than one person in the PNR, the trip duration is greater than 3 days, and the advance purchase time period is greater than 21 days. Airlines could also create cross-sell opportunities based on destination. For example, they could offer hotel transfers or shuttle services for beach destinations.

Getting a little more sophisticated, relevant cross-sell and upsell offers could also be created based on traveler shopping and purchase history. If a consumer has purchased meals on past trips, the airline could and should continue to offer meals to that particular customer. On the other hand, if a consumer continually rejects the offer of a rental car, then the airline should minimize offers of rental cars for that consumer in the future to avoid frustrating the traveler.

Similarly to the way Nordstrom utilized faceted navigation to narrow a selection of 582 coats down to 12, airlines could use advanced search and filter techniques to narrow down the number of flight options offered, creating a unique, personalized list of flight options—a set of—more-relevant products that the consumer would actually have a greater proclivity to purchase. The airline could let the user select desired options on a flight such as a nonstop morning flight with a waiver on one checked bag and a premium seat with extra leg room. Instead of returning hundreds of options, the consumer would get a personalized list of options that matched his or her search criteria. Figure 9.9 gives an example of potential options for advanced search criteria.

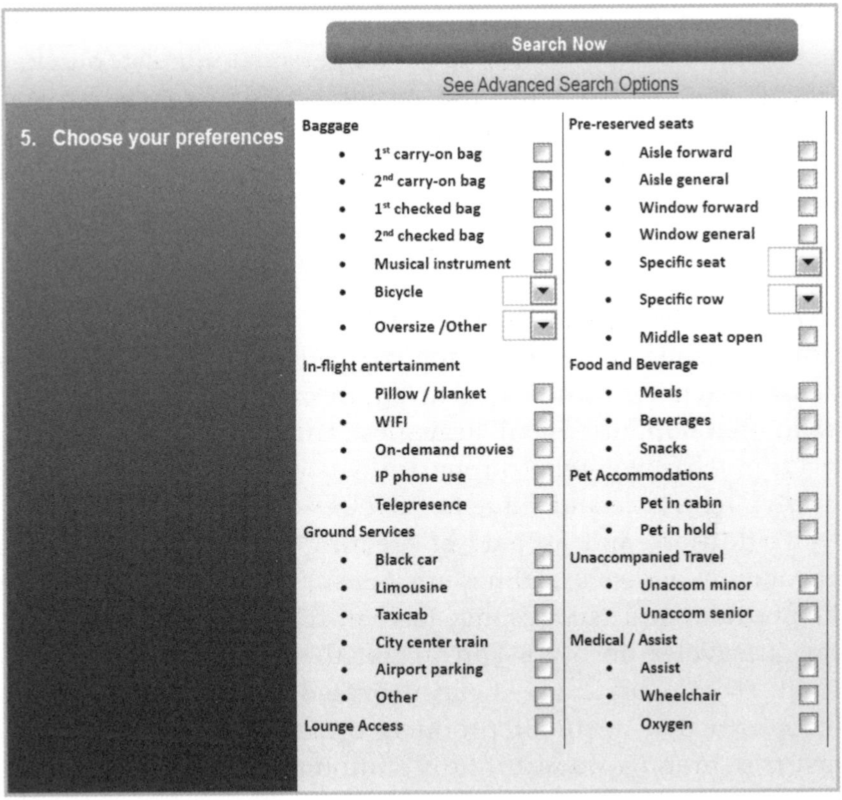

Figure 9.9   Advanced search criteria options

End-to-End Customer Experience

Effective retailers identify customer segments and create marketing programs specific to those segments. They also ensure a consistent brand experience across all channels. Their products live up to their brand promise, regardless of where it is sold. Successful retailers recognize the customer throughout the shopping experience, and they personalize the experience without appearing to harass or overwhelm the consumer.

The Kindle, for example, offers three products with different feature sets and price points to appeal to a broad consumer base.

To apply end-to-end customer experience retail principles to the airline industry, airlines can invest in personalization and ancillary integration throughout the travel life cycle.

To create personalized offers, advanced customer profiles that include demographics, lifestyle, personal interest, purchase history, market segment, and customer value can be created. Personalization data should be used to enhance cross-sell and upsell opportunities at appropriate points in the user experience — in those places where consumers are more apt to purchase — again, think "right time" for the offer.

Implications for Airlines Currently, an abundance of data is captured while consumers shop for and book travel. However, that data is not typically structured, formatted, and accessible in a way that supports retail strategies. Therefore, airlines need to invest in technology that supports the use of this rich data source to drive relevance and value to travelers.

In addition, and as part of creating a positive, end-to-end customer experience, airlines must ensure that customers receive the products and services they have purchased, even in the event that a traveler does not end up on their originally scheduled flight. This can be achieved via integrated, automated operations. To ensure that ancillary products don't negatively impact an airline's brand promise, fully automated reaccommodation tools for ancillaries will emerge, similar to what exists today for flight inventory, ensuring that *all* consumer expectations are addressed.

The new technology will include automated fulfillment of all ancillaries throughout operations, as well as automated exchanges and refunds of any product or service. To streamline these processes, inflight, check-in, loyalty, redemption, and revenue accounting systems will be enhanced with retail capabilities.

Revenue Optimization

Profitable retailers create specific marketing goals for each marketing campaign. Included in their campaigns are different marketing goals, such as higher total revenue, unit margin, or volume dependent on the campaign. These goals likely vary by season, product, distribution channel, or customer segment. They generally use tools to drive revenue optimization supported by upselling efforts, trial-and-error testing, and A/B testing.

Lucrative retailers experiment with verbiage, layout and design, product offers, and pricing.

Collaborative filtering, perfected by Amazon, the world's largest online retailer, is a common form of upselling. The capability simply recommends to shoppers additional products based on purchases made by others who have bought the same item.

Collaborative filtering makes cross-sell and upsell recommendations based on someone else's purchases. Amazon enhanced its basic cross-sell capabilities with the Amazon Betterizer, giving it the ability to cross-sell and upsell based on personal preferences.

Amazon Betterizer presents multiple products in multiple product segments to consumers who then simply select products they like by touching a "like" icon. This information is stored in consumers' personal profiles and later used to make personal product recommendations. This enables Amazon to create personal, targeted product offers without seeming overly invasive to the consumer.

Implications for Airlines   Most consumer products retailers actually view the travel industry broadly, and the airline industry more specifically, to be way out in front on the application of revenue optimization. Still, to apply revenue optimization retail principles to the airline industry, traditional revenue management algorithms can be enhanced with retail-centric capabilities, and airlines can follow the lead of companies like Amazon by implementing collaborative filtering for their customers.

Moreover, airlines currently use highly sophisticated revenue management techniques to support revenue optimization. However, revenue management strategies deployed by airlines today do not incorporate retail and customer-centric modeling within current algorithms. To improve on existing revenue management techniques and generate more incremental revenue, choice models can be enhanced to forecast revenue for different types of customer segments.

Potential segmentation opportunities include trip type (for example, extended leisure, day trip, overnight business, and so on), customer demographics, and purchase history. Similarly, customer lifetime value could also be incorporated to forecast revenue based on the expected value that a particular customer will bring over the course of his or her entire life with the airline as opposed to only forecasting revenue for a specific transaction at a specific point in time.

Choice models can also be enhanced to include ancillary revenues. Customer willingness to pay is a revenue management concept that represents the maximum amount a person is willing to pay to receive a good or service or avoid something negative.

Today, traditional revenue management algorithms don't include customer willingness to pay for ancillaries. However, airline revenue may be further optimized by opening and closing flight inventory based on forecasted revenue from air ancillaries or travel extras that are also expected to be sold in addition to the flight inventory.

For example, an airline might offer an inventory class that is not currently available if it expects to make more from the sale of an ancillary than what it may lose by allowing a lower class of inventory to be purchased. For instance, $50 in revenue from the sale of a hotel or a premium seat may compensate for the fare differential associated with a lower booking class of inventory. Additionally, ancillaries, with limited physical inventory, could be overbooked based on no-shows and cancellations to further maximize airline revenue. Dynamic pricing of ancillary fees could also be utilized to stimulate or decrease demand based on market conditions.

As mentioned, there are also many opportunities to incorporate collaborative filtering into airline retailing to identify additional opportunities to cross-sell and upsell. Today, many revenue management systems use historical booking data across broad segments of travelers for predictive forecasting, as opposed to real-time shopping data and behaviors gathered from the current transaction, or even from the past behavior of a specific traveler.

For example, if a customer looked at hotel information on the airline's website during a shopping session, that information should be captured to help identify upsell opportunities. Customer purchase history could also be used for upsell offers, and, in the event an airline doesn't have customer purchase history, collaborative filtering could also be conducted based on segmentation variables such as trip type. In this instance, an airline may want to offer a lounge pass to an overnight business traveler with a long connection. However, the airline would not want to offer that person travel extras such as sight-seeing tours that are more suitable for the leisure traveler.

Right Systems

Thriving retailers invest in the right systems technology. They capture the right data across their entire organization. They use flexible systems that allow them to quickly adjust to changing market conditions. They often invest in best-in-class systems, saving costs associated with building, maintaining, and upgrading their own in-house system.

In the past, this was not typically the case. Systems that addressed the retailing needs of consumer products companies simply didn't exist or didn't meet the quickly evolving needs of the industry. However, during the past decade, this has changed. While a "build-it-here" mentality existed in the past, the retailers in our study universally indicated that they have moved to a "buy-it" approach to creating solutions. The systems have evolved, and the total cost of ownership, as well as the level of efficacy of those systems, have rendered build scenarios virtually extinct.

Implications for Airlines　　To apply right-systems retail principles to the airline industry, airlines must invest in data integration and technology that allows them to offer the right product at the right place at the right time based on a full view of the customer, which is obtained via the use of integrated data.

Today, many airlines tend to look at data in product silos such as air, car, hotel, premium seat, and so on, or in functional silos such as ticketing, PNR, and check-in. As a result, they typically don't have a full view of the customer or a complete understanding of his or her total value. Once airlines are able to create a full view of the customer with an understanding of his or her total lifetime value, this information should be deployed within systems that create targeted, compelling offers to the consumer at appropriate, relevant places in the travel retail life cycle.

In addition, revenue reporting across all pertinent areas is necessary to support the development of a full view of the customer.

Conclusion

As airline retailing emerges and airlines begin to adopt more traditional retail concepts and strategies to their business, more focus will be placed on optimizing product placement in various distribution channels and personalizing offers to the individual customer. Leveraging actionable, data-driven customer insights, as Figure 9.10 depicts, will enable airlines to offer the right product to the right customer at the right time across the customer journey.

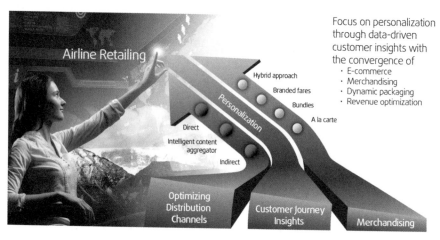

Figure 9.10   The emergence of airline retailing

Focusing on these key areas enables airlines to build a solid retailing strategy that drives additional revenue while boosting the customer experience. Once successfully in motion, customers will appreciate the ease of shopping with their preferred airline and look forward to making the selections that improve their overall travel experience, driving customer loyalty and enhancing the end-to-end customer experience.

Notes

1   Both ALDI groups of the two brothers Theo and Karl Albrecht together.

2   Global megatrends, 2013, PwC analysis (http://www.pwc.com/gx/en/annual-review/megatrends/index.jhtml) (accessed February 2014 online).

3   https://www.un.org/en/development/desa/population/publications/pdf/ageing/WorldPopulationAgeingReport2013.pdf (accessed February 2014 online).

4   http://www.iata.org/pressroom/pr/pages/2013–12–10–01.aspx (accessed February 2014 online).

5   Global megatrends, 2013, PwC analysis (http://www.pwc.com/gx/en/annual-review/megatrends/index.jhtml) (accessed February 2014 online).

6   "Building Trust in the Air," 2011, PwC publication (www.pwc.com/trustintheair) (accessed February 2014 online).

Index

About the Author

With a career that spans 45 years in the global airline industry, Nawal Taneja has worked for and advised major airlines and related businesses worldwide. Within the business sector his experience also includes the presidency of a small airline that provided schedule and charter service with jet aircraft, and the presidency of a research organization that provided consulting services to the air transportation community throughout the world. Within the academic community, he has served on the Faculties at the Massachusetts Institute of Technology (as an Associate Professor) and at The Ohio State University (first as a Professor, then as the Chairman of the Department of Aviation, and subsequently as the Chairman of the Department of Aerospace Engineering). Within the government sector, he has been recognized as an influential thinker and has advised worldwide Departments of Civil Aviation, Finance, Economics, and Tourism on matters relating to the role of governments for facilitating the development of the aviation sector to promote travel and tourism and enhance economic growth.

He has served on the Board of both public and private organizations, presents at industry conferences worldwide, and continues to advise senior executives in airlines and related businesses as well as senior government policy makers on managing the:

- dynamics of the global aviation industry relating to consumers, competitors, infrastructure, government policies, and technologies—aircraft, information, communications, analytics, social networks, mobile devices,
- evolution of the airline business based on: market fragmentation and segmentation; shift in the global economy and the center of gravity of the aviation activity; new-generation information and technologies, enabling and,

in some cases, driving business strategies; and best global business practices, and

- incremental and transformational strategies for profitable growth that is sustainable.

At the encouragement of, and for, practitioners in the global airline industry, he has authored seven other books in this series:

- *Driving Airline Business Strategies through Emerging Technology* (2002).
- *AIRLINE SURVIVAL KIT: Breaking Out of the Zero Profit Game* (2003).
- *Simpli-Flying: Optimizing the Airline Business Model* (2004).
- *FASTEN YOUR SEATBELT: The Passenger is Flying the Plane* (2005).
- *Flying Ahead of the Airplane* (2008).
- *Looking Beyond the Runway: Airlines Innovating with Best Practices while Facing Realities* (2010).
- *The Passenger Has Gone Digital and Mobile: Accessing and Connecting through Information and Technology* (2011).

All seven books have been published by Ashgate Publishing in the UK.

Nawal Taneja holds a Bachelor's degree in Aeronautical Engineering (First Class Honors from the University of London), a Master's degree in Flight Transportation from MIT's Department of Aeronautics and Astronautics, a Master's degree in Business Administration from MIT's Sloan School of Management, and a Doctorate in Air Transportation from the University of London.

Discar

AROUND
THE ALSTER

NEW TOWN

OLD TOWN

PORT AND
SPEICHERSTADT

0 kilometres   1
0 miles   1